ESSENTIALS OF
GRILLING

WILLIAMS-SONOMA

ESSENTIALS OF
GRILLING

RECIPES AND TECHNIQUES FOR SUCCESSFUL OUTDOOR COOKING

TEXT

DENIS KELLY

RECIPES

MELANIE BARNARD, BARBARA GRUNES, MICHAEL MCLAUGHLIN,
BOB AND COLEEN SIMMONS

GENERAL EDITOR

CHUCK WILLIAMS

PHOTOGRAPHY

JASON LOWE, MAREN CARUSO, HOLLY STEWART, DAVID MATHESON

ILLUSTRATIONS

MATHEW SQUILLANTE

Contents

Slowly rising wisps of fragrant smoke, sputtering fat hitting hot coals, thick, juicy steaks sizzling on the grill—these are the familiar smells, sounds, and sights of the backyard barbecue. As the hungry guests arrive, they fall into easy conversation around the fire, joking with the cook and always keeping one eye on the grill, admiring the food that will make up the feast.

Many of us recall scenes much like that, of family and friends on a warm day, all of them drawn by the promise of good company and a wonderful grilled meal. Indeed, my own memories of great food begin with the backyard barbecue. These days, the fare is more likely to be a spice-rubbed pork loin rotating on a spit above a hickory-scented fire, or a brined salmon slowly smoking over alder chunks, than the barbecued chicken or burgers of my youth. Yet the principle remains the same: cooking food on a grill delivers the most flavor and the most fun. It is a way to celebrate life and the outdoor table, and to participate in a timeless ritual that mimics the way our ancestors have cooked for centuries.

Grilling has come a long way from the days when the menu was limited to steaks, chicken, and burgers. Those old favorites are still delicious, of course, but cooks today, at home and in restaurants, feel free to toss a wide array of items—meat, poultry, fish, seafood, vegetables, even breads and pizzas—on the grill. In addition, these open-fire enthusiasts readily draw on grilling traditions that span the world, turning out everything from Bistecca alla Fiorentina (page 54) to Carne Asada with Blackened Corn (page 77), Spit-Roasted Piri-Piri Chicken (page 165) to Tea-Smoked Duck Breasts (page 192), Grilled Whole Striped Bass (page 224) to Barbecued Oysters (page 230).

Yes, grilling has changed—the foods are more varied, the recipes are more international, the equipment is fancier—but the basics have not: a grill, some fuel, and something to cook are all that are necessary. Everything the grill cook, novice or old hand, needs to know can be found in the following pages, including detailed descriptions of charcoal and gas grills, hardwood charcoal and briquettes, direct heat and indirect heat, barbecuing, and more. Then comes a parade of mouthwatering recipes—dishes guaranteed to be among your favorites.

Now, go out and light the grill and get started on making some new backyard memories.

Denis Kelly

Grilling Equipment

Modern manufacturers provide the grill cook with dozens of options, from elaborate gas grills with multiple burners to small cast-iron hibachis that can hold only a few handfuls of briquettes. This wealth of choices has made grilling possible in every season and for every occasion. The following guidelines will help you choose the right grill for your needs.

GRILL TYPES

This book concentrates on the two most popular types of outdoor grills: a medium-sized kettle-type charcoal grill and a propane- or natural gas–fueled gas grill. These grills will work with all the recipes that follow, including those that call for direct-heat grilling, indirect-heat grilling, and smoking (you'll find a detailed explanation of the different cooking methods on page 14). The differences in equipment come down to whether the grill has a cover, and to matters of size, sturdiness and durability, types of fuel used, and optional features. All of these will affect the cost of the product you choose.

Charcoal Grills

Consisting of a metal pan that holds a bed of glowing coals beneath a metal rack, charcoal grills come in many shapes and sizes. These include the small Japanese hibachi and the flat-bottomed, uncovered grill, which brings to mind the backyard barbecues of the 1950s. Nowadays, the more popular—and versatile—choice is a kettle-type grill whose deep, hemispherical base and domed cover make it fuel efficient and suitable for cooking with direct or indirect heat. Vents on the base and cover allow control of the temperature within for indirect-heat grilling and smoking.

The smallest charcoal grills, such as square or rectangular Japanese-style hibachis, are easily portable and are especially convenient for balcony or patio use. Bear in mind that

The most popular types of outdoor grills: a KETTLE-TYPE CHARCOAL GRILL and a PROPANE-FUELED COVERED GAS GRILL.

they will limit the quantity and size of the foods you cook and that the smallest ones lack a cover to allow for indirect-heat cooking. These compact grills are also sometimes made of less durable materials than their larger cousins and may not last beyond one or two grilling seasons. If you are an avid outdoor cook and plan to use the grill regularly, it's wise to invest in a large, sturdy model that will last for many grilling seasons.

Options for kettle grills include wheels, removable ash catchers, wire shelves, and cart frames. Some models feature gas ignition systems to make lighting charcoal a snap.

Gas Grills

Whether fueled by propane in refillable tanks or a natural-gas line that connects to the house, a gas grill emits flames that heat a bed of ceramic briquettes, heat-absorbent crushed lava rock, or stainless-steel or enameled metal baffles (devices to regulate the flow of gas), which in turn cook food placed on a rack above them.

A gas grill gives off the same kind of heat as glowing coals, although most models can't achieve the high temperatures and produce the smoky flavor possible with hardwood and charcoal. Yet many backyard grillers are attracted to gas grills for their ease of cooking and cleanup. Drippings are vaporized to create smoke, and excess grease is channeled off to prevent flare-ups. Also appealing is the ability to regulate heat with the turn of a dial. Most models include multiple controls, allowing only parts of the grill to be heated, which is useful for indirect-heat grilling.

Gas grill options include separate burners for cooking sauces or heating griddles, rotisseries for spit-roasting, and metal boxes that hold wood chips for smoking. The high

grill hood allows for indirect-heat grilling, for barbecuing, and for smoking.

Good-sized covered grills can easily handle enough food to feed a crowd and are commonly designed to handle the cooking of a big cut of meat or whole bird by indirect heat. If cared for properly, they will last season after season. When selecting a gas grill, look for one with more than one heat element so that it can be used for indirect-heat cooking.

Other Grills

In theory, indoor electric grills and grill pans can be used in the same manner as outdoor gas grills, but because they don't include a cover, their use is limited to direct-heat cooking. Most recipes for direct-heat grilling successfully make the move to this indoor equipment. The timing may be longer, however, as these grills generally do not get

as hot as outdoor gas or charcoal grills. Watch for visual clues that let you know the food is done. Be sure your kitchen has adequate ventilation to whisk away smoke and odors.

Two-sided electric grills call for a cooking technique that is markedly different from that of a conventional, one-sided grill, whether gas, electric, or charcoal. Since the heat comes from both sides of the grill unit, and the food is compressed between the two grilling plates, food preparation and timing are unique to the unit. Consult recipes written specifically for this equipment.

Above all, whether choosing a small hibachi for cooking on a fire escape or a deluxe back-yard gas model with all the bells and whistles, always look for a grill that requires a minimum or no assembly and has solidly welded parts. A warranty issued by a respected manufacturer is also an assurance of quality.

CARING FOR YOUR GRILL

Grills are low-maintenance tools, but they do require some attention. With regular care, high-quality grills will cook efficiently and cleanly for many years.

■ Before you begin to cook, brush the grate with oil to help keep food from sticking and to make cleanup easier.

■ After cooking, while the grill is still hot, use a long-handled wire brush to scrape off any food particles stuck to the rack. Cover the grill and allow the heat of the dying coals or gas flames to burn off the residue.

■ Don't let ashes accumulate in a charcoal grill. Clean out the fire bed frequently. Wait until the ash is completely cold, scoop it out, and discard it in a nonflammable container.

■ After a gas grill has completely cooled, sort through its lava rocks or ceramic briquettes, dislodging and removing any bits of food that could clog the gas jets. Replace the rocks or briquettes if they are heavily soiled and no longer heat efficiently. Do not wash the rocks with detergent. Clean gas jets by scraping off accumulated grease and ash with the scraper end of a grill brush or other metal scraper.

■ Never line the fire bed or cooking grate with any material. Grills get very hot, and any foreign substance presents a risk of catching fire. Lining a grill with aluminum foil hinders the necessary flow of air.

■ Protect your grill with a waterproof cover or store it indoors.

■ Always consult the owners' manual that comes with the grill before cooking on it for the first time. Be sure to note the cleaning instructions as well.

GRILLING ACCESSORIES

Cookware shops and hardware stores offer a vast array of tools and gadgets designed to make grilling easier. A few are essential, some are useful, and others are just plain fun. Shown here are a handful of accessories to consider acquiring for your outdoor kitchen.

Thermometers

An instant-read thermometer quickly measures the doneness of meat or poultry. Insert it into the grilled item near the end of cooking to

Skewers

Grilling kabobs requires a good set of skewers. If you've been frustrated by food spinning on traditional round skewers, you'll appreciate flat-edged metal ones that keep items in place when you turn them on the grill. Long skewers are also helpful for stabilizing large pieces of meat, such as a butterflied leg of lamb, on the grill. If you use wooden or bamboo skewers, submerge them in water and soak for at least 30 minutes before threading food onto them to prevent the skewers from burning.

handful of wood chips or herbs to the center. Fold the foil around the wood or herbs, making a compact packet. Tear open the packet or perforate it in several places with a fork or the tip of a knife to allow the smoke to escape during grilling.

Grill Baskets, Screens, and Plates

Made in a variety of shapes and sizes, grill baskets, essentially two hinged wire grids that can be latched shut, simplify grilling delicate foods like fish fillets or whole fish

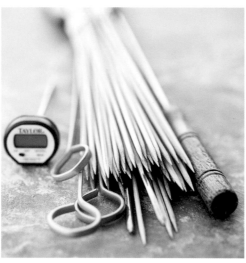  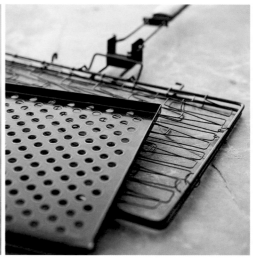

determine when it should come off the grill. When inserting the thermometer, do not allow it to touch a bone, which will skew the reading, and do not leave it in the food while it is still on the grill. Some covered grills come with a built-in thermometer. If your grill does not, for long cooking over low heat, insert an instant-read thermometer with a long probe through the vent opening to monitor the temperature inside the grill without opening the lid. A specialized grill thermometer or an oven thermometer can be attached to the grill rack to measure surface temperature.

Smoker Box

A small, vented metal smoker box is useful for holding wood chips or herbs in a gas grill. The smoker box is placed directly over a heat element, creating flavorful and aromatic smoke. The box prevents small particles from clogging the grill's fuel ports. A drawback to using a smoker box is that the wood chips may fail to ignite at low heat levels. If this happens, or if you don't have a smoker box on hand, you can fashion one out of heavy-duty aluminum foil: Place a large piece of heavy-duty foil on a work surface and add a

that can sometimes stick to the grill rack or are difficult to turn. Use the baskets, too, for grilling small foods such as shrimp (prawns), cherry tomatoes, and asparagus that could fall through the grill grate into the fire. Choose grill baskets with long, heatproof handles to facilitate safe turning. To help prevent sticking, brush or spray the inside surfaces of baskets with oil before using.

Grill screens, another versatile tool, are ideal for cooking any foods that might otherwise fall through the rack into the fire. This can include shrimp (prawns), scallops, or small pieces of vegetables. Made of fine wire mesh held together by a sturdy frame, the screens are placed directly on top of the grate. Brush or spray them with oil to keep foods from sticking, then let them heat for a minute or two before adding the food.

Perforated metal grill plates are also used for grilling small pieces of seafood, fish, or vegetables to prevent them from falling through the rack. They come in a variety of shapes and sizes and are evenly pierced with small holes. Coat with oil before using.

marinades or sauces while they cook. Select brushes with long natural bristles that are solidly attached to a sturdy handle, which will keep your hand away from the grill's heat.

A two-pronged fork is handy for spearing and moving large or awkwardly shaped foods. Be judicious in spearing, however, as you don't want to lose juices.

Choose a sturdy spatula with an extra-long, well-insulated handle to turn and move food around on the grill while keeping hands and arms at a safe distance from the heat.

Flame Source

Use a long match or gas wand to light the newspaper or coals of a charcoal grill. Many gas grills come equipped with a spark igniter. If yours does not have one, use a long match or gas wand to light the flame.

Cast-Iron Frying Pans

Dust off your heirloom cast-iron pan for the grilling season for cooking shellfish and for simmering sauces and gravies right on the grill. Cast-iron heats evenly, holds heat well,

Grill Tools

Designed specifically for cleaning grills, a long-handled grill brush has rustproof metal bristles and a stainless-steel scraper. Use it while the grill is hot, before or after cooking, to scrape off any food particles stuck to the rack. Look for wooden handles; plastic handles are prone to melting.

No grill cook should be without extra-long tongs. Use them when placing food on the grill, turning and moving food, and removing food when it is done. Long-handled brushes make it easy and safe to coat foods with

Chimney Starter

A metal cylinder with vents on the bottom and and a handle on the side, a chimney starter is a safe, efficient, and environmentally friendly way to start a fire in a charcoal grill. Available in different sizes, chimneys should be chosen to accommodate an amount of charcoal large enough to fill your grill. A large, 5-qt (160–fl oz/5-l) chimney (about 7 1/2 inches/ 19 cm in diameter and 12 inches/30 cm tall) holds enough charcoal to make a medium-hot fire in a medium or large kettle grill. Look for a chimney starter with a sturdy, wide handle.

and lasts a lifetime. Other types of frying pans can be used if they can withstand the high heat from the grill, and if you don't mind the possible blackening of the surface.

Protective Gear

An oven mitt and a pot holder made of heavy, quilted cotton can help protect your hands from intense heat during grilling. A leather grill glove, with an extension that shields the cook's forearm from the heat, provides maximum protection. A full-length, heavy-duty apron guards against splatters on clothing.

Fuel Types and Flavoring Materials

The outdoor cook faces an array of choices when it comes to fuels and flavoring materials. Knowing about different types will help you make the best selection for your grill and for the food you're cooking. Be sure to consult the owners' manual for specifics on your type of grill.

FUELS FOR CHARCOAL GRILLS

The most readily available fuel for a charcoal grill is briquettes. These compact, uniform, square-pillow-shaped lumps are made by compressing pulverized charcoal with binding agents and additives that facilitate lighting and burning. Charcoal briquettes make a good fire, are easy to use, and provide steady, spark-free heat, but the binding agents they include can give the grilling food an unpleasant taste. Pass up briquettes containing nitrates, petroleum, sand, or clay as fillers, and always avoid self-igniting briquettes, which violate air-quality control standards in some areas. Store all types of briquettes in a dry place. Briquettes are a good choice for indirect grilling, as they burn at a steady temperature and remain ignited for a long time.

Hardwood charcoal chunks make a hotter, cleaner-burning fire than charcoal briquettes, and impart a subtle smoke flavor to grilled food. These irregular-sized lumps of fragrant hardwood—mesquite is the most common, but you can also find hickory, alder, oak, apple, and pecan—have already been burned until they are charred to almost pure carbon. Before lighting the fire, break large chunks of the hardwood charcoal into smaller, more uniform pieces for more even heat. Keep a careful eye on the fire, as the charcoal will throw off some sparks at first. Like briquettes, hardwood charcoal should be stored in a dry place. This is the fuel of choice for many master grillers for the intense heat and quick smoke flavor it provides to direct-grilled foods.

CHARCOAL BRIQUETTES are the most readily available fuel for a charcoal grill.

HARDWOOD CHARCOAL adds subtle smoke flavor to grilled food.

PROPANE is an easy-to-use, clean-burning fuel for a gas grill.

FUELS FOR GAS GRILLS

For most gas grills, propane is the best fuel to use. You can find already-filled tanks of this clean-burning gas in hardware stores and specialty-grill stores. One tank will last for many hours of cooking, but it's always a good idea to keep a spare tank on hand.

Refills of propane can be found at some gas stations or home-supply stores. Look for propane dealers who refill empty tanks or exchange filled ones for empty ones at a reasonable price.

When propane tanks are not in use, store them away from direct sunlight, but keep them out of garages or other enclosed storage areas. Read and follow all storage precautions printed on the tank.

It is also possible to hook up a gas grill to a natural-gas line in your patio. Be aware that gas grills need to be adapted mechanically to burn natural gas efficiently and provide adequate cooking heat. Have a professional do the hookup and adaptation for you.

Some grilling purists object to propane or natural gas for grilling because it doesn't impart the same distinctive smoke flavor to food that charcoal does. This can be remedied by putting wood chips or other flavoring materials in the grill's smoker box (or in a perforated foil packet) during grilling. Even foods grilled over direct heat can benefit from the flavor of wood smoke on a gas grill. See page 13 for specifics on using wood chips and dried herbs to flavor food.

Another potential drawback to cooking with gas fuel is that it doesn't get as hot as a grill piled high with hardwood charcoal chunks. While a professional grill chef may notice a difference between the amount of heat generated by gas and charcoal, it should not trouble the average backyard griller.

FLAVORING MATERIALS

Grilling contributes some flavor in the form of smoke that rises from small flare-ups caused by fat and juices dripping into the fire. More flavor can be added through the smoke from aromatic wood chunks or chips, as well as from dried herbs or grapevine cuttings.

Hardwoods are available as chunks or chips. Burning easily and evenly, wood chips are the best choice for home grilling, working well for normal use on both charcoal and gas grills.

The most common hardwoods for grilling and smoking have flavors ranging from intense and wood flavored (hickory, mesquite, oak, and pecan) to moderate and fruity (apple, cherry, and plum) to mild (alder). Resinous soft woods, such as those from the pine family, should not be used to flavor grilled foods; they

impart an undesirable piney, sooty flavor to foods, and they could damage and/or discolor the grill.

For a charcoal grill, soak wood chips, herbs, or grapevine cuttings in water for 30 minutes, then drain before using. If using aromatics in a gas grill, do not soak them before use, as they are sometimes difficult to ignite. Scatter aromatic herb sprigs or grapevine cuttings directly over the coals of a charcoal grill. On a gas grill, place the flavoring materials in a smoker box or perforated foil packet (page 27) and place them over a heat element to ignite, releasing their aromatic smoke.

Before using any wood chips, herb sprigs, grapevine cuttings, or similar materials, consult the owners' manual for your particular grill for specific instructions on flavoring food.

WOOD AND HERB FLAVORING OPTIONS

Wood chips

Dried basil stems

Dried rosemary

Mixed herbs

Grapevine cuttings

Choose aromatic additions to enhance food in the same way that you choose spices or herbs.

ALDER CHIPS marry well with salmon and other fish and light meats.

APPLE CHIPS enhance chicken and game birds, pork, salmon, sweet glazes, and fruit sauces.

CHERRY CHIPS are similar to apple and complement poultry and seafood.

HICKORY CHIPS deliver a slightly nutty flavor to pork, chicken, and turkey.

MESQUITE CHIPS enhance fish, chicken, turkey, and pork.

OAK CHIPS complement pork and beef.

PECAN CHIPS are similar to hickory and pair well with chicken and pork.

DRIED BASIL STEMS infuse a wide variety of foods with a sweet herbal scent.

DRIED ROSEMARY SPRIGS give a pleasantly woodsy flavor to beef, lamb, pork, chicken, and meaty fish fillets or steaks.

MIXED HERBS create fragrant smoke that suits a wide variety of foods; they are sometimes sold in tea-bag-type packages.

GRAPEVINE CUTTINGS, a by-product of wine making, add fruity flavor to such grilled foods as beef, lamb, chicken, and fish.

Grilling Methods

While there are many models of grills on the market, there are only two methods for cooking on a grill: direct and indirect heat. The recipes in this book are clearly labeled. If using recipes from other sources, follow these guidelines to determine which method you should use.

DIRECT-HEAT GRILLING

This intense, high-heat method is used for searing and for cooking small or thin food items that are ready in 25 minutes or less, including steaks, chops, burgers, sausages, some poultry pieces, fish fillets, all types of kabobs, and vegetables.

For direct-heat grilling, foods are placed directly over the hot coals of a charcoal grill, or directly over the preheated heat elements of a gas grill. The surface of the food sears and caramelizes over the high heat, while the juices are sealed inside. Though direct-heat grilling is usually done with an uncovered grill, some cooks prefer to cover the grill to prevent flare-ups and to control temperatures.

INDIRECT-HEAT GRILLING

Indirect heat cooks foods by reflected heat, much like roasting in an oven. This method is used for cooking larger pieces of food, such as a pork loin or a whole chicken or turkey, that take longer than 25 minutes to cook. Indirect heat is also used for smoking and barbecuing.

For indirect-heat grilling, heat circulates inside the grill to cook the food slowly and evenly. While the food can be left unattended for much of the time, you may need to turn the food partway through the grilling time to ensure uniform doneness, or several times for barbecue. The grill should be kept covered throughout the cooking. Every time you lift the lid, heat escapes, increasing the grilling time.

HYBRID GRILLING

Some foods benefit from using a combination of direct- and indirect-heat grilling, and/or by using 2 or 3 levels of heat. This can be accomplished in a charcoal grill by creating different heat zones, or in a gas grill by setting the heat elements at different levels.

Bone-in chicken pieces, for example, do well when cooked using a combination of direct and indirect heat over a two-level fire. The chicken pieces are started over the high, direct-heat zone to brown and grill-mark their surface. Then, it is moved to the area with no heat and the grill is covered to finish cooking it over indirect heat.

Three levels of heat are useful for grilling very large items or several elements of a single meal. For example, foods can be seared quickly over high heat. Moved to lower heat, or to the area with no heat, they finish cooking directly over lower heat, or indirectly over the no-heat zone inside the covered grill.

DIRECT
Steaks, chops, burgers, lamb racks, butterflied meats and poultry, pork tenderloin, sausages, boneless poultry pieces, fish fillets and steaks, small whole fish, shellfish, kabobs, most vegetables

INDIRECT
Bone-in lamb legs, whole poultry, large whole fish, large fish fillets, winter squash

BARBECUE
Beef rib roast, beef brisket, pork roasts, pork shoulder, beef and pork ribs

HYBRID
Bone-in poultry pieces, mixed vegetables

The Art of Grilling

Just like any new skill, learning to grill takes practice. In addition to cooking the food, you must learn how to season and prepare it before grilling, and how to detect the moment when it is perfectly done. Learn these skills and you'll be well on your way to becoming a master.

PREPARING FOOD FOR GRILLING

One of the keys to successful grilling is to add flavor to food by seasoning it before grilling. Old grilling recipes warned cooks not to salt meat before cooking, or it would dry out. In today's thinking, salt, pepper, herbs, and other seasonings applied before grilling not only contribute flavor, but also form a savory, caramelized crust that keeps meat, poultry, and fish juicy and tender.

With the exception of fattier cuts (pork shoulder, spareribs), and of foods that have marinated in an oil-based marinade, it is a good idea to coat food with oil before grilling it. You can rub or brush on oil or use an oil spray (if you are using an oil spray, do not use it near a lighted grill). Apply salt, pepper, herbs, and/or spices after coating with oil.

Oiling the grill rack, in addition to oiling the food, is essential when cooking fish and shellfish, most vegetables, and lean meats and poultry. Use an oil spray (*away* from the fire) or a paper towel saturated with vegetable oil to coat the grill.

For best results, make sure that the grill is clean before cooking. While the grill is hot, before and after cooking, scrub it well with a stiff wire grill brush to remove bits of charred food and residual grease. (It is best to consult your owners' manual for the preferred way to clean your grill.)

Brining foods before cooking over indirect heat or smoking imparts flavor and enhances juiciness, especially in large cuts of meat and whole poultry. Brining a turkey before grilling helps the white meat stay moist.

CHECKING FOR DONENESS

The variable intensity of a grill's heat and the simple change of scene from kitchen to backyard can sometimes cause uncertainty over how long to cook some foods. Always bear in mind that times will vary with the particular type of grill and fuel you use, and with the size, thickness, and temperature of the ingredients you are grilling.

Determining when food is done comes with experience. Learn to follow visual clues with the help of a thermometer, and knowing when foods are done will soon become second nature. In most of the recipes in this book, estimated cooking times are provided in a range of 5 or 10 minutes. These ranges are guidelines and should not be taken to mean that the food will be done in exactly this number of minutes. Use an instant-read thermometer to check the food and follow the recommended temperatures. If you don't have a thermometer, cut into the food and check the interior visually, following the cues provided in the recipes.

MAKING GOOD GRILL MARKS

Marking your grilled foods with professional-looking cross-hatching is easier to do than you might think, and the distinctive marks create an attractive presentation.

1 Prepare the grill for direct-heat grilling, the higher the heat the better.

2 Clean the grill grate well, oil it generously, and place the food directly over the coals or heat elements, arranging the pieces so that they line up in the same direction.

3 After one-fourth of the total cooking time has elapsed, use a spatula or tongs to rotate

each piece 45 or 90 degrees, depending on whether you prefer diagonal or square grill marks, and continue to the halfway point.

4 At the halfway point, turn over the food pieces, keeping them lined up, and proceed to grill the food.

5 Repeating steps 2 and 3, finish cooking the food.

6 To preserve the cross-hatching, it is best not to move the food again. If you must turn it, however, try to keep it in the same relative position and angle.

Charcoal Grilling

Charcoal grilling is considered by many to be the purest form of grilling because you must learn how to master fire. The first step is to start the fire; then you must learn to manage it, which is perhaps the most challenging and rewarding task of all.

STARTING THE FIRE

The best way to start a charcoal fire is to use a chimney starter, a metal cylinder with vents, a handle, and a grate at the bottom. Newspaper is stuffed into the bottom of the chimney to create kindling, then charcoal briquettes or hardwood charcoal chunks are piled on top. When the newspaper is lit, the flame burns upward inside the chimney, igniting the charcoal. When the charcoal is fully ignited, it is poured onto the fire bed, more coals are added to the bed if needed, and in about 20 minutes you are ready to cook. Chimney starters can be found in outlets that carry charcoal grills, grilling equipment, and/or grilling fuels.

To avoid unpleasant fumes that can permeate food, do not use starter fluid or charcoal that has been presaturated with starter fluid. A chimney starter and a proper arrangement of coals make starter fluid unnecessary. If you choose to employ the fluid, allow it to burn off completely before grilling food, about 45 minutes.

The most important thing to keep in mind about preparing a charcoal fire is to allow enough time for the fire to get hot. To make sure the fire is ready, light the charcoal about 30 minutes before you want to begin cooking.

If you don't have a chimney starter, you can use a starting aid, such as an electric-coil starter, to ignite the charcoal: Move the grill to a location that is near an electrical outlet. Position the coil of the fire starter in the fire bed. Arrange a compact pyramid of charcoal pieces on top, using enough to cover the fire bed eventually according to your needs. Plug the starter into the electrical outlet to light the charcoal. When the charcoal is fully ignited, carefully remove the fire starter from under the coals and move it to a heatproof location to cool completely.

1 Place the chimney starter upside down on the fire bed. Crumple newspaper and stuff it under the grate in the bottom of the chimney. Turn the chimney right side up and fill with charcoal. Center the chimney on the fire bed.

2 Light the paper with a long wooden fireplace match or gas wand. The flames burning upward inside the chimney will ignite the coals. Let them burn for 10 to 15 minutes to ensure that all of the coals are lit.

3 You can tell at a glance when the coals are fully ignited: they will be glowing brightly and starting to turn gray. As they burn, the briquettes will shrink somewhat. To pour the ignited coals into the fire bed, see page 18.

CONTROLLING THE HEAT

Regulating the heat properly is the key to successful charcoal grilling, resulting in food perfectly seared—not burned—on the outside and juicy and tender—not dry and tough—on the inside.

Managing the heat on charcoal grills can seem complicated and imprecise to the inexperienced, but becomes relatively easy with a little practice. The trick, whether for direct-heat grilling or indirect-heat grill-roasting, is to create two or three heat levels in the fire by varying the depth of the coals, and then to move the food around on the grill as needed.

Vents also help to control the heat level of a charcoal grill. Open the vents on the grill to feed oxygen to the fire, thus increasing the cooking temperature. Partially close the vents for less heat. Before you start cooking on a charcoal grill, make sure the air vents are fully open. If they are closed when the grill is covered, the fire may die.

There are two low-tech ways to gauge the level of heat on a charcoal grill: look at the coals, noting both their appearance and ash layer; or hold your hand about 4 inches (10 cm) above the fire, or at the point where the food will be cooking. Keep your hand there as long as you comfortably can and count. Refer to the chart at right for the approximate temperature.

For a more precise measurement, use a special grill thermometer that clips onto the grill, an instant-read thermometer inserted into one of the top vents, or an oven thermometer inside a covered grill (page 10). High heat is about 400°F (200°C); medium-high heat is about 375°F (190°C); medium heat is about 350°F (180°C); medium-low heat is about 325°F (165°C); and low heat is about 300°F (150°C).

HEAT LEVEL	APPEARANCE OF COALS	HAND TEST
Very high	Glowing brightly	less than 1 second
High	Glowing brightly	1 or 2 seconds
Medium-high	Glowing brightly; faint coating of ash	2 or 3 seconds
Medium	Glowing; light coating of ash	3 or 4 seconds
Medium-low	Faint glow; moderate coating of ash	4 or 5 seconds
Low	Barely glowing; thick coating of ash	5 seconds or more

Direct-Heat Grilling with Charcoal

When people think of grilling, they are probably thinking of direct-heat grilling: a quick, high-heat method of cooking small pieces of food over a hot fire. Done over charcoal, direct-heat grilled foods gain an appealing charred exterior and slightly smoky flavor.

The easiest way to set up a direct-heat fire in a charcoal grill is to use long-handled tongs to spread hot coals evenly across the area of the fire bed directly below where the food will sit. As you become comfortable with grilling, it is wise to build three heat zones, creating one area with medium to high heat, one area with low to medium heat, and one area with no heat. If you have a grill with an adjustable grate, move it closer to the coals for high heat, farther away for medium heat.

You will want to start most foods cooked by direct heat over the highest heat, and move them to lower-heat areas as they brown.

For foods such as fish or shellfish that you want to cook only on very high heat, you can arrange the fire into two zones: one with very high heat, the other with no heat. However, many grill chefs prefer the three-level fire for more heat control even for these foods.

While the grill is heating, make sure the food you are planning to cook is properly prepared and seasoned. Trim any excess skin from fish and remove any small bones remaining in fillets with needle-nose pliers. Prior to cooking meat, trim off and discard most of the external fat. Internal fat, or marbling, promotes tenderness and flavor, but external fat causes flare-ups as it melts and drips into the fire. Remove external fat from poultry pieces for the same reason. Some cooks skin chicken before grilling to cut down on fat, but skin protects delicate meat, keeping it from drying out, and adds flavor during cooking. It's better to keep the skin on during cooking and remove it afterward, if desired. Most vegetables don't need to be peeled before grilling; just cut them into convenient shapes and sizes.

Grilling foods over direct heat can often cause flare-ups, which happens when dripping fat comes in contact with flame. Some cooks control the fire by dousing it with water from a spray bottle, which can cause steam burns. A better method of halting flare-ups is to move the food to a cooler part of the fire and, if needed, to cover the grill and close its vents to prevent oxygen from fueling the flames.

1 Ignite the coals using a chimney starter (page 16). When fully lit, dump the coals in the fire bed. If needed, pour in more coals; they will ignite from the heat of the already-lit coals.

2 Spread the coals two or three layers deep in one-third of the fire bed, one or two layers deep in another one-third of the fire bed, and leave one-third of the fire bed free of coals.

3 Position the grill rack in its slots over the coals. Be sure the grill rack is well oiled before placing food on it, to prevent the food from sticking.

Indirect-Heat Grilling with Charcoal

The grill is transformed into an oven for indirect-heat grilling, which utilizes low heat and a cover to move the heat over all sides of the food. Smoke-scented air circulates around large pieces of food, resulting in juicy, aromatic flesh and a golden brown exterior.

For indirect-heat grilling, the charcoal is arranged on either side of a drip pan placed in the center of the fire bed. The drip pan sits below the food to collect the dripping juices and fat, preventing flare-ups. The air circulating inside the covered grill "roasts" the foods as if they were in an oven. For barbecuing or smoking, the fire is set up the same way, but fewer coals are needed and wood chips are added to the coals just before cooking begins.

Make sure that the handles of the grill grate are placed over the coals. If you are going to be cooking food for longer than an hour, add charcoal through the holes under the handles as needed to maintain the temperature (break up hardwood charcoal, if necessary). Some grills come with hinged cooking grates. Position the hinged areas over the coals and add coals as needed during cooking.

Keep in mind that you may need to turn the food or rotate it for even cooking. Just as there are hot spots in your kitchen oven, so too may there be areas of higher heat in the covered grill.

SMOKING WITH CHARCOAL

Cooking on the grill infuses food with some smoke flavor, but you can add more flavor and aroma in the form of wood chips or chunks, fresh or dried herbs, or grapevine cuttings. See page 13 for a description of wood chips and other flavoring materials.

Add the drained, soaked wood pieces or herbs directly to the coals while the food cooks, timing the addition so the flavor of the smoke they generate heightens, but does not dominate, the flavor of what you are cooking. Robust meats, for example, can take longer smoking, while just a few minutes of smoke toward the end of cooking is enough for mild seafood.

If you are grilling large items, such as a whole bird or roast, which spend a lot of time on the grill, you may need to add additional smoking materials during cooking. Keep some wood chips or other aromatics soaking, then drain them and toss them onto the coals as they are needed.

1 Ignite the coals using a chimney starter (page 16). When fully lit, dump the coals in the fire bed. If needed, pour in more coals; they will ignite from the heat of the already-lit coals.

2 Arrange the coals into 2 equal piles on either side of the fire bed and place a foil drip pan in the center, leaving the middle of the grill without heat. Pour water into the pan and replace the rack with its handles over the coals.

3 For even cooking, tie or truss the food into a compact shape (page 290). Put the food on the center of the grill rack directly over the drip pan and cover the grill.

Gas Grilling

Many people are attracted to gas grills because of their convenience and ease in cleanup. Gas grilling alone produces less smoky flavors than charcoal, but you can add aromatics to generate the smoke flavors. And, managing the heat during grilling is a snap.

STARTING THE GRILL

Before starting a fire in a gas grill, it is very important that you read the owners' manual and become familiar with all of the parts of the grill and how they work. If your grill has a propane hookup, be sure also to read the instructions on the propane tank thoroughly. If the grill has a natural-gas hookup, read the literature that came with it when it was installed. Make sure your grill is in a location where it has adequate ventilation, such as on an outdoor deck or patio.

Starting the fire in a gas grill is a much simpler matter than in a charcoal grill. First, open the grill lid and make sure that the burner controls are turned off. If you are using fuel from a propane tank, make sure the tank has fuel in it, then simply turn on the valve. Immediately light the grill following the manufacturer's instructions, which usually call for pushing the spark igniter to ignite the gas jets. If your gas grill does not have an automatic spark-inducing ignition button, use a long wooden fireplace match or a gas wand

to ignite the gas jets. Turn the knobs to adjust the heat level to high, then close the lid. It is important to light the grill 10 to 15 minutes in advance of cooking so that its lava-rock or ceramic briquette bed or metal baffles have time to heat up fully. Once this has been done, you can adjust the heat elements to the level appropriate for what you are going to grill.

Always turn off the grill after you have finished cooking. First, turn off all of the heat elements, rotisserie motors, and side burners. Then, make sure that the propane or natural gas valve is turned securely to the off position. Clean the grill thoroughly to remove any grease and charred bits of food. After cleaning the grill, and after the grill has cooled down completely, place a protective cover over it or move it to a protected area for storage.

1 Open the grill lid and make sure that the burner controls are turned off. If you are using fuel from a propane tank, make sure the tank has fuel in it. Then, turn the fuel valve on the propane tank so that it is all the way open.

2 Turn on all heat elements to the high heat setting. Light the grill by depressing the automatic spark igniter. If your gas grill does not have an automatic spark igniter, use a long wooden fireplace match or a gas wand to ignite the gas jets.

3 Close the grill lid and let the bed of lava rock, ceramic briquettes, or metal baffles heat until the temperature in the covered grill reaches at least 350°F (180°C). This will take 10 to 15 minutes. When ready to cook, turn the knobs to the desired heat level.

CONTROLLING THE HEAT

As with a charcoal grill, the secret to cooking foods perfectly on a gas-fueled grill lies in regulating the heat properly. Learn this key skill and your food will have juicy, tender interiors and browned and crisped exteriors.

On a gas grill, regulating the heat is simple: Turn the knobs to regulate the heat element underneath the portion of the grill you wish to heat. An added benefit with many gas grills is a built-in thermometer that tells you the temperature inside the covered grill, much like an oven thermometer. If you don't have a thermometer, hold your hand about 4 inches (10 cm) above the fire, or at the point where the food will be cooking. Keep your hand there as long as you can and count. Refer to the times and temperatures in the chart below.

Once you begin cooking, changing the heat level is as easy as adjusting the heat on your kitchen stove. If the food is cooking too fast, turn the heat element down. If you need more heat, turn the heat element up. If you wish to keep foods warm, turn the heat element off; the residual heat will be enough to keep the food at a pleasing temperature.

As you become more familiar with using the gas grill, try building at least two different heat zones by varying the heat level of the burners, and then move the food around on the grill as needed.

To create heat zones in a gas grill, after the grill has preheated for 10 to 15 minutes, turn down the heat in one-third of the fire bed, and turn off the heat in another one-third of the fire bed. You will now have one area with medium to high heat, one area with low or medium heat, and one area with no heat. If your grill has only two heat elements, place already-cooked foods that need to stay warm in a pan positioned near the grill.

HEAT LEVEL	TEMPERATURE	HAND TEST
Very high	450°F (230°C) and higher	less than 1 second
High	400°–450°F (200°–230°C)	1 or 2 seconds
Medium-high	375°–400°F (190°–200°C)	2 or 3 seconds
Medium	350°–375°F (180°–190°C)	3 or 4 seconds
Medium-low	300°–350°F (150°–180°C)	4 or 5 seconds
Low	200°–300°F (95°–150°C)	5 seconds or more

Direct-Heat Grilling with Gas

Grilling directly over the high heat of a gas grill makes quick work of dinner, whether it be steaks or chops, poultry or fish, or even vegetables. If the heat is too high and the food starts to char, simply turn down the heat elements or move the food to a cooler part of the grill.

To set up for direct-heat cooking in a gas grill, turn on all the heat elements to high. The grill rack will be preheated in 10 to 15 minutes. Adjust the heat level to the temperature that is specified in the recipe and place the food directly over the heat elements to cook.

As you become more comfortable with the way your gas grill works, it is a good idea to work with a three-zone fire, creating one area with medium to high heat, one area with low to medium heat, and one area with no heat. This is easy to do on a gas grill: simply reduce one of the heat elements on the preheated grill to medium, and turn the other heat element off. Start foods over the highest heat, move them to the more moderate area as they sear or if flare-ups occur, and then to the area with no heat to keep warm.

If your grill has only two heat elements, turn one of the heat elements to low, then position a foil pan or similar vessel near the grill for keeping foods warm.

For foods you want to cook only on very high heat, such as fish or seafood, arrange the fire into two areas only: one with very high heat, the other with no heat.

If you wish to employ a combination of cooking methods in a gas grill, there is no need for a special setup. Because of the way the gas grill is constructed, it is easy to change the levels of heat whenever you wish. For example, if your food is cooking too fast, or you want to convert from direct-heat grilling to indirect-heat grilling, simply turn the appropriate burner down or off, depending on your needs.

While the grill is heating, make sure the food you are planning to cook is properly prepared and seasoned. Trim excess skin and remove small bones from fish. Trim off most of the external fat from meat and poultry prior to cooking; it can cause flare-ups as it melts and drips into the fire. Cut vegetables into desired shapes and sizes.

Flare-ups caused by melting and dripping fat are common when grilling over direct heat. The best and easiest way to control them is to move the food to a cooler part of the grill.

1 Light the gas grill according to the instructions on page 20. Turn on all the heat elements to high, close the grill lid, and let the grill heat for 10 to 15 minutes.

2 Create two or three heat zones in the grill. For a three-burner grill, turn one heat element to medium and the other off. For a two-burner grill, turn the second burner to medium.

3 Start foods over the highest heat, and move them to a more moderate area as they sear or if flare-ups occur. Keep foods warm over the area with no heat or in a pan set to the side.

Indirect-Heat Grilling with Gas

An indirect-heat fire in a gas grill is ideal for cooking whole birds or roasts. Cooking them on the grill can be even better than roasting them in a conventional oven, especially during the warm-weather months when you want to keep the kitchen cool.

For indirect-heat grilling on a gas grill, one or more of the heat elements is turned off after preheating. The food is placed over the zone with no heat and the grill is covered. Air circulating inside the covered grill mimics an oven and cooks the food. The results are much like what happens when roasting in an oven—juicy, tender flesh and a golden brown exterior—with the added benefit of smoke flavor from the grill.

To create an indirect-heat fire, first preheat the grill using all of the burners, then turn off the burner directly below where the food will sit. Gas grills come with a drip pan to collect the grease. Put the food over the no-heat zone and adjust the burners on either side of the food to provide equal amounts of heat, or to one side of the food if using a two-burner grill. Turning the food or rotating it periodically ensures even cooking.

SMOKING WITH GAS

Indirect-heat cooking goes hand-in-hand with smoking, which infuses food with flavor. Wood chips are the most popular flavoring material to use when smoking, but you can also use a variety of herbs and other aromatics (page 13). Unlike for a charcoal grill, do not soak wood chips, dried herbs, grapevine cuttings, or other aromatics if you are using them in a gas grill, as soaking can hinder their ability to ignite. Add flavoring materials to a smoker box (page 27). Place the box directly over a heat element to ignite the wood chips or aromatics. The smoke will begin to emerge in a few minutes.

If you don't have a smoker box, make a perforated aluminum foil packet to hold the smoking materials (page 27). Place the foil packet directly over a heat element and the smoke will begin to rise in a few minutes.

If you are cooking a roast or whole bird that requires considerable time in a covered grill, replenish the smoker box with flavoring materials, or add new foil packets as needed. When replenishing the smoking materials, take care not to leave the grill cover open for too long or the heat will dissipate.

1 After preheating the grill (page 20), create two heat zones by turning off one heat element. For a three-burner grill, the area with no heat should be in the center.

2 For even cooking, it is a good idea to tie or truss the food into a compact shape before cooking (page 290). Place the food over the area with no heat.

3 Cover the grill and let the food cook in the circulating heat. Check periodically to ensure that it is cooking evenly and is not browning too fast.

Barbecuing

Among American food lovers, the mere mention of the subject of barbecuing can provoke a pretty lively discussion, if not an all-out argument. While many people use the word "barbecuing" interchangeably with "grilling," aficionados are more precise about what they call barbecue.

Southerners in particular may swell up with indignation if they hear the word barbecue applied to anything other than pork (or beef if they are from Texas) cooked long and slow in a smoky fire of hickory, oak, or pecan wood.

When a large, tough cut—such as pork ribs or pork shoulder, beef brisket, or even a whole hog—is cooked for many hours at very low temperatures in savory smoke in a pit roaster, these tough cuts become luscious, velvety, and exquisitely tender. True barbecue lovers patiently await the brisket that slow-roasts overnight, or the pork shoulder pulled into shreds for sandwiches after spending many

hours in a smoky pit. Some will allow pork loin or beef ribs, but other barbecue fanatics would not consider these tender meats that cook in only an hour or two to be true barbecue.

Achieving the results of the professional pitman or the semi-pro barbecue aficionado requires specialized equipment such as a pit roaster or an offset smoker-cooker. However, with attention to temperatures and patient care, a delicious approximation of traditional Southern barbecue can be achieved in an ordinary charcoal grill or gas grill. For the purposes of this cookbook, we will define barbecuing as cooking food slowly over a

low- to medium low–heat indirect fire with the grill's lid closed, using wood chips or chunks to create smoke.

The basic strategy is to use a small number of coals (or the temperature dial of your gas grill) to create a low fire and to monitor the temperature with a thermometer, adding coals as needed to keep the heat level consistent. A drip pan filled with water helps keep the environment inside the grill moist, while wood chips supply the smoke. The meat may be seasoned with a rub, marinated, brined, or mopped with sauce during cooking, or some combination of these flavoring techniques may be used. Cuts that need to cook for several hours may be wrapped in foil for part of the cooking to prevent them from drying out. This helps ensure flavorful, tender meat without the extra low temperatures and long cooking times required for traditional barbecue.

1 After arranging a small number of hot coals on either side of the fire bed with tongs, place a drip pan in the center and fill it with water. This will keep the food moist as it cooks.

2 To create fragrant smoke to imbue your barbecue with flavor, sprinkle soaked, drained hickory wood chips or chunks directly onto the hot coals. Keep extra chips on hand.

3 Replace the grate, positioning its hinged sides over the coals, and place the food to be barbecued in the center, directly over the drip pan. Cover the grill.

BARBECUING WITH CHARCOAL

The first step to barbecuing in a charcoal grill is to set up the grill for cooking over indirect heat at low to medium-low temperatures (page 19; *right*). This means you will either arrange a relatively small number of hot coals from a chimney starter into two piles on either side of the grill, or rake the coals into piles once they are hot and ashy if you are using starter fluid. After the coals are arranged, place a drip pan in the center of the fire bed and fill it with water. This will keep the environment inside the grill moist. Have ready at hand an instant-read thermometer, preferably with a long probe, a specialized grill thermometer, or an oven thermometer. For the best barbecue results, the temperature inside the grill should remain constant and on the low side of its range. You will need to add coals and wood chips during cooking to maintain a constant heat level and source of smoke inside the grill.

Using a Chimney Starter for Barbecue

The best way to start a fire for slow-cooking food is with a chimney starter. The cylinder of a large (5-quart/5-l) chimney starter can serve as a measuring cup for coals to create the right heat level. To start a low fire, fill the chimney one-quarter of the way up with briquettes. You will need approximately 20 briquettes. For a medium-low fire, fill the chimney a scant halfway up. You will need about 45 coals.

The chimney can also be used to start new coals to replenish the fire. While adding unlit coals is easier, there is a time lag before the coals ignite and raise the temperature. Adding hot coals will keep the temperature inside the grill even. While barbecuing, maintain a supply of hot coals in a chimney starter kept in another grill or on a stone or cement surface. Use tongs to handle hot coals.

HEAT LEVEL	TEMPERATURE	BRIQUETTE COUNT
Very high	450°F (230°C) and higher	1 1/2 large chimneys (145 coals)
High	400°–450°F (200°–230°C)	1 1/4 large chimneys (110 coals)
Medium-high	375°–400°F (190°–200°C)	1 large chimney (about 90 coals)
Medium	350°–375°F (180°–190°C)	3/4 large chimney (about 65 coals)
Medium-low	300°–350°F (150°–180°C)	1/2 large chimney (about 45 coals)
Low	200°–300°F (95°–150°C)	1/4 large chimney (about 20 coals)

Smoking with Charcoal

Most barbecue recipes call for adding flavor with smoke. Soak hardwood chips for at least 1/2 hour before starting the fire and wood chunks for at least 1 hour. When your coals reach the white ash stage, add the chunks or chips directly onto the hot coals. Keep more wood chips on hand, soaking, to replenish the smoke source as needed.

Controlling the Heat

Once the coals and any wood chips or chunks are in place, replace the rack with the handles over the coals and place the food to be cooked over the drip pan. Cover the grill and check the temperature. It should be between 200° and 325°F (95° and 165°C) for barbecuing.

Newer-model kettle grills come with a built-in temperature gauge, but some of these are wildly inaccurate. Most are placed in the top of the unit, and since hot air rises they are in fact gauging the hottest part of the grill. The temperature can vary greatly between this part of the grill and the rack where your food is located. Some home barbecue cooks use a candy thermometer with a long probe that is inserted into a top vent to get a better idea of the temperature inside the grill. You can also use an oven thermometer, which you can place on the grate next to the meat and check each time you replenish the wood or add more coals. Try not to open the lid more than is necessary while barbecuing, since this causes the temperature to fluctuate.

Plan to stoke the fire with soaked wood chips or chunks about every half hour and to replenish the fire with coals every hour or so. If you plan to do much barbecuing, buy a hinged grill rack that flips up on both sides. This makes it much easier to add more coals.

As the fire burns down, add more briquettes, a few at a time—use hot coals from a chimney for the best results—and more wood chips.

In addition to adding hot coals, you can maintain the ideal temperature range in your grill by adjusting the dampers and vents on the bottom and top of your kettle grill. The dampers and vents should be open when you start the fire. Partially closing the dampers and vents will starve the fire and cool it down. If you check the temperature and find it is too high, close all but one of the bottom dampers and all but one of the top vents. Position the open dampers and vents opposite each other so that smoke will be drawn across the meat in the center. Wait a few minutes and check the temperature again. If it is too low, open some of the dampers and vents. With practice, you'll learn to regulate the heat and smoke levels throughout the cooking period.

1 Check the temperature inside the grill when first adding food and every 45 minutes or so thereafter. The temperature should remain as constant as possible.

2 When the temperature starts to drop too low, add more coals. Keep a supply of hot coals burning in a chimney starter, and add just a few at a time to keep the temperature steady.

3 You can also control the heat level inside the grill using the vents and dampers. Open the vents for more oxygen and a hotter fire, or close them partially to lower the temperature.

BARBECUING WITH GAS

Gas grills have advantages as well as disadvantages when it comes to barbecuing. The advantage is that you can regulate the heat level with a turn of the dial; the downside is that it is often difficult to maintain the low temperatures recommended for low, slow barbecue in a gas grill—and if you succeed in getting the burners turned down low enough, it's hard to keep the wood chips smoking long enough to add much flavor. But with a little care, very tasty barbecue can be prepared in a gas grill.

To barbecue successfully in a gas grill, prepare the grill for indirect cooking over low to medium-low heat by turning two burners on low or medium-low and leaving the central burner unlit. Place a drip pan under the unheated portion of the grill, fill it with water, replace the grate, and place the meat directly above the drip pan. As in a charcoal grill, meat will be seasoned with a rub, marinade, brine, and/or sauce; sometimes wrapped for part of the cooking time in heavy-duty foil to prevent drying; and roasted at low heat levels for up to several hours.

Smoking with Gas

If you have a smoker box attached to your gas grill (recommended if you like smoke flavors), put dry hardwood chips in the box. If the smoker box has a water well, fill it with water. You can also purchase stand-alone smoker boxes. If you do not have a smoker box, make a foil packet by spreading out a rectangle of heavy-duty foil and placing a handful of dry hardwood chips in the center. Fold and seal the foil and use the tip of a knife to cut an X in the top of the packet and peel back the edges, or puncture the top and bottom of the packet in 5 or 10 places. Place the foil pack directly on top of one of the burners. A trick to get the dry wood chips smoking in a gas grill is to preheat the grill on high heat with dry chips in the smoker box or foil packet. Leave the lid up on the smoker box to help the chips to ignite quickly. When the smoke starts to billow up, close the lid on the smoker box, turn the heat down to low, and add the meat to the unlit center over a pan half filled with water. Replace the chips in the smoker box or add other foil packets as needed during cooking. If you like, you can top your ignited dry wood chips with a small handful of soaked chips for additional smoke.

Controlling the Heat

To maintain low to medium-low heat in a gas grill, check the thermometer often as the meat cooks and adjust the burner dials as needed.

1 To add smoke flavor on a gas grill, enclose dry hickory chips in a smoker box and heat it on a burner. Some grills feature an attached smoker box with a water well.

2 If you don't have a smoker box, you can create a makeshift one from aluminum foil Fold a rectangle of foil in half and place the dry chips in the center.

3 Seal the 3 open sides and tear open the top. Place the packet on a burner and heat until the chips ignite. Once lit, you can top the dry chips with soaked ones for extra smoke.

Rotisserie Grilling

Rotisserie grilling, or spit-roasting, is a popular way to cook large items of food such as roasts and whole birds. A rotisserie is available as an attachable accessory for most gas grills and for some charcoal grills. Look for a rotisserie attachment in a store that sells grilling supplies.

A rotisserie consists of a large spit that, powered by an electric motor, slowly rotates at a constant speed above the fire bed. Held securely in place with adjustable pronged forks that clamp firmly to the spit, a large roast or whole bird will cook slowly and evenly on a rotisserie. When shopping for a rotisserie, look for a model with a strong, reliable motor and sturdy counterweight system.

The key to using a rotisserie is to balance food as evenly as possible on the spit. If the food is not well balanced, the motor will strain and jerk, resulting in uneven cooking, lost juices, and undue stress to the motor. Most rotisseries come with a counterweight system that can be adjusted to compensate for the awkward shape of certain foods.

To cook foods on a rotisserie, first prepare a charcoal or gas fire for indirect-heat cooking (page 19 or 23). Use sturdy cotton or linen kitchen string to truss whole poultry (page 290) or to tie roasts into compact shapes. Following the manufacturer's instructions or the directions below, thread the food onto the spit. Place the spit in the rotisserie mechanism according to the manufacturer's instructions (this will vary considerably depending on the type and brand of the grill) and position the food over the drip pan, if using charcoal. Turn on the rotisserie motor, cover the grill, and cook the food according to the recipe or until done to your liking.

Be sure to check the food with an instant-read thermometer, or cut into it to check for doneness. For poultry, the bird is done when the juices run clear when the thickest part of the thigh is pierced with a knife. For red meat, it will appear pinkish-red to grayish brown when cut into, depending on whether you prefer medium-rare or medium-well meat, respectively.

If desired, baste the food occasionally using basting sauces or drippings from the pan, although the turning motion self-bastes the food as it grills.

Many foods that are cooked over indirect heat can also be cooked on a rotisserie. The timing will be about the same.

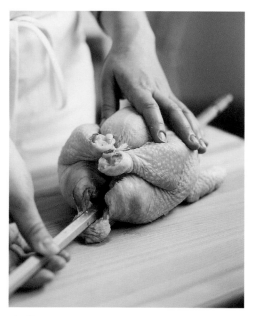

1 Thread a trussed bird onto the spit through the cavity. Pierce a leg of lamb or roast with the sharp end of the spit and carefully push it through the center of the meat.

2 Insert the prongs of the fork nearest the handle securely into the meaty parts of the food. Carefully center the food on the spit and twist the nut on the fork to secure it.

3 Thread the second pronged fork onto the spit and insert the prongs securely into the meaty parts of the food on the opposite end. Twist the nut on the fork to secure it.

Safety Issues

GRILL SAFETY

Cooking with fire, whether with a charcoal or gas grill, can be a dangerous sport. Follow these guidelines for safe outdoor cooking:

■ Never spray starter fluid, oil, or another flammable liquid on already-lit charcoal.

■ From the moment you ignite the charcoal to the moment you dispose of the cooled ashes, never leave your grill unwatched or unattended.

■ Always keep children and pets safely away from the grill.

■ Do not wear loose clothing when grilling, and tie back long hair.

■ Always use your grill in the open air on a level surface, well clear of enclosures, overhangs, or anything combustible.

■ Use only fire starters specifically designed for grill use and store them in a safe, secure place away from the grill. Never store any combustible fuels, such as kerosene or gasoline, anywhere near an outdoor grill.

■ Do not use chimney or electric-coil starters with self-igniting briquettes.

■ If using a chimney starter, as soon as the coals have been poured into the fire bed, remove it and place it on a fireproof surface, well clear of anything flammable or of anyone who might touch it, until it cools completely.

■ Take care when using a spray bottle to control flare-ups, as the steam created from the water can cause burns. Instead, squelch flare-ups by moving the food to a cooler spot on the grill or covering the grill until the flames subside.

■ Keep a fire extinguisher and a water hose handy in case of a threatening fire.

FOOD SAFETY

Grilling goes hand in hand with warm summer weather. Unfortunately, so do food-borne illnesses. But the risk is present year-round. To guard against them, keep the following guidelines in mind:

■ If the food you plan to cook is frozen, thaw it completely in the refrigerator or microwave, not at room temperature. Uncooked food should never sit out for more than 2 hours, or 1 hour during hot weather.

■ Check sell-by and use-by dates on food packaging. Throw out anything that looks or smells in any way suspicious.

■ Always wash your hands with plenty of warm, soapy water, especially before and after handling raw meat, poultry, or seafood.

■ Do not return cooked foods to the unwashed platter or plates on which they sat when raw, especially if they were soaking in a marinade. If you are basting with a marinade in which raw food sat, bring the liquid to a boil in a saucepan for 2 minutes before using, or stop using the basting liquid at least 5 minutes before finishing cooking.

■ Using hot, soapy water, wash and rinse brushes that were used on raw food before using them on cooked food.

■ Purchase a high-quality instant-read thermometer to measure internal temperatures of grilled food. Follow suggested temperatures to be sure any bacteria has been killed.

■ Cool all hot items completely before refrigerating. A hot sauce in the refrigerator could cause the temperature inside to rise to a level that encourages bacteria to grow in other stored items.

Starters

About Starters

Use the grill to create delicious appetizers and first courses while the main dish cooks. The smoky flavors and aromas of the grill stimulate appetites and ready guests' palates for the main dish to come. And, cooking starters on the grill keeps the kitchen cool on warm summer evenings.

Whenever guests gather for a grilled meal, their appetites are heightened the moment they catch their first whiff of smoke rising from the fire. The best way to appease their hunger while you finish cooking the main course is to offer up some tasty grilled starters to launch the feast.

Smoky grilled vegetable- or cheese-based dips, spreads, and toppings are good vehicles for the irresistible aroma and flavor of the grill. Bread, polenta, and pizza take beautifully to the fire, too, all of them benefitting from the unique flavor and texture that the grill delivers.

Crisp, juicy chicken wings and tender satay are standard backyard fare, longstanding crowd pleasers that guests recognize and consume quickly. But other less common candidates for the grill, such as delicately breaded crab cakes and spice-rubbed sea scallops, are no less successful when treated to the natural wonders of a smoky fire.

The secret to cooking more than one course on the same grill is to create heat zones. A three-level fire in a charcoal grill (page 18), or a gas grill with two or more burners turned on, makes a versatile stage for cooking different elements of the meal. Here is how to use that stage effectively.

If you are cooking a whole turkey or other large item over indirect heat, a time-consuming process, quickly lift the grill cover and sneak an appetizer over the hottest part of the grill while the bird finishes cooking. When the appetizer is done, use its vacated space to cook vegetables or other side dishes.

If you are cooking steaks, chops, or thin cuts of poultry over direct heat, use high heat to sear and brand them with grill marks, then move the items to a cooler part of the grill and quickly grill the appetizers over the now-free high heat. Finish cooking the main course over high heat while your guests are enjoying the appetizers.

When you're planning the menu, keep in mind mood, color, flavor, and texture, and try to strike a balance among these elements. Pair elegant appetizers with upscale main dishes. Or choose a casual finger food to begin a backyard barbecue. Pay attention to temperatures, too. For example, keep salad greens very cold and serve on chilled plates, then top them with a hot grilled morsel. The contrast is very appealing.

Improvising Starters

Don't feel limited to opening your meal with only the recipes in this chapter. Many additional ideas for starters can be found in the other chapters of the book. Cut into a different shape or served in smaller portions, the following recipes can be transformed into wonderful appetizers.

Beef

Steak Chimichurri (page 62), cut into cubes, skewered onto toothpicks, and served with the extra *chimichurri* as a dipping sauce

Steak au Poivre (page 64), seared rare, thinly sliced, and served with a baby greens salad

Stuffed Flank Steak (page 73), placed on a platter and served as part of an appetizer buffet

Caper-Rosemary Sirloin (page 80), thinly sliced and served on grilled bread

Sirloin with Thai Flavors (page 81), cut into strips and served with an extra portion of the marinade made specifically to be a dipping sauce

Alehouse Beef-and-Potato Skewers (page 82)

The Best Burger (page 87) made into miniatures

Herbed Tenderloin with a Trio of Summer Sauces (page 89), with the beef thinly sliced and served on crostini

Korean-Style Short Ribs (page 90)

Creole Smoked Beef Ribs (page 273), cut into bite-sized sections

Lamb

Rib chops held by the bone with fingertips for easy eating

Skewers of *Souvlakia* (page 116) with *tzatziki* for dipping

Moroccan-Spiced Lamb Burgers (page 119), made into miniatures, placed on a platter, and served with toothpicks for easy handling

Pork

Marinated Pork Tenderloins (page 148), thinly sliced and served warm with a dipping sauce

Sesame-Hoisin Baby Back Ribs (page 151)

Grilled sausages, cut into pieces and served with toothpicks for easy handling

Poultry

Hickory Grill-Smoked Chicken (page 162), the breast carved off the bone into thin slices

Asian Chicken Salad (page 178)

Turkey Burgers (page 188), made into miniatures, with cranberry relish as an accompaniment

Orange-Glazed Duck Breasts (page 191), thinly sliced and served on *crostini* with orange sections

Tea-Smoked Duck Breasts (page 192), cut into chunks, speared onto toothpicks, and served with *Sweet and Sour Sauce* (page 287) for dipping

Seafood

Salmon Burgers (page 211), made into miniatures

Chunks of *Plank-Grilled Salmon* (page 214), with the dill sauce for dipping

Grill-Smoked Salmon (page 217) set on a buffet with lemon slices, capers, finely chopped red onion, the horseradish sauce, and miniature bagels

Swordfish Kabobs with Romesco Sauce (page 219)

Cilantro Pesto Shrimp (page 226), served with toothpicks for easy handling

Shrimp and Scallop Skewers (page 227)

Barbecued Oysters (page 230)

Grill-Roasted Mussels (page 231)

Vegetables

Mixed Grill of Summer Vegetables (page 236) with the finishing sauce described in the head note used for dipping

Mixed Grill of Winter Vegetables (page 239), cut into bite-sized pieces and served with aioli for dipping

Grilled asparagus (page 241 or 242) with aioli for dipping

Ginger-Soy Eggplant (page 248), cut into bite-sized pieces and threaded on skewers before grilling

Fennel and Orange Salad (page 250) divided among individual plates and offered as a first course

Honey-Lime Sweet Potatoes (page 252)

Balsamic Portobello Steaks (page 253)

Smoky Potatoes with Cumin Rub (page 258), served with the sour cream-based companion sauce for dipping

Grill-Roasted Red Pepper and Garlic Dip

6 large cloves garlic, peeled but left whole

3 tablespoons olive oil

3 red bell peppers (capsicums)

3 tablespoons fresh lemon juice

1½ teaspoons sweet paprika

½ teaspoon ground coriander

Salt and freshly ground pepper

1 crustless slice coarse country bread, 2 by 2½ by 1 inch (5 by 6 by 2.5 cm), torn into small pieces

1 English (hothouse) cucumber, peeled if desired and cut crosswise into thirds, then pieces quartered lengthwise

1 fennel bulb, trimmed and cut lengthwise into slices ½ inch (12 mm) thick

4 carrots, peeled and thickly sliced on the diagonal

MAKES ABOUT 2 CUPS
(16 FL OZ/500 ML) DIP;
6 SERVINGS

Prepare a CHARCOAL or GAS grill for DIRECT grilling over MEDIUM-HIGH heat (page 18 or 22). Oil the grill rack. Slide the garlic cloves, spacing them slightly apart, onto a metal skewer. Brush with 1 teaspoon of the oil.

CHARCOAL: Place the bell peppers and skewered garlic on the grill rack over the hottest part of the fire. Cover the grill. Cook the garlic, turning it once, until the cloves are browned, about 2½ minutes per side. Cook the peppers, rotating them as necessary, until the skin chars and blisters evenly, 15–20 minutes.

GAS: Place the bell peppers and the skewered garlic on the grill rack directly over the heat elements. Cover the grill. Cook the garlic, turning it once, until the cloves are browned, about 2½ minutes per side. Cook the peppers, rotating them as necessary, until the skin chars and blisters evenly, 15–20 minutes.

While the peppers are still hot, slip them into a paper bag, seal the top, and let steam for 5 minutes. Then, remove the peppers from the bag and, using your fingers or a paring knife, peel away the skin. Cut off the stem and remove and discard the seeds. Coarsely chop the peppers. Slide the garlic off the skewer and coarsely chop.

In a food processor, combine the bell peppers, garlic, lemon juice, the remaining 2 tablespoons plus 2 teaspoons olive oil, the paprika, coriander, 1 teaspoon salt, and ½ teaspoon ground pepper. Using pulses, process briefly. Add the torn bread and process, stopping once or twice to scrape down the sides of the work bowl, until thick and smooth. Transfer to a bowl and let stand at room temperature for 1 hour to develop the flavors. Adjust the seasoning with salt and pepper.

Serve the dip accompanied with the cucumber, fennel, and carrots for dipping.

This flavorful blend is also delicious for dipping grilled shrimp or for spreading on grilled fish or chicken. Grilling the garlic mellows its bite, making for addictive eating. Use the grill-roasted garlic on its own as an easy spread for grilled bread or to embellish flavored butter (page 289) or grilled poultry or vegetables.

Charred-Tomato Bruschetta

1 lb (500 g) ripe tomatoes

18 baguette slices, about ¹/₄ inch (6 mm) thick

¹/₃ cup (3 fl oz/80 ml) olive oil

3 tablespoons finely chopped fresh basil, plus whole leaves for garnish

2 teaspoons balsamic vinegar

1 clove garlic, minced

Salt and freshly ground pepper

MAKES 18 TOASTS; 6 SERVINGS

Prepare a CHARCOAL or GAS grill for DIRECT grilling over MEDIUM-HIGH heat (page 18 or 22). Brush the tomatoes and bread slices lightly and evenly with the oil.

CHARCOAL: Grill the tomatoes over the hottest part of the fire, turning often, until charred on all sides and starting to soften, 5–8 minutes. Transfer to a cutting board. Grill the bread slices, turning once, until crisp and lightly branded with grill marks, 3–4 minutes total.

GAS: Grill the tomatoes directly over the heat elements, turning often, until charred on all sides and starting to soften, 5–8 minutes. Transfer to a cutting board. Grill the bread slices, turning once, until crisp and lightly branded with grill marks, 3–4 minutes total.

Core the tomatoes, then chop them and their charred peels. Transfer to a bowl. Stir in the chopped basil, vinegar, garlic, and salt and pepper to taste. Let stand for 30–60 minutes to develop the flavors.

Top the bread slices with the tomatoes and garnish with basil leaves.

The crisp Italian-style toast known as *bruschetta* is never better than when the toasting is done on the grill. Prepare the zesty topping in advance, and you will have something you can quickly assemble for guests to nibble while the rest of the meal cooks on the grill.

Spiced Eggplant Dip

Eggplant's neutral nature makes it a fine foil for the lively seasonings of Morocco and the smoke of the grill. Serve the dip with grilled pita bread triangles.

Prepare a CHARCOAL or GAS grill for DIRECT grilling over HIGH heat (page 18 or 22). Brush the eggplant slices evenly on both sides with 4 tablespoons (2 fl oz/60 ml) of the oil.

CHARCOAL: Grill the eggplant slices over the hottest part of the fire, turning once, until tender, about 5 minutes per side.

GAS: Grill the eggplant slices directly over the heat elements, turning once, until tender, about 5 minutes per side.

Transfer the eggplant to a cutting board, stacking the slices. Let them steam until cool. Chop the eggplant.

In a food processor, combine the eggplant, tomato, lemon juice, the remaining 2 tablespoons oil, the garlic, cinnamon, cumin, pepper flakes, and salt and pepper to taste. Process until fairly smooth. (Bits of peel will remain.) Cover and let stand at room temperature for 1 hour to develop the flavors, then serve.

2 lb (1 kg) eggplant (aubergine), cut into slices 1 inch (2.5 cm) thick

6 tablespoons (3 fl oz/90 ml) olive oil

1 cup chopped tomato

3 tablespoons lemon juice

2 cloves garlic, chopped

$3/4$ teaspoon cinnamon

$1/2$ teaspoon each ground cumin and red pepper flakes

Salt and black pepper

MAKES ABOUT 3 CUPS (24 FL OZ/ 750 ML) DIP; 8 SERVINGS

Mint-and-Cumin Chicken Satay

For the Peanut Sauce

1 cup (10 oz/315 g) creamy peanut butter

$^2/_3$ cup (5 fl oz/150 ml) chicken broth

$^1/_3$ cup (3 fl oz/80 ml) fresh orange juice

2 tablespoons soy sauce

1 tablespoon fresh lemon juice

$^1/_2$ teaspoon Asian sesame oil

3 cloves garlic, chopped

1 tablespoon peeled and minced fresh ginger

1 small habanero or jalapeño chile, seeded and chopped

3 tablespoons chopped fresh mint

2 tablespoons finely chopped fresh mint

1 tablespoon ground cumin

$^1/_4$ teaspoon ground cayenne pepper

Salt and freshly ground black pepper

2 lb (1 kg) boneless, skinless chicken breasts, cut lengthwise into 30 strips $^1/_2$ inch (12 mm) wide and longest strips halved crosswise

30 long bamboo skewers, soaked (page 10)

MAKES 6–8 SERVINGS

To make the peanut sauce, in a food processor, combine the peanut butter, broth, orange juice, soy sauce, lemon juice, sesame oil, garlic, ginger, and chile. Process, stopping several times to scrape down the sides of the work bowl, until smooth. Let stand at room temperature for 1 hour, or cover and refrigerate for up to 24 hours to develop the flavors. If refrigerated, return to room temperature. Stir in the chopped mint just before serving.

In a small bowl, stir together the finely chopped mint, cumin, cayenne pepper, and $^1/_4$ teaspoon each salt and black pepper. Weave the chicken strips lengthwise onto the skewers. Sprinkle the chicken with the mint-cumin mixture, patting it into the meat.

Prepare a CHARCOAL or GAS grill for DIRECT grilling over MEDIUM-HIGH heat (page 18 or 22). Oil the grill rack.

CHARCOAL: Grill the skewers over the hottest part of the fire, turning once or twice, until the chicken is lightly marked by the grill and opaque throughout but still moist, about 4 minutes total.

GAS: Grill the skewers directly over the heat elements, turning once or twice, until the chicken is lightly marked by the grill and opaque throughout but still moist, about 4 minutes total.

Arrange the skewers on a serving platter. Drizzle the chicken with some of the peanut sauce. Serve immediately with the remaining sauce on the side.

Traditional Indonesian satay, skewered chicken strips grilled and served with a peanut dipping sauce, is the inspiration for this recipe. But this starter heads to the eastern Mediterranean and the Caribbean for its bold seasonings, proving the universal appeal of the dish.

Pomegranate Chicken Wings

**2 cups (16 oz/500 g)
plain yogurt**

2 tablespoons lemon juice

2 tablespoons olive oil

**4 teaspoons finely chopped
fresh oregano**

2 cloves garlic, minced

Salt and ground pepper

**24 chicken drumettes, about
3 lb (1.5 kg), rinsed and dried**

**1 bottle (10 oz/315 g)
pomegranate molasses**

MAKES 6 SERVINGS

Set a fine-mesh sieve over a bowl. Pour in the yogurt and let drain for 1 hour. Discard the whey in the bowl. Turn the thickened, drained yogurt into the bowl and stir in the lemon juice, oil, oregano, garlic, a pinch of salt, and a generous grinding of pepper. Cover and let stand at room temperature for 1 hour.

Prepare a CHARCOAL or GAS grill for DIRECT grilling over MEDIUM heat (page 18 or 22). Oil the grill rack.

CHARCOAL: Grill the drumettes over the hottest part of the fire, turning them every 3–4 minutes and brushing them with the molasses after the first 10 minutes, until tender and glazed, 20–25 minutes.

GAS: Place the drumettes directly over the heat elements, turning them every 3–4 minutes and brushing them with the molasses after the first 10 minutes, until tender and glazed, 20–25 minutes.

Arrange the drumettes on a platter and season lightly with salt and pepper. Serve at once, accompanied with the yogurt sauce for dipping.

Here is an unusual, but tasty, Middle Eastern–inspired recipe for chicken wings, featuring pomegranate molasses. The ruby-colored juice of the pomegranate, boiled down to a thick syrup, has a berrylike tartness that is unique. The meatier third segments of chicken wings are often sold separately; usually labeled "drumettes," they are the best choice here.

Grilled Bread Salad

This appealing hot-weather dish will recall several bread-based salad cousins (*panzanella* in Italy, *fattoush* in Egypt) while adding the extra flavor of the grill. The bread chunks function like oversize croutons, soaking up the tangy dressing and the tomatoes' juices while providing starchy contrast to the crisp vegetables and salty olives. Chopped fresh mint makes a good addition.

Prepare a CHARCOAL or GAS grill for DIRECT grilling over MEDIUM-HIGH heat (page 18 or 22). Brush the bread on both sides with half of the oil.

CHARCOAL: Grill the bread over the hottest part of the fire, turning once, until toasted, 8–10 minutes total.

GAS: Grill the bread directly over the heat elements, turning once, until toasted, 8–10 minutes total.

Remove the bread slices from the grill and, while still hot, rub them on both sides with the halved garlic clove; set aside. Thinly slice the cucumber and onion. Cut each tomato into 8 wedges. In a bowl, combine the tomatoes, cucumber, onion, vinegar, the remaining oil, 3/4 teaspoon salt, and a grinding of pepper. Let stand, stirring occasionally, until juicy.

Cut the bread into 3/4-inch (2-cm) cubes. Crumble the feta. Add the bread to the salad and toss well. Add the olives, feta, and pepper to taste and toss gently. Serve immediately.

3 slices coarse white bread

2/3 cup (5 fl oz/150 ml) olive oil

1 clove garlic, halved

1/2 cucumber, peeled

1 small red onion, halved

1 1/2 lb (750 g) tomatoes

1/4 cup (2 fl oz/60 ml) balsamic vinegar

Salt and ground pepper

5 oz (155 g) feta cheese

3/4 cup (4 oz/125 g) olives

MAKES 6 SERVINGS

Grilled Polenta with Fennel Salad

For this recipe, polenta is cooked, spread in a pan to cool and firm up, and then cut into triangles and grilled. The cornmeal becomes a crisp, golden counterpoint to a cool and crunchy fennel salad. You can also use the grilled polenta triangles as a base for savory toppings, such as sautéed mushrooms, melted Gorgonzola cheese, or the charred tomato topping for *bruschetta* on page 36.

To make the polenta, measure the cornmeal and place in a deep saucepan. Gradually whisk in the water. Whisk in 1¼ teaspoons salt. Place over medium heat and bring to a simmer, whisking often. Reduce the heat to low and cover partially. Cook at a very slow simmer, stirring often, until the polenta is very thick and pulls away from the sides of the pan, about 25 minutes. Remove from the heat and season generously with pepper.

Lightly brush an 8-inch (20-cm) square baking pan with oil. Spoon the hot polenta into the pan and smooth it evenly to the edges with the back of a spoon dipped in water to ease spreading. Let cool completely, cover, and refrigerate for about 24 hours.

Invert the pan of polenta onto a cutting board and rap the bottom to release the polenta. With a long knife, trim the edges even. Cut into 4 squares, then cut each square in half on the diagonal, making 8 triangles. Pat dry with paper towels.

To make the fennel salad, trim off the stalks and fronds from the fennel bulbs. Finely chop and reserve 2 tablespoons of the fronds. Trim away any bruised outer layers from the bulbs. Using a mandoline, sharp knife, or a box grater-shredder with a slicing blade, thinly shave the fennel bulbs and then the onion.

In a bowl, toss together the fennel, onion, olives, reserved fennel fronds, vinegar, oil, sugar, and ¼ teaspoon salt. Season generously with pepper.

Prepare a CHARCOAL or GAS grill for DIRECT grilling over MEDIUM-HIGH heat (page 18 or 22). Oil the grill rack. Brush the polenta triangles lightly all over with oil.

CHARCOAL: Grill the polenta triangles over the hottest part of the fire, carefully turning once with a large spatula, until crisp and well branded with grill marks on both sides, about 5 minutes per side.

GAS: Grill the polenta triangles directly over the heat elements, carefully turning once with a large spatula, until crisp and well branded with grill marks on both sides, about 5 minutes per side.

Place 1 triangle on each small individual plate. Spoon the fennel salad over or alongside the polenta triangles, dividing it evenly. Serve immediately.

For the Polenta

1½ cups (7½ oz/235 g) polenta or yellow cornmeal

4 cups (32 fl oz/1 l) water

Salt and freshly ground pepper

Olive oil for brushing

For the Fennel Salad

2 small fennel bulbs

1 small red onion

⅔ cup (3½ oz/105 g) coarsely chopped, pitted Kalamata olives

3 tablespoons red wine vinegar

3 tablespoons olive oil

½ teaspoon sugar

Salt and freshly ground pepper

MAKES 8 SERVINGS

Smoky Sea Scallops with Avocado-Corn Salsa

For the Avocado-Corn Salsa

2 ears corn, grilled (page 244)

2 ripe avocados, halved, pitted, peeled, and chopped

1 yellow onion, minced

1 tomato, peeled, seeded, and coarsely chopped

1 jalapeño chile, seeded and chopped

2 cloves garlic, minced

$^1/_3$ cup ($^1/_2$ oz/15 g) chopped fresh cilantro (fresh coriander)

3 tablespoons fresh lime juice

Salt

2 canned chipotle chiles in adobo sauce, mashed

1 cup ($1^1/_2$ oz/45 g) chopped fresh cilantro (fresh coriander)

$^1/_3$ cup (3 fl oz/80 ml) fresh orange or lime juice

1 teaspoon ground cumin

Garlic powder

Salt

2 lb (1 kg) sea scallops, side muscle removed

Vegetable oil for brushing

3 cups plum, peach, or cherry wood chips, soaked if using charcoal (page 13)

MAKES 6 SERVINGS

To make the avocado-corn salsa, steady the stalk end of 1 ear of corn on a cutting board. Using a sharp knife, cut down along the cob to strip off the kernels, rotating the cob a quarter turn with each cut. Put the corn kernels in a bowl and repeat with the second ear. Add the avocados, onion, tomato, jalapeño chile, garlic, and cilantro to the corn and toss to mix. Add the lime juice, mix well, and season to taste with salt. Cover lightly and refrigerate until ready to serve; the salsa can be made several hours in advance. Toss again just before serving.

In a bowl, stir together the chipotle chiles, cilantro, orange juice, cumin, and garlic powder and salt to taste.

Brush the scallops on both sides with the oil and then rub with the chipotle mixture. Cover and refrigerate for 30 minutes.

Prepare a CHARCOAL or GAS grill for DIRECT grilling over MEDIUM-HIGH heat (page 18 and 22). Oil the grill rack or a fish- or vegetable-grilling basket.

CHARCOAL: Sprinkle the wood chips on the coals. Arrange the scallops on the rack or in the basket over the hottest part of the fire. Cook the scallops, turning once, until they are opaque throughout but still moist in the center when tested with a knife, 4–5 minutes per side.

GAS: Put the wood chips in a smoker box or perforated foil packet (page 10). Arrange the scallops on the rack or in the basket directly over the heat elements. Cover the grill and cook the scallops, turning once, until they are opaque throughout but still moist in the center when tested with a knife, 4–5 minutes per side.

Divide the scallops evenly among warmed individual plates and place a spoonful of the salsa alongside. Serve immediately.

Scallops are available year-round, but the supply is more plentiful in the summer, when the corn for the hot-weather salsa that accompanies them here is also abundant. Chipotle chiles, which are smoked dried jalapeños, are commonly available packed in cans in a vinegary chile sauce called adobo. They will add a pleasantly piquant and smoky accent to summertime's plump grilled scallops.

Pizza with Bacon and Tomatoes

Grilling pizza produces a deliciously smoky effect, similar to that of pizza baked in a wood-burning oven. Once you've mastered the basic technique, feel free to improvise your own adventurous topping combinations.

To make the dough, in a large bowl, whisk together the water and yeast. Let stand until foamy, about 5 minutes. Whisk in 1 cup (5 oz/155 g) of the flour and the salt. Stir in enough flour, about 2 cups (10 oz/315 g), to form a sticky dough. Turn the dough out onto a well-floured work surface and knead, adding more flour as needed, until smooth and satiny, about 5 minutes. Put 1 tablespoon oil in each of 2 bowls. Cut the dough in half, shape each into a ball, and put 1 ball in each bowl. Turn the dough to coat with oil and cover each bowl with a kitchen towel. Let rise at room temperature until doubled in bulk, about 2 hours.

Prepare a CHARCOAL or GAS grill for INDIRECT grilling over HIGH heat (page 19 or 23). Oil the grill rack.

Brush a work surface with the remaining 1 tablespoon oil. Transfer 1 dough ball to the oiled surface and pat and stretch the dough into a round about 12 inches (30 cm) in diameter. Transfer the dough to a baker's peel that has been lightly dusted with cornmeal.

CHARCOAL: Slide the pizza off the peel onto the grill rack away from the fire. Cook until the bottom of the crust is lightly marked by the grill but not crisp, 4–6 minutes. Using 2 spatulas, turn the crust grilled-side up. Working quickly, sprinkle half of the cheese over the crust. Scatter half of the bacon and half of the tomatoes over the cheese, then sprinkle half of the basil evenly over the top. Cook, rotating once or twice, until the cheese is melted and the crust is crisp and brown at the edges, 8–10 minutes longer.

GAS: Slide the pizza off the peel onto the grill rack away from the heat elements. Cook until the bottom of the crust is lightly marked by the grill but not crisp, 4–6 minutes. Using 2 spatulas, turn the crust grilled-side up. Working quickly, sprinkle half of the cheese over the crust. Scatter half of the bacon and half of the tomatoes over the cheese, then sprinkle half of the basil evenly over the top. Cook, rotating once or twice, until the cheese is melted and the crust is crisp and brown at the edges, 8–10 minutes longer.

Transfer the pizza to a cutting board, cut into wedges or squares, and serve at once. Repeat with the remaining ingredients to make a second pizza.

For the Dough

1¹/₂ cups (12 fl oz/375 ml) warm water (105°–115°F/ 41°–46°C)

1 package (2¹/₂ teaspoons) active dry yeast

About 3¹/₂ cups (17¹/₂ oz/ 545 g) bread flour

1¹/₂ teaspoons salt

3 tablespoons olive oil

Cornmeal for dusting

³/₄ lb (375 g) low-moisture, part-skim mozzarella cheese, coarsely shredded

4 slices thick-cut bacon, about 6 oz (185 g) total weight, cut crosswise into ¹/₂-inch (12-mm) pieces and cooked until crisp

16 cherry tomatoes, halved

12 large fresh basil leaves, torn into 1-inch (2.5-cm) pieces

MAKES 6–8 SERVINGS AS AN APPETIZER, 4–6 SERVINGS AS A MAIN COURSE

Beef

About Beef

Nothing epitomizes the joy of outdoor cooking more than the sight of a steak sizzling over a bed of glowing coals. In fact, many knowledgeable cooks insist there is no better way to cook most cuts of beef than over a smoky direct- or indirect-heat fire.

Tender porterhouse and T-bone steaks are ideally suited to grilling over direct heat. Little adornment—coarse salt and freshly cracked pepper or a flavored butter—is all that's needed. The beefy flavor of rib-eye and strip steaks stands alone beautifully, too, but it also holds its own with zesty marinades and robust sauces.

Elegant, lean, and mild-flavored, the filet mignon is perhaps the most versatile of steaks, pairing equally well with assertive spice rubs and herb or olive pastes as it does with simple compound butters. Serve it whole or sliced.

Less tender, but no less flavorful, cuts from the belly of the steer, such as skirt, flank, and hanger steaks, are wonderful when bathed in a tangy marinade or coated with a bold dry rub, lightly charred over high, direct heat, and thinly sliced across the grain. Served with spicy Latin or Asian accompaniments, they give backyard barbecues an international accent. Sirloin and flatiron steaks are perfect vehicles for a variety of global flavorings, too, from intriguing Southeast Asian–style sauces to assertive Mediterranean flavors to a hearty English ale-based marinade.

Kabobs made from beef cubes, either marinated or rubbed with spice pastes before grilling, are a quick way to satisfy a beef craving and are a fitting centerpiece for a casual alfresco dinner party. Add some vegetables to the skewers for vibrant color.

At the other end of the size and time spectrum, large rib roasts and whole tenderloins, rubbed with a spice mixture or fresh herb paste and then grilled relatively slowly over indirect heat, transform the grill into a backyard oven, and free you to enjoy the outdoors with your guests. Beef ribs, tri-tip, or brisket, barbecued in a smoky grill, make great fare for a family cookout. (Turn to page 262 for true barbecue recipes.) If you're short on time, short ribs can be quick-grilled using a Korean technique.

Veal chops cook quickly on the grill and will impress guests at a company dinner. Garnish them simply with fresh herbs and lemon, or stuff them with a savory mixture before cooking. And, of course, no grilling repertory would be complete without the secret to a superb hamburger: freshly ground, boldly seasoned, and lightly handled. Lay out a buffet of condiments, garnishes, and grilled side dishes and your work is finished.

Working with Beef

SHOPPING FOR BEEF

With the exception of flank, skirt, and hanger steaks, which come from the belly of the steer, steaks are cut from the back of the animal, usually from the loin and rib portions. Most steaks are tender enough to grill over direct heat, which creates a caramelized crust and juicy interior. The less tender steaks from the belly tend to have a "beefier" flavor than those from the less used muscles along the back; these steaks benefit from a marinade before grilling to increase their tenderness.

When choosing steaks, seek out bright red meat with light marbling (internal fat), a fine texture, and nearly white outer fat. The exterior fat should be minimal, although you can always trim it later. The more marbling, the more tender and juicy the beef will be, so keep this in mind when you are balancing a meal for health reasons. Look for many small deposits of fat, which resemble the light streaks in a dark marble floor, rather than a few large globs.

Use the same criteria for choosing meat for kabobs or for choosing ribs as you would for steaks: vibrant red meat with good marbling. Pass up beef that is turning brown or has large pieces of fat. For best results with kabobs, choose a large piece of meat and cut it into cubes just before using.

When selecting ground (minced) beef, seek out a nice piece of chuck with 15 to 20 percent fat, ask the butcher to grind it for you, and then cook it the same day. Better yet, if you have access to a meat grinder, grind it yourself just before you plan to use it. Not only will this create a flavorful burger, but it will also reduce the likelihood that a breeding ground for dangerous bacteria will develop. When choosing beef for your burgers, don't skimp on the fat. The right amount of fat in the meat will create a juicy and flavorful burger that holds together well, a result worth the calorie splurge.

When shopping for roasts, look for well-trimmed external fat and a good amount of internal marbling. The meat should appear slightly moist and be a good, even red color. Smell the meat to make sure that it has a clean, fresh aroma with no off odor. Most large cuts will appear fine-grained, with the exception of brisket and tri-tip, which will have a coarser texture.

Whether buying steaks, burgers, roasts, or ribs, pass up meat that is wet or sticky and has purple discoloration. Also avoid meat with yellow or brown fat or any meat that smells stale, sour, or otherwise unpleasant. For the best quality, cultivate a relationship with a reliable, high-volume butcher who will cut meats to your specifications.

PREPARING BEEF FOR GRILLING

Prior to cooking beef, trim off most of the external fat and discard it. Internal fat or marbling promotes tenderness and flavor, but external fat causes flare-ups as it melts and drips into the fire.

Beef should be salted before it goes on the grill, which is contrary to the old thinking that salting before cooking draws out juices and produces dried-out meat. Be prepared to salt beef more than you think necessary. A generous sprinkling will bring out the true flavor of the meat and keep it nice and juicy.

TESTING BEEF FOR DONENESS

To judge the doneness of grilled beef visually, cut into the thickest part. Rare beef will look reddish in the center, and medium will have a trace of pink. Cooking beef beyond medium causes it to dry out and become tough. Burgers are the exception; for safety's sake, they should be cooked to no less than medium (145°F/63°C), and many health experts say it is wisest to cook them to at least medium-well (160°F/71°C). For a more exact test, insert an instant-read thermometer into the thickest part of a piece of meat away from the bone.

All beef should rest for 3 to 15 minutes after grilling, depending on size, to allow the juices to redistribute throughout the meat, thus ensuring juiciness and full flavor. The internal temperature could rise as much as 5° to 10°F (3° to 6°C) as the meat sits. Keep this in mind and remove beef from the grill when it is some degrees shy of the desired temperature. You can always cook beef a little more if needed.

DONENESS	COLOR	TEMPERATURE °F	TEMPERATURE °C
Rare	Red	120° to 125°	49° to 52°
Medium-rare	Pinkish red	130° to 135°	54° to 57°
Medium	Trace of pink	140° to 145°	60° to 63°
Medium-well	No trace of pink	150° to 155°	65° to 68°
Well	Grayish brown	160° and higher	71° and higher

Beef Cuts for Grilling

U.S. butchers divide the steer into eight primal sections, seen below. Most cuts from the top of the steer are tender enough to grill over direct heat. Less tender cuts from the bottom of the steer need tenderizing before grilling. Cuts from the round section are usually not tender enough to grill.

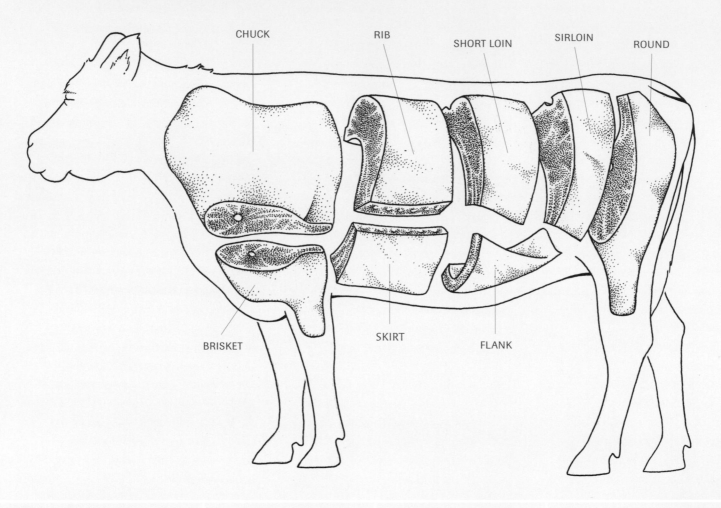

CHUCK   RIB   SHORT LOIN   SIRLOIN   ROUND

BRISKET   SKIRT   FLANK

CHUCK

Flatiron steak

Short Ribs

BRISKET

Brisket Roast

SKIRT

Skirt Steak

FLANK

Flank Steak

Hanger Steak

SIRLOIN

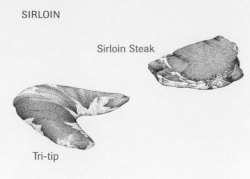

Sirloin Steak

Tri-tip

SHORT LOIN

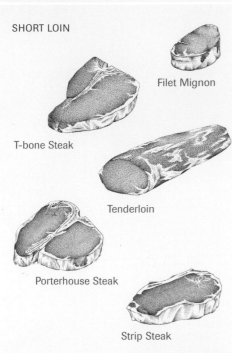

Filet Mignon

T-bone Steak

Tenderloin

Porterhouse Steak

Strip Steak

RIB

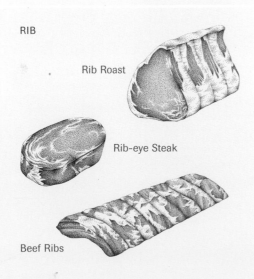

Rib Roast

Rib-eye Steak

Beef Ribs

BEEF CUTS FOR GRILLING

Some of the best beef cuts for grilling come from the less exercised areas of the steer, the short loin, sirloin, and rib sections. Less tender cuts of meat from other parts of the animal can also be grilled successfully, but they may need a marinade or long, slow cooking to render them tender.

Flatiron Steak

Cut from the chuck, this steak is very tender. Cut out the small line of gristle running through the meat before or after grilling.

Short Ribs

Usually cut from the chuck portion of the steer, short ribs are rectangles of beef about 2 inches (5 cm) by 3 inches (7.5 cm).

Brisket Roast

An inexpensive, tough cut of meat, brisket benefits from long, slow, smoky roasting.

Skirt and Flank Steaks

These are thin, fibrous steaks cut from the steer's underbelly. A bath in a marinade and slicing across the grain after grilling heightens their tenderness.

Hanger Steak

A chewy cut from the belly of the steer, hanger steak has a deep, rich, beefy flavor. Thinly slice it across the grain for the best presentation.

Sirloin Steak

Sirloin is the most popular retail steak. Pick top sirloin over other types for guaranteed tenderness. Sirloin is also a great choice for cutting into cubes and threading onto skewers to make kabobs.

Tri-Tip

Also called triangle roast, this lean, tender roast cut from the bottom sirloin is extremely tasty beef at a reasonable price. It makes a nice roast, or is perfect for cutting into kabobs and threading on skewers.

Filet Mignon

A boneless cut of meat from the tenderloin, filet mignon is expensive, but worth it for its versatility and unmatched tenderness.

Tenderloin

Sometimes referred to as Chateaubriand, this elegant cut makes a meltingly tender boneless roast.

T-bone and Porterhouse Steaks

Both steaks boast a firm, meaty strip steak and a soft, succulent tenderloin attached to a T-shaped bone. The T-bone has a smaller tenderloin portion.

Strip Steak

Cut from the little-exercised short loin section of the steer, this tender steak is perfect for a special occasion.

Rib Roast

A special-occasion cut from the prized rib portion of the steer. The ribs, when left in, further give the roast deep, meaty flavor.

Rib-Eye Steak

A boneless steak from the rib section, this is an excellent-quality, tender cut of meat.

Beef Ribs

Cut from the rib roast, beef ribs are quick cooking, meaty, and inexpensive—a good option for feeding a crowd.

Bistecca alla Fiorentina

2 porterhouse steaks, each about 1¹/₂ lb (750 g) and at least 1 inch (2.5 cm) thick

5 tablespoons (2¹/₂ fl oz/ 75 ml) extra-virgin olive oil

Coarse sea or kosher salt and freshly ground coarse pepper

4 lemon wedges

Arugula (rocket) leaves for garnish

MAKES 4 SERVINGS

Prepare a CHARCOAL or GAS grill for DIRECT grilling over HIGH heat (page 18 or 22). Brush both sides of the meat with about 1¹/₂ tablespoons of the oil. Season liberally with salt and pepper, patting it into the meat.

CHARCOAL: Grill the steaks over the hottest part of the fire until they are nicely charred and cooked to your liking, 4–6 minutes per side for medium-rare.

GAS: Grill the steaks directly over the heat elements until they are nicely charred and cooked to your liking, 4–6 minutes per side for medium-rare.

Transfer the steaks to a platter and let rest for 3–5 minutes before cutting into servings. Drizzle the meat with the remaining oil. Spoon the oil and meat juices that collect in the bottom of the platter over each serving. Accompany with the lemon wedges and garnish each portion with arugula leaves.

This is the classic steak preparation of Tuscany, Italy's best-known beef region. Like most fine Italian food, it is simplicity itself, and its success relies on quality ingredients. In other words, buy the biggest and best steaks you can find, and that usually means porterhouse, a T-bone with the added bonus of the tenderloin tail.

T-Bone with Blue Cheese Butter

You can use porterhouse, strip steak, fillet, or even a tender sirloin for this ultra-easy preparation. A tender cut of beef needs little adornment, but a dab of blue cheese butter can send a good steak into greatness. Serve it with garden-fresh green beans.

In a small bowl, mix together the butter, blue cheese, and chives until well blended. Use immediately, or cover and refrigerate, for up to 24 hours. If refrigerated, return to room temperature before using.

Prepare a CHARCOAL or GAS grill for DIRECT grilling over HIGH heat (page 18 or 22). Oil the grill rack. Season the steaks on both sides with salt and pepper.

CHARCOAL: Grill the steaks over the hottest part of the fire until they are nicely charred and cooked to your liking, 4–6 minutes per side for medium-rare.

GAS: Grill the steaks directly over the heat elements until they are nicely charred and cooked to your liking, 4–6 minutes per side for medium-rare.

Top each steak with a dollop of the blue cheese butter, then let rest for 3 minutes. Serve the steaks hot.

2 tablespoons unsalted butter, at room temperature

2 tablespoons blue cheese, preferably Maytag blue, at room temperature

1 tablespoon snipped fresh chives

4 T-bone steaks, each 10–12 oz (315–375 g) and about 1 inch (2.5 cm) thick

Salt and freshly ground pepper

MAKES 4 SERVINGS

Steak with Grilled Thyme Potatoes

4 T-bone steaks, each 10–12 oz (315–375 g) and about 1 inch (2.5 cm) thick

2 tablespoons chopped fresh summer savory or thyme

2 tablespoons chopped fresh marjoram

Coarse sea or kosher salt and freshly ground coarse pepper

2 large baking potatoes, about ³/₄ lb (375 g) each

2 tablespoons olive oil

2 tablespoons chopped fresh thyme, plus sprigs for garnish

MAKES 4 SERVINGS

T-bone steak has the best of everything: a richly marbled strip steak, considered by many to be the best steak for flavor; a tenderloin that lives up to its name; and a big T-bone that holds the two together and imparts its own meaty flavor. Because of its natural qualities, this steak needs little extra flavoring on the grill, so here it is treated to summery herbs, salt, and pepper and nothing more. Potatoes are steak's perfect partner, and again fresh herbs are the simple seasoning.

Sprinkle the steaks evenly on both sides with the savory, marjoram, and ¹/₂ teaspoon each salt and pepper. Pat the seasonings so that they adhere. Let the steaks stand at cool room temperature for up to 1 hour.

Prepare a CHARCOAL or GAS grill for DIRECT grilling over MEDIUM-HIGH heat (page 18 or 22). Oil the grill rack.

While the grill is heating, prepare the potatoes: Cut the unpeeled potatoes lengthwise into slices slightly less than ¹/₄ inch (6 mm) thick. Place the slices on a baking sheet, brush the top side with half of the oil, then sprinkle with half of the thyme, a scant ¹/₂ teaspoon salt, and ¹/₄ teaspoon pepper. Turn the slices over, brush with the remaining oil, and sprinkle with the remaining thyme and the same amounts of salt and pepper.

CHARCOAL: Grill the potato slices in a single layer over the hottest part of the fire, turning once with a spatula, until the slices are golden and lightly charred on the edges, 5–6 minutes per side. Transfer the potatoes to a warm platter and sprinkle with additional salt and pepper if desired. Grill the steaks over the hottest part of the fire until nicely charred and cooked to your liking, 4–6 minutes per side for medium-rare.

GAS: Grill the potato slices in a single layer directly over the heat elements, turning once with a spatula, until the slices are golden and lightly charred on the edges, 5–6 minutes per side. Transfer the potatoes to a warm platter and sprinkle with additional salt and pepper if desired. Grill the steaks directly over the heat elements until nicely charred and cooked to your liking, 4–6 minutes per side for medium-rare.

Let the steaks rest for about 3 minutes before serving. Serve the potatoes next to the steaks, or serve the steaks topped with the potatoes so that they soak up some steak juices. Garnish with thyme sprigs.

Kansas City Strip Steaks

Every U.S. city has its own food specialties, and Kansas City is known for some of the country's best steak sauces. It also is home to some of the best steaks, so it is natural to combine the two. That said, it might be a good idea to make a double batch of sauce for steak another day or for using on chicken or pork chops. Serve these tender strip steaks with your favorite steak-house side dishes, such as baked potatoes and a salad of small, sweet pear tomatoes.

To make the Kansas City steak sauce, in a saucepan over medium heat, warm the oil. Add the onion and celery and cook, stirring, until softened, about 4 minutes. Add the aniseeds and celery seeds and cook, stirring, for 1 minute. Stir in the mustard until dissolved, then stir in the ketchup, chili sauce, vinegar, honey, and Worcestershire sauce. Bring to a boil, reduce the heat to medium-low, and simmer uncovered, stirring often, until lightly thickened, 10–15 minutes. Use the sauce immediately, or cool, cover, and refrigerate for up to 1 month. If refrigerated, remove from the refrigerator 30 minutes before using.

Prepare a CHARCOAL or GAS grill for DIRECT grilling over HIGH heat (page 18 or 22). Oil the grill rack. Season the meat on both sides with salt and pepper. Pour about $1/2$ cup (4 fl oz/125 ml) of the sauce into a small bowl for brushing on the steaks.

CHARCOAL: Grill the steaks over the hottest part of the fire for 3 minutes, brush with the sauce, and turn. Grill for another 3 minutes, brush again with the sauce, and turn. Continue grilling until the steaks are nicely charred and cooked to your liking, 2–3 minutes more for medium-rare.

GAS: Grill the steaks directly over the heat elements for 3 minutes, brush with the sauce, and turn. Grill for another 3 minutes, brush again with the sauce, and turn. Continue grilling until the steaks are nicely charred and cooked to your liking, 2–3 minutes more for medium-rare.

Discard any sauce that had been used for brushing the meat. Pass the reserved sauce at the table, warmed if desired, for spooning over the steaks.

For the Kansas City Steak Sauce

1 tablespoon vegetable oil

1 small yellow onion, finely chopped

1 small celery stalk, finely chopped

1 teaspoon aniseeds, lightly crushed

$1/2$ teaspoon celery seeds

$1 1/2$ teaspoons dry mustard

$1/2$ cup (4 fl oz/125 ml) tomato ketchup

$1/2$ cup (4 fl oz/125 ml) bottled chili sauce

$1 1/2$ tablespoons cider vinegar

$1 1/2$ tablespoons honey

1 tablespoon Worcestershire sauce

4 strip or rib-eye steaks, each $1/2$–$3/4$ lb (250–375 g) and about $3/4$ inch (2 cm) thick

Salt and freshly ground pepper

MAKES 4 SERVINGS

Strip Steak with Grilled Mushrooms and Onions

For this hearty dish, grill the mushrooms and onions before the steaks; they take longer and call for a cooler fire. These large, tender steaks can be sliced before serving, or if you have just four robust appetites at your table, you can serve them whole.

To make the marinade, select a shallow, nonreactive dish just large enough to hold the mushrooms in a single layer. Combine the oil, vinegar, mustard, thyme, $^1\!/_2$ teaspoon salt, and $^1\!/_2$ teaspoon pepper in the dish and whisk well.

Cut off each mushroom stem even with the base of the cap and brush the caps clean. Add the mushrooms to the dish and turn several times to coat evenly. Let stand at room temperature for 1 hour, or cover and refrigerate for up to 3 hours.

Remove the steaks from the refrigerator about 30 minutes before grilling. Lightly brush the onion slices and the steaks with olive oil. Season the steaks and onion slices on both sides with salt and pepper. Drain the mushrooms, discarding the marinade, just before grilling.

Prepare a CHARCOAL grill for DIRECT grilling over two levels of heat, one MEDIUM and the other HIGH (page 18). Or prepare a GAS grill for DIRECT grilling over MEDIUM heat (page 22). Oil the grill rack.

CHARCOAL: Grill the mushrooms and onions directly over the medium coals, turning several times, until nicely browned and soft throughout, about 10 minutes for the mushrooms and 12–14 minutes for the onions. Transfer the vegetables to a large sheet of heavy-duty aluminum foil, wrap loosely, and place at the edge of the coals to keep warm while grilling the steaks. Grill the steaks over the hottest part of the fire, turning once, until they are nicely charred and cooked to your liking, 4–5 minutes per side for medium-rare steaks.

GAS: Grill the mushrooms and onions directly over the heat elements, turning several times, until nicely browned and soft throughout, about 10 minutes for the mushrooms and 12–14 minutes for the onions. Transfer the vegetables to a large sheet of heavy-duty aluminum foil, wrap loosely, and place on an area with lower heat to keep warm while grilling the steaks. Raise the heat to high. Grill the steaks directly over the heat elements, turning once, until nicely charred and cooked to your liking, 4–5 minutes per side for medium-rare.

Let the steaks rest for 3–4 minutes. Leave the steaks whole or thinly slice across the grain. Serve with the mushrooms and onions.

For the Marinade

2 tablespoons extra-virgin olive oil

1 tablespoon red wine vinegar

$^1\!/_2$ teaspoon Dijon mustard

$^1\!/_2$ teaspoon fresh thyme leaves

Salt and freshly ground pepper

$^1\!/_2$ lb (250 g) large cremini mushrooms, each about 2 inches (5 cm) in diameter

4 strip or rib-eye steaks, each 8–10 oz (250–315 g) and 1–1$^1\!/_4$ inches (2.5–3 cm) thick

3 sweet onions such as Vidalia, cut crosswise into slices $^1\!/_2$ inch (12 mm) thick

Extra-virgin olive oil for brushing

Salt and freshly ground pepper

MAKES 4–6 SERVINGS

Steak Chimichurri

For the Chimichurri

⅔ cup (5 fl oz/150 ml) sherry vinegar

¼ cup (2 fl oz/60 ml) olive oil

¾ cup (1 oz/30 g) chopped fresh flat-leaf (Italian) parsley

3 tablespoons chopped fresh oregano

6 large cloves garlic, chopped

½ teaspoon red pepper flakes

Salt

4 strip or rib-eye steaks, each ½–¾ lb (250–375 g) and ¾ inch (2 cm) thick

MAKES 4 SERVINGS

To make the *chimichurri*, select a shallow, nonreactive dish just large enough to hold the meat in a single layer. Add the vinegar, oil, parsley, oregano, garlic, pepper flakes, and ¾ teaspoon salt to the dish and mix well. Pour off and reserve ⅓ cup (3 fl oz/80 ml) of the *chimichurri*. Add the steaks to the dish and turn to coat both sides. Cover and refrigerate for at least 2 hours or for up to 6 hours, turning occasionally. Remove from the refrigerator 30 minutes before grilling.

Prepare a CHARCOAL or GAS grill for DIRECT grilling over HIGH heat (page 18 or page 22).

CHARCOAL: Grill the steaks over the hottest part of the fire, turning once, until nicely charred and cooked to your liking, 3½–5 minutes per side for medium-rare. Brush with the marinade when turning.

GAS: Grill the steaks directly over the heat elements, turning once, until nicely charred and cooked to your liking, 3½–5 minutes per side for medium-rare. Brush with the marinade when turning.

Let the steaks rest for 2–3 minutes. Serve with the reserved *chimichurri* for drizzling over the top.

Chimichurri, a deceptively simple mixture of parsley, garlic, oil, and vinegar, is the melodic name of a classic marinade-sauce of Argentina, a country famous for its beef. Like most great dishes, *chimichurri* depends on quality ingredients, so be selective and look for crisp, dark green flat-leaf parsley with a peppery fragrance, and choose garlic that is firm and unblemished.

Steak au Poivre with Grilled Leeks

6 filets mignons, each 5–6 oz (155–185 g) and about 1¹/₂ inches (4 cm) thick

Salt and freshly cracked pepper

6 slender leeks, each ³/₄-1 inch (2–2.5 cm) in diameter

2 tablespoons olive oil

1 tablespoon chopped fresh thyme

MAKES 6 SERVINGS

Season the steaks lightly on both sides with salt, then firmly pat 1¹/₂ tablespoons pepper on both sides, distributing it evenly.

Trim the leeks, leaving about 1 inch (2.5 cm) of the tender green tops intact. Halve each leek lengthwise, rinse thoroughly under running cold water, and dry well. Brush the leeks with the oil, then sprinkle with half of the thyme.

Prepare a CHARCOAL or GAS grill for DIRECT grilling over HIGH heat (page 18 or 22). Oil the grill rack.

CHARCOAL: Grill the steaks over the hottest part of the fire until they are lightly charred and cooked to your liking, 5–6 minutes per side for medium-rare. While the steaks are cooking, place the leeks at the edges of the grill where the heat is less intense. Grill the leeks, turning them 2 or 3 times, until softened and golden, 6–9 minutes total. Sprinkle with the remaining thyme.

GAS: Grill the steaks directly over the heat elements until they are lightly charred and cooked to your liking, 5–6 minutes per side for medium-rare. While the steaks are cooking, place the leeks on an area with lower heat. Grill the leeks, turning them 2 or 3 times, until softened and golden, 6–9 minutes. Sprinkle with the remaining thyme.

Serve the steaks on top of the leeks or with the leeks crisscrossed over the top.

Filet mignon, that most elegant and tender of beef steaks, is also the cut with the mildest, most elusive taste. That's why it is well suited to a sharply flavored, crunchy crust of cracked pepper that will punch up the flavor and deliver a textural counterpoint to the tender meat. Leeks, the most elegant of the onion family, are full of natural sweetness that caramelizes beautifully on the grill. This recipe is ideal for entertaining; adjust it to serve as many or as few as you like.

Filets Mignons with Pesto and Grilled Tomatoes

The steak is also wonderful stuffed with prepared *tapenade*, a Provençal olive-anchovy-caper condiment, or with *caponata*, a Sicilian sweet-and-sour eggplant relish. The pesto recipe here makes more than you will need, but the extra can be refrigerated or frozen. If you like, thin the leftover pesto with a little white wine and brush it on chicken just as it comes off the grill. A simple baby lettuce salad alongside the filets mignons is all you need to complete the meal.

To make the pesto, engage the motor of a food processor and drop the garlic cloves through the feed tube. When the garlic is minced, turn off the motor and add the basil and pine nuts. Process until finely chopped. With the motor running, pour in the oil in a steady stream to make a smooth, thick paste. Transfer the pesto to a small bowl and stir in the cheese by hand. You will have about 1 cup (8 fl oz/250 ml) pesto. Measure 6 tablespoons (3 fl oz/90 ml) for stuffing the steaks; reserve the remainder for another use.

Prepare a CHARCOAL or GAS grill for DIRECT grilling over MEDIUM-HIGH heat (page 18 or 22). Oil the grill rack.

Using a small, sharp knife, make a horizontal cut into one side of each steak, forming a pocket almost to the edges of the steak; take care not to cut all the way through. Using a small spoon, stuff 1 tablespoon of the pesto into each pocket. If necessary, secure the pocket with toothpicks. Brush both sides of the steaks and tomato slices with the olive oil, then season with salt and pepper.

CHARCOAL: Grill the steaks over the hottest part of the fire, turning once, until nicely charred and cooked to your liking, 5–6 minutes per side for medium-rare. While the steaks are cooking, place the tomatoes at the edges of the grill where the heat is less intense. Grill the tomato slices, turning once with a spatula, until just softened and lightly charred, 2–4 minutes per side.

GAS: Grill the steaks directly over the heat elements, turning once, until nicely charred and cooked to your liking, 5–6 minutes per side for medium-rare. While the steaks are cooking, place the tomatoes on an area with lower heat. Grill the tomato slices, turning once with a spatula, until just softened and lightly charred, 2–4 minutes per side.

To serve, place each steak on a plate on or next to a tomato slice.

For the Basil Pesto

3 cloves garlic

2 cups (2 oz/60 g) loosely packed fresh basil leaves

3 tablespoons pine nuts, lightly toasted

1/2 cup (4 fl oz/125 ml) olive oil

1/2 cup (2 oz/60 g) grated Parmesan cheese

6 filets mignons, each 5–6 oz (155–185 g) and about 1 1/2 inches (4 cm) thick

6 toothpicks, soaked in water for 10 minutes and drained (optional)

6 slices beefsteak tomato, each about 1/2 inch (12 mm) thick

2 tablespoons olive oil

Salt and freshly ground pepper

MAKES 6 SERVINGS

London Broil Salad

For the Mustard-Herb Vinaigrette

³/₄ cup (6 fl oz/180 ml) extra-virgin olive oil

¹/₃ cup (3 fl oz/80 ml) balsamic vinegar

1¹/₂ tablespoons chopped fresh thyme

1¹/₂ tablespoons chopped fresh marjoram

1¹/₂ tablespoons Dijon mustard

2 large cloves garlic, finely chopped

Salt and freshly ground pepper

1 flank steak, about 1¹/₂ lb (750 g) and 1–1¹/₂ inches (2.5–4 cm) thick

1 large head romaine (cos) lettuce, leaves torn into bite-sized pieces

3 tomatoes, cut into wedges

1 wedge pecorino romano cheese

MAKES 6 SERVINGS

To make the mustard-herb vinaigrette, in a small bowl, whisk together the oil, vinegar, thyme, marjoram, mustard, garlic, and ³/₄ teaspoon each salt and pepper. Place the meat in a shallow nonreactive dish just large enough to hold it flat. Pour half of the vinaigrette over the meat and turn to coat both sides. Cover and refrigerate for at least 4 hours or for up to 24 hours, turning occasionally. Cover and refrigerate the remaining vinaigrette. Remove the meat from the refrigerator 30 minutes before grilling.

Prepare a CHARCOAL or GAS grill for DIRECT grilling over HIGH heat (page 18 or 22). Remove the meat from the marinade, reserving the marinade.

CHARCOAL: Grill the meat over the hottest part of the fire, turning once or twice and brushing with the reserved marinade for up to 5 minutes before the meat is done, until nicely charred and cooked to your liking, 10–12 minutes total for medium-rare.

GAS: Grill the meat directly over the heat elements, turning once or twice and brushing with the reserved marinade for up to 5 minutes before the meat is done, until nicely charred and cooked to your liking, 10–12 minutes total for medium-rare.

Let the meat rest for about 5 minutes. Thinly slice across the grain, reserving any meat juices that accumulate.

Toss the lettuce with the reserved vinaigrette, then divide the lettuce evenly among individual plates. Arrange the meat over the lettuce, then arrange the tomato wedges around the meat, again dividing evenly. Drizzle the steak with any accumulated meat juices. Using a vegetable peeler or paring knife, shave the cheese, sprinkle the shavings over the salad, and serve.

London broil, contrary to supermarket meat labels, is not a cut of beef, nor is it British. Rather, it is a classic American way to prepare a large, flat steak, which can be anything from sirloin to round to flank. Since the steak needs to be sliced thinly, flank is the perfect choice, as it is full flavored but must be tenderized by marinating and thinly slicing across the grain.

Ginger-Soy Flank Steak
with Grilled Green Onions

For the Marinade

¹/₂ cup (4 fl oz/125 ml) soy sauce

2 tablespoons vegetable oil

1 teaspoon Asian sesame oil

2 tablespoons firmly packed golden brown sugar

2 cloves garlic, finely chopped

1 teaspoon peeled and grated fresh ginger

1 flank steak, 1¹/₄–1¹/₂ lb (625–750 g)

12 green (spring) onions

1 teaspoon vegetable oil

MAKES 4 SERVINGS

To make the marinade, select a shallow, nonreactive dish just large enough to hold the steak. Combine the soy sauce, vegetable oil, sesame oil, brown sugar, garlic, and ginger in the dish and stir until the sugar dissolves. Put the steak in the dish and turn to coat both sides. Marinate the steak at room temperature, turning occasionally, for 20–30 minutes.

Trim the root ends and the straggly tops from the green onions. Coat the onions lightly with the vegetable oil. Set aside.

Prepare a CHARCOAL or GAS grill for DIRECT grilling over HIGH heat (page 18 or 22). Oil the grill rack. Remove the meat from the marinade; discard the marinade.

CHARCOAL: Grill the steak over the hottest part of the fire, turning once, until nicely charred and cooked to your liking, 4–5 minutes per side for medium-rare. Grill the onions, turning once or twice, until softened and lightly browned, 3–4 minutes.

GAS: Grill the steak directly over the heat elements, turning once, until nicely charred and cooked to your liking, 4–5 minutes per side for medium-rare. Grill the onions, turning once or twice, until softened and lightly browned, 3–4 minutes.

Let the steak rest for about 5 minutes. Thinly slice across the grain and at an angle to the cutting board, reserving any meat juices that accumulate. Divide the slices among warmed individual plates and spoon the juices over the top. Serve on a bed of the grilled green onions.

Flank steak is a versatile cut, serving equally well as an easy dinner main course, a sandwich filling at lunchtime, or an accompaniment to scrambled eggs for a hearty breakfast. Here, it is marinated with soy sauce, ginger, and garlic and cooks in less than 10 minutes. Grilled whole green onions add an aromatic accompaniment.

Stuffed Flank Steak

This flavor-packed steak is reminiscent of *braciole*, an Italian-American favorite in which steak, often flank steak, is butterflied or thinly sliced, rolled around a savory bread crumb, meat, and cheese filling, and then braised. In this grilled version, the rolled steak is wrapped in aluminum foil and cooked over indirect heat, which allows the meat to tenderize and simmer in its own juices while absorbing the smokiness of the slow-burning coals. Serve with grilled polenta and a simple green salad. You can butterfly the meat yourself, or ask the butcher to do it.

In a bowl, combine the bread crumbs, cheese, salami, pine nuts, garlic, anchovies, parsley, and oregano. Mix well.

To butterfly the steak, lay it flat on a work surface. Using a long-bladed knife, cut it horizontally almost in half lengthwise, taking care not to cut all the way through or to make holes in the meat. Open the meat to lie flat on a piece of heavy-duty aluminum foil that is at least 3 inches (7.5 cm) larger on all sides than the meat.

Season the meat, top and bottom, with salt and pepper. Brush the side of the meat that will be grilled with the oil, then place it, oiled side down, on the foil. Distribute the stuffing evenly on the opened side of the butterflied steak, leaving a 1/2-inch (12-mm) border on all sides. Using the foil as an aid, roll up the steak jelly-roll fashion. Completely wrap the rolled steak in the foil, twisting the ends and tying the roll with kitchen string if necessary. Let the meat stand for 30 minutes at room temperature, or refrigerate for up to 4 hours. If refrigerated, remove from the refrigerator 30 minutes before grilling.

Prepare a CHARCOAL or GAS grill for INDIRECT grilling over MEDIUM heat (page 19 or 23).

CHARCOAL: Place the foil-wrapped meat on the grill away from the coals. Cover the grill and cook, turning 4 or 5 times, until the meat is very tender when pierced with a fork, about 2 hours total.

GAS: Place the foil-wrapped meat on the grill away from the heat elements. Cover the grill and cook, turning 4 or 5 times, until the meat is very tender when pierced with a fork, about 2 hours total.

Let the meat rest in the foil for 15 minutes. Unwrap and cut crosswise into slices no more than 1/2 inch (12 mm) thick. Arrange on a platter and pour any accumulated meat juices in the foil over the slices. Serve at once.

1/2 cup (1 oz/30 g) fresh white bread crumbs

1/3 cup (11/2 oz/45 g) grated Romano or Parmesan cheese

1/3 cup (2 oz/60 g) chopped salami, preferably Genoa

3 tablespoons coarsely chopped toasted pine nuts

3 large cloves garlic, finely chopped

2 anchovy fillets, mashed

1/4 cup (1/3 oz/10g) chopped fresh flat-leaf (Italian) parsley

2 tablespoons chopped fresh oregano

1 flank steak, 11/2 –13/4 lb (750–875 g)

Salt and freshly ground pepper

2 tablespoons olive oil

MAKES 6-8 SERVINGS

Steak Fajitas

2 large cloves garlic, finely chopped

1 or 2 jalapeño chiles, seeded and finely chopped

$^1/_4$ cup (2 fl oz/60 ml) fresh lime juice

3 tablespoons olive oil

1 tablespoon chili powder

1 teaspoon ground cumin

1 large skirt or flank steak, 1–1$^1/_2$ lb (500–750 g)

1 large red bell pepper (capsicum), quartered lengthwise and seeded

1 large yellow bell pepper (capsicum), quartered lengthwise and seeded

6–8 green (spring) onions, trimmed, including 4 inches (10 cm) of tender green tops

12 flour tortillas, each 7–8 inches (18–20 cm) in diameter

Pico de gallo (page 288)

Guacamole (page 289)

1$^1/_2$ cups (12 fl oz/375 ml) sour cream

1$^1/_2$ cups (6 oz/185 g) shredded Monterey jack cheese

MAKES 4–6 SERVINGS

To prepare the marinade, select a shallow, nonreactive dish just large enough to hold the steak. Add the garlic, chile(s), lime juice, oil, chili powder, and cumin to the dish and mix well. Add the steak and turn to coat both sides. Let stand at room temperature for at least 15 minutes, or cover and refrigerate for up to 1 hour. If refrigerated, remove from the refrigerator 30 minutes before grilling.

Prepare a CHARCOAL or GAS grill for DIRECT grilling over HIGH heat (page 18 or 22). Oil the grill rack.

Remove the steak from the marinade. Add the bell peppers and green onions to the marinade and stir to coat well.

CHARCOAL: Place the meat over the hottest part of the fire. Place the vegetables at the edges of the grill where the heat is less intense. Grill the meat and vegetables, turning once or twice, until the meat is nicely charred and medium-rare, and the vegetables are tender and lightly charred, 5–8 minutes total.

GAS: Place the meat directly over the heat elements. Place the vegetables on an area with lower heat. Grill the meat and vegetables, turning once or twice, until the meat is nicely charred and medium-rare, and the vegetables are tender and lightly charred, 5–8 minutes total.

Let the meat rest for 5 minutes. Meanwhile, wrap the tortillas in aluminum foil and heat on the grill for about 2 minutes. Thinly slice the meat across the grain, then thinly slice the vegetables. Toss the vegetables with the meat and any accumulated juices.

To serve the fajitas, heap the meat and vegetables on a platter. Serve the tortillas, pico de gallo, guacamole, sour cream, and cheese in separate dishes. Encourage diners to make their own fajitas by wrapping the ingredients in the tortillas.

Although today fajitas can be made with anything from chicken to shrimp to tofu, they built their reputation on steak. You can use skirt steak or flank steak, both flat, tough steaks that turn juicy, tender, and flavorful after they are marinated briefly, cooked quickly on the grill, and then sliced across the grain. Tradition holds that everyone assembles his or her own fajita at the table.

Carne Asada with Blackened Corn

Carne asada, a specialty of Mexico, translates simply as "grilled meat," and how it is presented differs greatly from town to town. In this version, both the steak and corn are treated to a marinade seasoned with the classic chili powder of the Hill Country of Texas, just north of San Antonio.

To make the chili powder marinade, in a small dish, stir together the ground chile, paprika, cumin, oregano, $^1/_2$ teaspoon salt, cayenne to taste, and garlic. Stir in the oil and lime juice. Pour $^1/_4$ cup (2 fl oz/60 ml) of the marinade into a shallow, nonreactive dish just large enough to hold the steak. Cover the remaining marinade and set aside. Add the steak to the dish and turn to coat both sides with the marinade. Let the steak stand at room temperature for 30 minutes.

Prepare a CHARCOAL or GAS grill for DIRECT grilling over two levels of heat, one MEDIUM-HIGH and the other HIGH (page 18 or 22). Remove the meat from the marinade. Brush the corn with some of the reserved marinade.

CHARCOAL: Grill the corn over the medium-hot coals, turning occasionally, until just tender, 10–12 minutes total. The corn will char. Grill the steak over the hottest part of the fire, turning once, until nicely charred and cooked to your liking, 3–4$^1/_2$ minutes per side for medium-rare.

GAS: Grill the corn over the medium-hot elements, turning occasionally, until just tender, 10–12 minutes total. The corn will char. Grill the steak over the hottest elements, turning once, until nicely charred and cooked to your liking, 3–4$^1/_2$ minutes per side for medium-rare.

Let the meat rest for about 3 minutes. Thinly slice the meat across the grain. Brush the grilled corn and drizzle the meat with any remaining marinade.

For the Chili Powder Marinade

1 tablespoon ground ancho chile

1$^1/_2$ teaspoons hot or sweet paprika

1 teaspoon ground cumin

$^3/_4$ teaspoon dried oregano

Salt

$^1/_8$–$^3/_4$ teaspoon ground cayenne pepper

2 cloves garlic, finely chopped

$^1/_4$ cup (2 fl oz/60 ml) olive oil

2 tablespoons fresh lime juice

1 skirt or hanger steak, about 1$^1/_2$ lb (750 g)

4 ears corn, shucked

MAKES 4 SERVINGS

Flatiron Steak with Grilled Pepper Salad

For the Marinade

Grated zest of 1 orange

$^1/_3$ cup (3 fl oz/80 ml) fresh orange juice

2 tablespoons extra-virgin olive oil

2 tablespoons red wine vinegar

2 cloves garlic, minced

2 teaspoons fresh oregano leaves or 1 teaspoon dried oregano

Salt and freshly ground black pepper

2 flatiron steaks, each about 1 lb (500 g) and 1 inch (2.5 cm) thick

5 bell peppers (capsicums), preferably a mix of colors

MAKES 4 OR 5 SERVINGS

To make the marinade, in a small bowl, whisk together the orange zest and juice, oil, vinegar, garlic, oregano, $^1/_2$ teaspoon salt, and $^1/_2$ teaspoon pepper. Remove 3 tablespoons of the marinade and reserve to dress the bell peppers. Choose a shallow, nonreactive dish just large enough to hold the steak and place the steak in it. Pour the marinade over the steak and turn the steak to coat both sides. Let stand at room temperature for 30 minutes.

Cut each bell pepper in half through the stem end, following a section line. Slice off the stem portion from each half and then remove and discard the seeds. Lightly flatten each pepper half with the heel of your hand.

Prepare a CHARCOAL or GAS grill for DIRECT grilling over HIGH heat (page 18 or 22). Oil the grill rack. Remove the steak from the marinade; discard the marinade.

CHARCOAL: Grill the peppers, skin sides down, over the hottest part of the fire until the skins are nicely charred, 4–5 minutes. Transfer the peppers to a plate, cover with foil, and let steam for 10 minutes. Grill the steaks over the hottest part of the fire, turning once, until nicely charred and cooked to your liking, 4–5 minutes per side for medium-rare steaks.

GAS: Grill the peppers, skin sides down, directly over the heat elements until the skins are nicely charred, 4–5 minutes. Transfer the peppers to a plate, cover with aluminum foil, and let steam for 10 minutes. Grill the steaks directly over the heat elements, turning once, until nicely charred and cooked to your liking, 4–5 minutes per side for medium-rare.

Let the steaks rest for 5 minutes. Meanwhile, using your fingers or a paring knife, peel the skins from the peppers, and cut the peppers lengthwise into strips $^3/_8$ inch (9 mm) wide. Place the pepper strips in a bowl, add the reserved 3 tablespoons marinade, and toss to coat the peppers evenly.

Thinly slice the steaks across the grain and at an angle to the cutting board. Serve hot, warm, or at room temperature with the roasted pepper salad.

A combination of classic Mediterranean flavors—olive oil, garlic, oregano, and orange juice—marinates this lean, flavorful cut. A colorful salad of grilled sweet red, yellow, and, if desired, pungent green bell peppers is served alongside the thinly sliced steak. The flatiron, also known as a boneless top blade steak, has two sections separated by a line of tough gristle. Removing the gristle yields a pair of good-sized steaks. Grill the peppers first and allow them to steam for a few minutes for easier removal of their charred skins.

Caper-Rosemary Sirloin

²/₃ cup (5 fl oz/150 ml) Chianti or other dry red wine

3 tablespoons balsamic vinegar

2 tablespoons olive oil

3 tablespoons capers

2 tablespoons chopped fresh rosemary

2 cloves garlic, minced

1 sirloin steak, 1³/₄–2 lb (875 g–1 kg) and 1 inch (2.5 cm) thick

Freshly ground pepper

MAKES 4 SERVINGS

Select a shallow, nonreactive dish just large enough to hold the steak. Add the wine, vinegar, oil, capers, chopped rosemary, and garlic to the dish and mix well. Season the steak generously with pepper. Add the steak to the dish and turn to coat both sides. Cover and refrigerate, turning the meat occasionally, for 2–6 hours. Remove from the refrigerator 30 minutes before grilling.

Prepare a CHARCOAL or GAS grill for DIRECT grilling over HIGH heat (page 18 or 22). Oil the grill rack. Remove the meat from the marinade; discard the marinade.

CHARCOAL: Grill the meat over the hottest part of the fire, turning once or twice, until nicely charred and cooked to your liking, 8–12 minutes total for medium-rare.

GAS: Grill the meat directly over the heat elements, turning once or twice, until nicely charred and cooked to your liking, 8–12 minutes total for medium-rare.

Let the steak rest for 5 minutes. Cut into portions or slices.

Because of its robust, beefy flavor, sirloin is an excellent choice for this assertive marinade, but flank steak would do well, too. For extra rosemary flavor, soak 4 or 5 rosemary branches in water for about 5 minutes, drain, and toss them on the coals or on the grill rack away from the heat source just before grilling the steak. Serve the steak Tuscan style with herbed white beans.

Sirloin with Thai Flavors

This recipe takes advantage of the many excellent bottled Asian sauces now on market shelves. Seasoned with fresh ginger and lime juice and zest, this simple marinade will also complement pork, chicken, and shrimp (prawns). Serve this dish with grilled fresh vegetables, such as baby bok choy and sweet bell peppers (capsicums).

Select a shallow, nonreactive dish just large enough to hold the steak. Add the lime juice, fish sauce, hoisin sauce, chile sauce, ginger, and lime zest to the dish and mix well. Add the steak and turn to coat both sides. Cover and refrigerate for at least 2 hours or for up to 8 hours, turning the meat occasionally. Remove from the refrigerator 30 minutes before grilling.

Prepare a CHARCOAL or GAS grill for DIRECT grilling over HIGH heat (page 18 or 22). Oil the grill rack. Remove the steak from the marinade; discard the marinade.

CHARCOAL: Grill the steak over the hottest part of the fire until it is nicely charred and cooked to your liking, 4–6 minutes per side for medium-rare.

GAS: Grill the steak directly over the heat elements until it is nicely charred and cooked to your liking, 4–6 minutes per side for medium-rare.

Let the meat rest for 3–5 minutes. Cut into slices to serve.

6 tablespoons (3 fl oz/90 ml) fresh lime juice

3 tablespoons fish sauce

3 tablespoons hoisin sauce

3 tablespoons Asian hot-chile sauce

3 tablespoons peeled and grated fresh ginger

1 teaspoon grated lime zest

1 sirloin or flatiron steak, 1³/₄–2 lb (875 g–1 kg) and 1 inch (2.5 cm) thick

MAKES 6 SERVINGS

Alehouse Beef-and-Potato Skewers

**1 lb (500 g) small
red-skinned or Yukon gold
potatoes, each about
1¹/₂ inches (4 cm) in
diameter or cut if larger**

For the Alehouse Marinade

**³/₄ cup (6 fl oz/180 ml)
ale or beer**

**¹/₃ cup (3 fl oz/80 ml) beef
broth**

**¹/₃ cup (3 fl oz/80 ml) spicy
tomato juice**

**1 tablespoon Worcestershire
sauce**

**¹/₂-1 teaspoon hot-pepper
sauce such as Tabasco**

**1 tablespoon chopped fresh
thyme**

**1 tablespoon chopped fresh
oregano**

**2 fresh or dried bay leaves,
broken in half**

**1¹/₂ lb (750 g) boneless
sirloin, about 1¹/₂ inches
(4 cm) thick, cut into
1¹/₂-inch (4-cm) cubes**

MAKES 4 SERVINGS

Sirloin is an outstanding beef cut for kabobs. Use red-skinned or Yukon gold potatoes, or a combination, for a particularly attractive presentation. Mushrooms or parboiled carrot chunks would be good additions to the skewers.

Bring a saucepan three-fourths full of salted water to a boil. Add the potatoes and parboil just until they can be pierced with a knife but are not completely tender, 8–10 minutes. Drain well and set aside. (The potatoes can be parboiled up to 4 hours ahead of grilling and kept at room temperature.)

To make the marinade, select a shallow, nonreactive dish just large enough to hold the meat. Add the ale, broth, tomato juice, Worcestershire and hot-pepper sauces, thyme, oregano, and bay leaves to the dish and mix well. Add the meat and turn to coat on all sides. Cover and refrigerate for at least 1 hour or for up to 4 hours. Add the potatoes to the marinade during the last 30 minutes.

Prepare a CHARCOAL or GAS grill for DIRECT grilling over HIGH heat (page 18 or 22). Oil the grill rack. Remove the meat and potatoes from their marinade and discard the marinade. Dividing the ingredients evenly, thread the meat and potatoes alternately onto 8 metal skewers.

CHARCOAL: Grill the skewers over the hottest part of the fire, turning to char all sides, until the potatoes are browned and the meat is cooked to your liking, 7–9 minutes total for medium-rare meat.	GAS: Grill the skewers directly over the heat elements, turning to char all sides, until the potatoes are browned and meat is cooked to your liking, 7–9 minutes total for medium-rare meat.

Transfer the skewers to warmed individual plates and serve at once.

Sichuan Orange Beef Kabobs

2 navel oranges

¹/₄ cup (2 fl oz/60 ml) rice vinegar

¹/₄ cup (2 fl oz/60 ml) soy sauce

1¹/₂ tablespoons chile oil

2 tablespoons chopped ginger

4 small dried hot chiles

3 cloves garlic, sliced

1¹/₂ lb (750 g) boneless sirloin, cut into 1-inch (2.5-cm) cubes

8 long wooden skewers, soaked

2 green onions, shredded

MAKES 4 SERVINGS

Prepare a CHARCOAL or GAS grill for DIRECT grilling over HIGH heat (page 18 or 22). Oil the grill rack. Cut the peel from the oranges and cut into squares. Squeeze the juice from 1 orange and slice the other crosswise. Combine the vinegar, soy sauce, chile oil, ginger, chiles, garlic, and orange juice. Brush the orange slices with the marinade and set aside. Add the beef and orange peel to the marinade and let stand for 30 minutes. Thread the beef and orange peels onto the skewers.

CHARCOAL: Grill the skewers over the hottest part of the fire, turning from time to time, 6–8 minutes for medium-rare. Just before the skewers are ready, grill the orange slices over an area with lower heat, turning once.

GAS: Grill the skewers directly over the heat elements, turning from time to time, 6–8 minutes for medium-rare. Just before the skewers are ready, grill the orange slices over an area with lower heat, turning once.

Transfer the skewers to individual plates and sprinkle with the green onions. Arrange the orange slices alongside (cut into quarters if desired) and serve at once.

Orange beef, a peppery, deep-fried beef dish, is a perennial favorite on Chinese restaurant menus. This grilled version has the same appeal, with the addition of aromatic smoke and the omission of all that frying and extra fat. Serve the meat alone or on a bed of steamed rice.

DIRECT METHOD · HIGH HEAT · MARINATE UP TO 4 HOURS

The Ultimate Philly Cheese Steak

Philadelphians pride themselves on their cheese steak, a thinly sliced, panfried beefsteak topped with lots of melted cheese, sautéed onions, and juices in a long, crusty bun. If that sounds good to you, imagine how much better it would be if the steak and onions were grilled. Hanger steak, cut from the underside of the steer, is similar to skirt steak or flank steak, both of which make good substitutes here.

Combine the oil, vinegar, oregano, garlic, and ¹/₂ teaspoon each salt and pepper. Add the steak and marinate at room temperature for 30 minutes, or cover and refrigerate for up to 4 hours. Prepare a CHARCOAL or GAS grill for DIRECT grilling over HIGH heat (page 18 or 22). Oil the grill rack. Add the onion slices to the marinade and turn to coat both sides. Split the rolls lengthwise.

CHARCOAL: Grill the steak and onions over the hottest part of the fire, turning once, 6–8 minutes total for medium-rare steak and 10–14 minutes for the onions. While the meat rests, toast the rolls, cut sides down.

GAS: Grill the steak and onions directly over the heat elements, turning once, 6–8 minutes total for medium-rare steak and 10–14 minutes for the onions. While the meat rests, toast the rolls, cut sides down.

Slice the meat against the grain and heap onto the roll bottoms with the cheese and onions. Let stand for 1 minute before cutting each sandwich in half to serve.

¹/₄ cup (2 fl oz/60 ml) olive oil

3 tablespoons vinegar

2 tablespoons minced oregano

2 large cloves garlic, minced

Salt and ground pepper

1 hanger, skirt, or flank steak, 1¹/₂ lb (750 g)

2 Vidalia onions, thickly sliced crosswise

6 long, crusty sandwich rolls

1¹/₂ cups (6 oz/185 g) shredded cheddar cheese

MAKES 6 SERVINGS

The Best Burger

A good burger is an edible work of art: a nicely charred crust that gives way to a sublimely juicy interior, sandwiched in a roll that fits just right and has the perfect texture for soaking up some of the juices while retaining its own integrity.

Prepare a CHARCOAL or GAS grill for DIRECT grilling over HIGH heat (page 18 or 22). Oil the grill rack.

Divide the meat into 6 equal portions. Dampen your hands, then pat each portion into a patty 4–4^1/$_2$ inches (10–11.5 cm) in diameter and about ^{3}/$_4$ inch (2 cm) thick. Take care not to handle the meat more than necessary or to compact the patties too much. Season all sides with salt and pepper.

CHARCOAL: Grill the burgers over the hottest part of the fire, turning once, until nicely charred and cooked to your liking, 4^1/$_2$–6 minutes per side for medium. About 1 minute before the burgers are done, place the buns, cut sides down, at the edge of the grill where the heat is less intense and grill until lightly toasted.

GAS: Grill the burgers directly over the heat elements, turning once, until nicely charred and cooked to your liking, 4^1/$_2$–6 minutes per side for medium. About 1 minute before the burgers are done, place the buns, cut sides down, on an area of lower heat and grill until lightly toasted.

Assemble the burgers in the buns with the embellishments of choice. Serve at once.

2^1/$_4$ lb (1.1 kg) freshly ground (minced) beef chuck

Salt and freshly ground pepper

6 crusty rolls

Sliced cheese, such as mild cheddar or Monterey jack

Sliced mild onion

Sliced tomato

Sliced dill pickle

Cooked bacon slices

Tender leaf lettuce

Good-quality tomato ketchup

Dijon or whole-grain mustard

MAKES 6 SERVINGS

Herbed Tenderloin with a Trio of Summer Sauces

Easy and quick to grill, and even easier to slice, beef tenderloin is an ideal meat for a party. Ask the butcher to tie it into a compact shape for roasting. Almost any herb or combination of herbs can be used to season it, or you can treat it to a liberal sprinkling of coarse salt and freshly ground pepper and nothing more. You can also grill it ahead and serve it sliced at room temperature with any one, two, or all three of the sauces. The sauces are also excellent with plain steak or even hamburgers.

Prepare one or more sauces, as desired. To make the roasted pepper sauce, in a small bowl, stir together the sour cream and the roasted pepper purée. To make the mustard mayonnaise, in a small bowl, stir together the mayonnaise and mustard. Finally, to make the pesto sauce, in a small bowl, stir together the yogurt and pesto. Season all the sauces with salt and pepper to taste. Cover and refrigerate all the sauces for at least 30 minutes or for up to 24 hours. Remove the sauces from the refrigerator 30 minutes before using.

Rub the meat with the oil, then season with 1 teaspoon salt and 2 teaspoons coarse pepper. Sprinkle evenly with the parsley and thyme, patting them onto the meat. Let the meat stand at room temperature for 15 minutes, or cover and refrigerate for up to 2 hours. If refrigerated, remove from the refrigerator 45 minutes before grilling.

Prepare a CHARCOAL or GAS grill for DIRECT grilling over MEDIUM-HIGH heat (page 18 or 22). Oil the grill rack.

CHARCOAL: Place the meat directly over the fire, cover the grill, and cook for 5 minutes. Using tongs, turn the meat a quarter turn, re-cover, and continue to cook and turn every 5 minutes until all sides are seared and the meat is cooked to your liking, 30–35 minutes total for medium-rare.

GAS: Place the meat directly over the heat elements, cover the grill, and cook for 5 minutes. Using tongs, turn the meat a quarter turn, re-cover, and continue to cook and turn every 5 minutes until all sides are seared and the meat is cooked to your liking, 30–35 minutes total for medium-rare.

To test for doneness, insert an instant-read thermometer into the thickest part of the meat; it should register 130°F (54°C). The temperature will rise another 5°–10°F (3°–6°C) while the roast is resting.

Let the roast rest for 10–15 minutes. Slice across the grain and serve warm or at room temperature with the sauce(s) on the side.

For the Roasted Pepper Sauce

1/2 cup (4 fl oz/125 ml) sour cream

1/2 red bell pepper (capsicum), grill-roasted, peeled, and seeded (page 78), and puréed until smooth

For the Mustard Mayonnaise

1/2 cup (4 fl oz/125 ml) mayonnaise

1/4 cup (2 oz/60 g) Dijon mustard

For the Pesto-Yogurt Sauce

1/2 cup (4 oz/125 g) low-fat plain yogurt

1/4 cup (2 fl oz/60 ml) store-bought basil pesto

Salt and freshly ground pepper

1 beef tenderloin, about 5 lb (2.5 kg), trimmed and tied

2 tablespoons olive oil

Freshly ground coarse pepper

1/4 cup (1/3 oz/10 g) chopped fresh flat-leaf (Italian) parsley

2 tablespoons chopped fresh thyme or other herb of choice

MAKES 8 SERVINGS

Korean-Style Short Ribs

¼ cup (2 fl oz/60 ml)
soy sauce

3 tablespoons rice vinegar

3 tablespoons dry sherry

3 tablespoons Asian
sesame oil

1½ tablespoons peeled and
grated fresh ginger

1½ tablespoons honey

⅓ cup (1½ oz/45 g) sesame
seeds, toasted

3–4 lb (1.5–2 kg) beef short
ribs, crosscut flanken style
(see note)

Lettuce leaves

MAKES 4 SERVINGS

In a shallow, nonreactive dish just large enough to hold the meat in a single layer, stir together the soy sauce, vinegar, sherry, sesame oil, ginger, honey, and about ¼ cup (1 oz/30 g) of the sesame seeds. Add the ribs and turn to coat all sides. Cover and refrigerate for at least 3 hours or for up to 24 hours, turning occasionally. Remove from the refrigerator 30 minutes before grilling.

Prepare a CHARCOAL or GAS grill for DIRECT grilling over HIGH heat (page 18 or 22). Oil the grill rack. Remove the meat from the marinade, reserving the marinade.

CHARCOAL: Grill the ribs over the hottest part of the fire, turning once and brushing with the marinade for up to 5 minutes before the ribs are done, until nicely charred and cooked to your liking, 6–10 minutes per side for medium-rare.

GAS: Grill the ribs directly over the heat elements, turning once and brushing with the marinade for up to 5 minutes before the ribs are done, until nicely charred and cooked to your liking, 6–10 minutes per side for medium-rare.

Sprinkle the ribs with the remaining sesame seeds and serve with the lettuce.

Most Americans cook beef ribs over a slow, smoky fire. Koreans, who are famous for their beef ribs, take a different approach: they put them over a hot, direct fire to sear the outside and create a juicy, medium-rare interior, much like cooking a steak. The ribs are crosscut, also known as flanken style, and are much thinner than traditional American or English beef ribs. In Korea, these ribs are often sold as street food and are sometimes wrapped in lettuce leaves for an edible napkin.

Lemon-Tarragon Veal Chops

Lemon and tarragon have an affinity for each other, and both complement veal beautifully. Be sure to use the best olive oil on your pantry shelf. Delicious and relatively pricey, veal chops are worthy of the finest ingredients.

Cut 1 of the lemons into 8 crosswise slices. Grate enough zest from the remaining lemon to yield $3/4$ teaspoon, then squeeze 1 tablespoon juice. In a small bowl, combine the lemon zest and juice, oil, and chopped tarragon. Season the chops on both sides with salt and pepper, then brush with some of the lemon-tarragon mixture, reserving about 1 tablespoon of the mixture for the lemon slices. Let the chops stand at room temperature for 15 minutes, or cover and refrigerate for up to 3 hours. If refrigerated, remove from the refrigerator 30 minutes before grilling.

Prepare a CHARCOAL or GAS grill for DIRECT grilling over MEDIUM-HIGH heat (page 18 or 22). Oil the grill rack.

CHARCOAL: Grill the chops over the hottest part of the fire until nicely charred and cooked to your liking, 5–7 minutes per side for medium-rare. About 3 minutes before the veal is done, brush the lemon slices with the reserved 1 tablespoon lemon-tarragon mixture. Grill the lemon slices, turning once, until lightly charred and softened, 30–60 seconds per side.

GAS: Grill the chops directly over the heat elements until nicely charred and cooked to your liking, 5–7 minutes per side for medium-rare. About 3 minutes before the veal is done, brush the lemon slices with the reserved 1 tablespoon lemon-tarragon mixture. Grill the lemon slices, turning once, until lightly charred and softened, 30–60 seconds per side.

Serve the veal chops with the grilled lemon slices.

2 large lemons

2 tablespoons extra-virgin olive oil

$1^1/_2$ tablespoons chopped fresh tarragon

4 loin veal chops, each 10–12 oz (315–375 g) and 1–$1^1/_4$ inches (2.5–3 cm) thick

Salt and freshly ground pepper

MAKES 4 SERVINGS

Veal Chops with Sage and Sun-Dried Tomatoes

6 loin veal chops, each about $3/4$ lb (375 g) and $1^{1}/_{2}$ inches (4 cm) thick

$1/4$ cup (2 oz/60 g) chopped oil-packed sun-dried tomatoes

2 tablespoons chopped fresh sage, plus whole leaves for garnish

2 large cloves garlic, finely chopped

Salt and freshly ground pepper

6 toothpicks, soaked in water for 10 minutes and drained

MAKES 6 SERVINGS

Ask the butcher to cut a pocket in the veal chops, or do it yourself: Using a small, sharp knife, cut a deep, wide, horizontal pocket into each veal chop, cutting all the way to the bone, but taking care not to cut through the top or bottom of the chop.

To make the stuffing, in a small dish, mix together the sun-dried tomatoes, chopped sage, garlic, and $1/4$ teaspoon each salt and pepper. Using a spoon or your fingers, insert about 1 tablespoon of the filling into each pocket, then secure the pockets with the toothpicks. Season both sides of the chops with $1/2$ teaspoon each salt and pepper.

Prepare a CHARCOAL or GAS grill for DIRECT grilling over MEDIUM-HIGH heat (page 18 or 22). Oil the grill rack.

CHARCOAL: Grill the veal chops over the hottest part of the fire until they are nicely charred and cooked to your liking, 5–7$^{1}/_{2}$ minutes per side for medium-rare.

GAS: Grill the veal chops directly over the heat elements until they are nicely charred and cooked to your liking, 5–7$^{1}/_{2}$ minutes per side for medium-rare.

Serve the veal chops hot.

Veal chops are special-occasion meat, and they deserve special-occasion treatment. A veal chop needs little in the way of adornment. A simple stuffing of fresh sage leaves and sun-dried tomatoes is just enough.

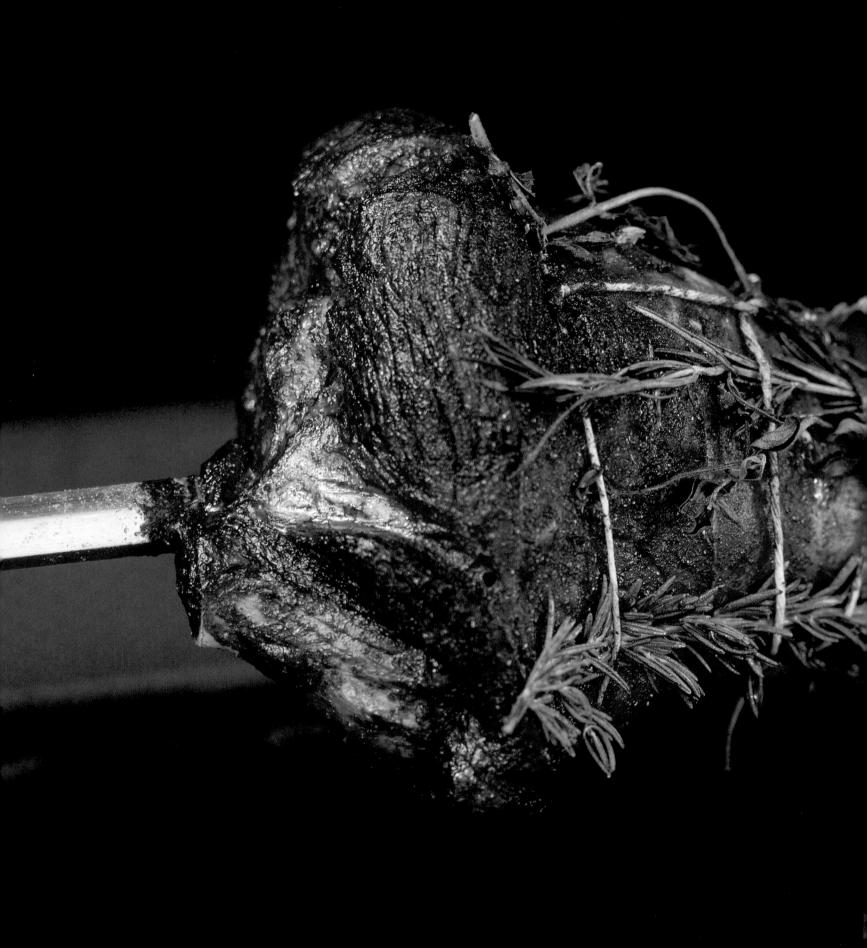

Lamb

About Lamb

Grill smoke marries well with the assertive, slightly gamy character of good lamb. A staple in Middle Eastern and Mediterranean countries, lamb is often embellished with such flavorings as garlic, oregano, mint, mustard, cumin, and paprika—the bolder, the better—before grilling.

Some people mistakenly believe that lamb has a strong smell and taste, qualities better attributed to young lamb's mature cousin, mutton. But you don't see much mutton in today's butcher shops or grocery stores. The young lamb on the market today has a unique, mild, slightly sweet flavor that pairs well with a variety of seasonings, from simple fresh herb pastes and marinades to complex exotic spice mixtures.

Racks of lamb take well to the grill's smoke flavors. Typically considered company fare, lamb racks prepared on an outdoor grill instead of in an oven allow you to entertain in the open air during the warm summer months without skimping on the menu.

Boned and butterflied leg of lamb is an impressive menu centerpiece for a festive get-together with friends. The even cut allows for relatively quick cooking. All it needs is an overnight soak in a simple marinade. For a conversation-sparking main course, spit-roast a bone-in leg for an outdoor dinner party. While your guests mingle in the yard sipping cocktails, they will smell the aroma of the lamb roasting over the fire and see its dramatic shape as it slowly turns on the spit.

Highly seasoned and briefly grilled, lamb chops from the loin or rib sections make a quick family main course in hot-weather months when the outdoor light lingers for hours. Versatile lamb chops can be flavored subtly or elaborately, taking well to a variety of treatments from cuisines around the globe.

Lamb kabobs, made in the style of Greece, India, or Italy, are ideal starting points for a themed menu. In addition, these exotic kabobs are easy to prepare and require minimal cleanup, leaving the cook free to spend time with friends and family, a big part of what makes grilling fun. If you have them, sturdy branches of fresh rosemary, about 8 inches (20 cm) long and soaked in water to cover for about 30 minutes, make aromatic and unusual skewers for simply seasoned lamb cubes.

At your next cookout, surprise guests with spiced lamb burgers in place of the usual beef burgers. Pita bread, yogurt sauce, and chopped vegetable garnishes can stand in for the predictable bun, ketchup, and lettuce-tomato-pickle topping. This new twist on an old favorite will convert even the most dubious diners to lamb's natural richness and flavor.

Working with Lamb

SHOPPING FOR LAMB

Full racks of lamb consist of eight ribs, but you can also find half racks of four ribs each. A good butcher will "french" the lamb rack for you, which means he or she will remove the flap of fat and meat surrounding the eye of the roast and to clean the ends of the rib bones. You can also do this yourself (see page 292). Frenching the meat makes a more attractive restaurant-style presentation.

A versatile cut of meat, lamb legs can be found both bone-in and boneless. A half-leg of bone-in lamb is a manageable cut of meat for cooking on the grill over indirect heat or roasting on a rotisserie spit. Boneless legs of lamb should be butterflied for even grilling. Ask the butcher to bone and butterfly the leg for you, as it can be a complicated process.

Whether from the loin or the rib, lamb chops are usually found on the bone. Loin chops are considered by many to be more flavorful than rib chops because they contain more internal fat (marbling).

Less expensive cuts of lamb can be used for kabobs, which are usually marinated in a bold mixture before grilling to tenderize them. The best cuts for kabobs are from the sirloin, shoulder, or leg; more expensive, tender cuts from the rib and loin can become mushy when marinated. For the tastiest results, pass up lamb that has already been cut into cubes; opt instead for a large piece of lamb and cut it yourself.

Most of the lamb available at the market comes from animals between five and twelve months of age. Lamb labeled as "spring lamb" is not necessarily an indication of quality, as lamb is now successfully raised year-round.

Choose lamb that is light red and finely textured; meat that is purplish or has dark spots could indicate that the lamb is old and has an undesirable flavor. If the lamb has bones, be sure that they are reddish and moist. When you smell the meat, you should detect no off odors. The fat should be creamy white, smooth, and well trimmed. Unlike beef, the tenderness of lamb does not rely on its marbling (streaks of internal fat), although lamb cuts with a generous amount of internal fat will be extra flavorful and juicy.

Avoid lamb with dark purple spots, dry, white bones, rough, yellowing fat, and a strong odor. As for any type of meat, it is best to foster a relationship with a reputable, high-volume butcher to ensure the purchase of a consistent, quality product.

PREPARING LAMB FOR GRILLING

For even cooking over direct heat, very large lamb cuts, such as the leg, must be boned and butterflied before grilling. Ask your butcher to do this for you. Bone-in leg of lamb can be cooked over indirect heat or roasted on a rotisserie spit.

Trim off as much of the external fat from lamb as possible, as it can taste and smell unpleasant when charred.

Be lavish with exotic seasonings and bold herbs and spices, such as rosemary, oregano, garlic, cumin, and mustard, which stand up well to lamb's earthy, slightly gamy flavors. Salting lamb generously before grilling brings out its natural flavors and nicely sets off powerful marinades and seasonings.

Be sure to serve lamb while the meat is still hot, as lamb fat is especially unappealing when cold. It's a good idea to warm plates or platters to ensure that the lamb stays warm and appealing throughout the meal.

TESTING LAMB FOR DONENESS

Treat lamb as you would beef, cooking it to no more than medium for the best flavor. Use a visual cue (cut into the thickest part and check the color) or an instant-read thermometer, following the chart below.

All lamb should sit for 3 to 15 minutes after grilling to allow the juices to redistribute throughout the meat, thus ensuring juiciness and full flavor. The internal temperature could rise 5° to 10°F (3° to 6°C) as the meat sits. Keep this in mind and remove lamb from the grill when it is some degrees shy of the desired temperature. Remember to keep the lamb warm at all times for the finest flavor and texture and to serve it on warmed plates as soon as possible after the lamb is cooked.

DONENESS	COLOR	TEMPERATURE °F	TEMPERATURE °C
Rare	Red	125° to 130°	49° to 54°
Medium-rare	Pinkish red	130°	54°
Medium	Trace of pink	140°	60°
Medium-well	No trace of pink	150°	65°
Well	Grayish brown	160° and higher	74° and higher

Lamb Cuts for Grilling

In the United States, lamb is divided into six primary cuts: the shoulder, forelegs and breast, belly, rib, loin, and leg. The lamb cuts suitable for direct-heat grilling come from the rib and loin, which are the tender and little-exercised parts of the animal. Less tender cuts from the leg can also be grilled but must be either boned and butterflied if grilled over direct heat, or indirect-heat grilled. Cuts from the shoulder, foreleg, breast, and belly are not as widely available as the other cuts, and are better suited to other types of cooking methods.

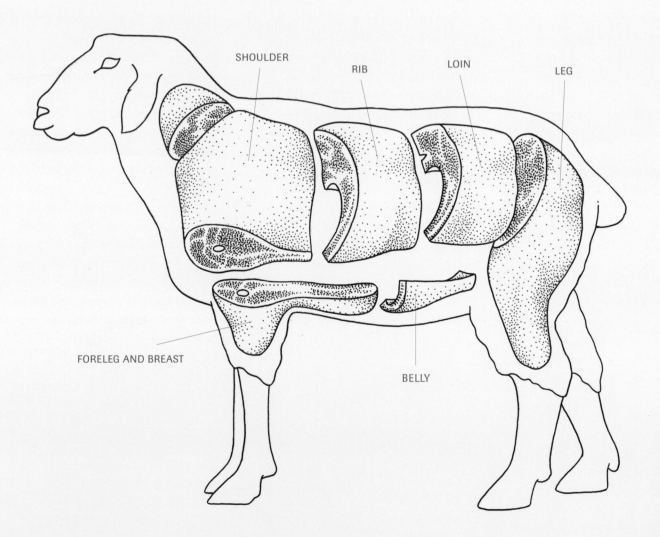

SHOULDER

RIB

LOIN

LEG

FORELEG AND BREAST

BELLY

RIB

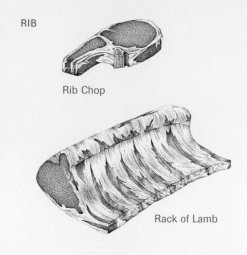

Rib Chop

Rack of Lamb

LOIN

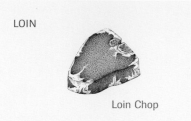

Loin Chop

LEG

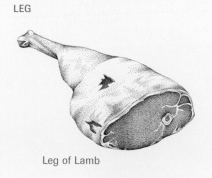

Leg of Lamb

Boned and Butterflied Leg of Lamb

LAMB CUTS FOR GRILLING

The cuts listed below are easy to find in a butcher shop or specialty food store. If you purchase your meat from a supermarket, pass up previously packaged meats and ask the butcher there to cut it for you fresh.

Rib Chops

Rib chops have more fat than loin chops, which means they boast a bit more flavor. They can be cut into either single thickness (one rib) or double thickness (two ribs). Opt for double-thick chops if you enjoy your lamb medium-rare to rare; thinner chops cook more quickly and are hard to pull from the fire in time. Slather rib chops with a bold spice paste, herb rub, or bread-crumb coating; quickly grill over direct heat; and serve with a chutney or relish. Long soaks in acidic marinades can overtenderize the meat.

Rack

Tender, juicy, and easy to cook, grill-roasted lamb racks hold their own with rich sauces and fruit garnishes. Lamb racks are versatile cuts of meat, and can be cooked over direct or indirect heat.

Loin Chops

Loin chops have the signature T-shaped bone of the loin and are the most expensive of the lamb chops. Flavor loin chops as you would rib chops.

Bone-in Leg

Cooked over indirect heat, a leg of lamb is a good grilling choice. Coat the leg with fragrant herbs and spices, grill-roast or spit-roast on a rotisserie, and then cut on the diagonal into thin slices.

Boned and Butterflied Leg

When boned and butterflied (ask the butcher to do this for you), a leg of lamb can be cooked relatively quickly over direct heat. Smear a butterflied leg with a mustardy paste or soak it in a flavorful marinade before grilling and slicing into serving portions.

Kabobs

Marinating lamb cubes carved from less tender cuts is easy on the budget and, when treated to the tenderizing and flavoring powers of the marinade, delicious at the table. For the best kabobs, choose lamb sirloin, shoulder, or leg; cut it into cubes; and marinate the cubes in an acidic citrus or yogurt-based marinade. Grill on skewers over a direct fire.

Burgers

It is wise to purchase a whole piece of lamb from the shoulder or leg and have the butcher grind it for you. Or, if you have access to a meat grinder, do it yourself at home. A high ratio of fat to meat is not an asset in lamb burgers, as lamb fat congeals at a lower temperature than beef fat and can be unappealing. Grill lamb burgers over a direct fire and serve them with your favorite condiments, exotic or traditional.

Provençal Rack of Lamb

A rack of lamb is special-occasion fare, and what better inspiration for a special occasion than Provence? The herbed mustard coating can also flavor chicken or meaty fish steaks, such as tuna or swordfish. Be sure to reserve some of the coating to use as a table sauce. Its flavor is completely different from that of the grilled coating on the meat. Serve with grilled or sautéed summer squash.

In a small nonreactive bowl, stir together the mustard, Cognac, oil, vinegar, mustard seeds, and 1 teaspoon pepper until well blended. Stir in the tarragon. Set aside ¼ cup (2 fl oz/60 ml) of the mixture to use as a table sauce. Brush the remaining mustard mixture over the meaty parts of the lamb racks. Let the lamb stand at room temperature for at least 20 minutes, or cover and refrigerate for up to 4 hours. If refrigerated, return to room temperature before grilling.

Prepare a CHARCOAL or GAS grill for DIRECT grilling over MEDIUM-HIGH heat (page 18 or 22). Oil the grill rack.

CHARCOAL: Place the lamb racks on their sides over the hottest part of the fire and cook, turning once, until nicely browned, crusty, and done to your liking, 10–13 minutes per side for medium-rare.

GAS: Place the lamb racks on their sides directly over the heat elements, turning once, until nicely browned, crusty, and done to your liking, 10–13 minutes per side for medium-rare.

To test for doneness, insert an instant-read thermometer into the thickest part of the rack away from the bone; it should register 130°F (54°C).

Let the lamb rest for about 5 minutes. Cut the racks in half or into chops to serve. Pass the reserved sauce at the table.

¼ cup (2 oz/60 g) Dijon mustard

3 tablespoons Cognac or brandy

3 tablespoons olive oil

1 tablespoon white wine vinegar

2 teaspoons mustard seeds

Freshly cracked pepper

3 tablespoons chopped fresh tarragon

2 racks of lamb, 1¼–1½ lb (625–750 g) each, frenched (page 292)

MAKES 4 OR 5 SERVINGS

Rack of Lamb with Mint Pesto Crust

For the Mint Pesto

1 cup (1 oz/30 g) lightly packed fresh mint leaves

²/₃ cup (1 oz/30 g) lightly packed fresh parsley sprigs

¹/₄ cup (1 oz/30 g) pine nuts

3 large cloves garlic, finely chopped

1 teaspoon grated lemon zest

1 tablespoon fresh lemon juice

Salt

¹/₄ teaspoon red pepper flakes

¹/₃ cup (3 fl oz/80 ml) extra-virgin olive oil

¹/₃ cup (1¹/₂ oz/45 g) grated Parmesan cheese

2¹/₂ cups (3¹/₂ oz/105 g) *panko* or coarse dried bread crumbs

2 racks of lamb, 1¹/₄–1¹/₂ lb (625–750 g) each, frenched (page 292)

MAKES 4-5 SERVINGS

To make the mint pesto, in a food processor, combine the mint, parsley, pine nuts, garlic, lemon zest and juice, ¹/₂ teaspoon salt, and red pepper flakes. Pulse until all the ingredients are finely chopped, then process, stopping to scrape down the sides of the work bowl once or twice, until a coarse purée forms. With the motor running, pour in the olive oil, processing until it is well incorporated, 5–10 seconds. Transfer to a bowl and stir in the cheese. Let the pesto stand at room temperature for 15 minutes, or cover and refrigerate for up to 24 hours before using.

Prepare a CHARCOAL or GAS grill for INDIRECT grilling over MEDIUM-HIGH heat (page 19 or 23). If using a charcoal grill, place a drip pan in the center of the fire bed. Oil the grill rack.

Spread the bread crumbs on a plate. Smear the pesto over the meaty part of each lamb rack, then dredge the lamb in the crumbs to cover the pesto coating. Pat extra bread crumbs onto any area that is not coated.

CHARCOAL: Place the lamb racks on their sides over the drip pan, cover the grill, and cook, turning once, until nicely browned, crusty, and done to your liking, 12–15 minutes per side for medium-rare.

GAS: Place the lamb racks on their sides on the grill rack away from the heat elements, cover the grill, and cook, turning once, until nicely browned, crusty, and done to your liking, 12–15 minutes per side for medium-rare.

To test for doneness, insert an instant-read thermometer into the thickest part of the rack away from the bone; it should register 130°F (54°C). The temperature will rise another 5°–10°F (3°–6°C) while it is resting.

Let the lamb rest for about 5 minutes. Cut the racks in half or into chops to serve.

Rack of lamb can be grilled either by direct or indirect heat. Indirect cooking is preferred when the lamb is coated with delicate mixtures, such as the mint pesto crust in this recipe. Indirect cooking takes a bit longer than direct, of course, but requires less attention, as the likelihood of flare-ups is lessened. Israeli couscous (pearl pasta) makes a nice side dish.

Panko are Japanese dried bread crumbs. If you can't find these coarse, flavorful crumbs, make your own by drying fresh bread crumbs in a 300°F (150°C) oven until they are golden and crisp.

Stuffed Boneless Leg of Lamb

In this recipe, a boned leg of lamb is treated to a flavorful stuffing. The lamb is laid flat, spread with a layer of heady Dijon mustard, topped with a mixture of red bell pepper, garlic, and shallot, and then rolled up, tied, and grilled. When the leg is carved for serving, each slice reveals a colorful stripe of stuffing, making for a particularly beautiful presentation.

Remove the lamb leg from the refrigerator 1 hour before grilling.

To make the stuffing, in a frying pan over medium heat, warm the olive oil. Add the bell pepper and sauté until slightly softened, 2–3 minutes. Add the garlic and shallots and sauté until the shallots are slightly softened and the garlic is fragrant, about 2 minutes. Add the vinegar and thyme, stir well, and cook for 1 minute. Season to taste with salt and pepper, remove from the heat, and let cool.

Remove the netting, if any, from the leg of lamb and unroll the lamb. Using a sharp knife, carefully trim away any visible fat from both sides of the lamb, and then lay it flat, boned surface up. Cover with a large sheet of plastic wrap and pound with a meat pounder to an even thickness. Spread the mustard evenly over the inside of the lamb and then sprinkle generously with salt and pepper. Distribute the cooled stuffing evenly over the mustard. Roll the lamb up starting from a long end and form into a compact roll. Using kitchen string, secure the roll at 2-inch (5-cm) intervals along its length. Then tie a piece of string lengthwise once or twice around the roll to help it keep its shape. Lightly brush the rolled leg with olive oil and season on all sides with salt and pepper.

Prepare a CHARCOAL or GAS grill for INDIRECT grilling over MEDIUM heat (page 19 or 23). Oil the grill rack.

CHARCOAL: Place a drip pan half full of water in the center of the fire bed. Grill the lamb over the hottest part of the fire for 5 minutes, turning once, to sear lightly. Turn the lamb over and place over the drip pan. Cover the grill and continue to cook until done to your liking, adding more hot coals as needed to maintain the temperature, 1¹/₄–1¹/₂ hours for medium.

GAS: Place a shallow pan half full of water at the edge of the grill rack. Grill the lamb directly over the heat elements for 5 minutes, turning once, to sear lightly. Turn the lamb over and place it away from the heat elements. Cover the grill and continue to cook until done to your liking, 1¹/₄–1¹/₂ hours for medium.

To test for doneness, insert an instant-read thermometer into the thickest part of the lamb; it should register 140°F (60°C). The temperature will rise another 5°–10°F (3°–6°C) while the meat is resting.

Let the lamb rest for 15–30 minutes. Remove the strings and cut the lamb roll crosswise into thin slices to serve.

1 boned leg of lamb, about 5 lb (2.5 kg)

For the Stuffing

1 tablespoon extra-virgin olive oil

1 red bell pepper (capsicum), seeded and finely chopped

3 cloves garlic, thinly sliced

2 shallots, thinly sliced (about 3 tablespoons)

1 tablespoon red wine vinegar

1 teaspoon fresh thyme leaves

Salt and freshly ground pepper

2 tablespoons Dijon mustard

Salt and freshly ground pepper

Olive oil for brushing

MAKES 8–10 SERVINGS

Tunisian-Spiced Leg of Lamb

For the Tunisian Spice Rub

1 tablespoon ground coriander

2 teaspoons ground cumin

Salt

$^1/_2$ teaspoon ground cinnamon

$^1/_4$ teaspoon ground cloves

$^1/_4$ teaspoon ground cayenne pepper

$^1/_2$ bone-in leg of lamb, 4–5 lb (2–2.5 kg)

8 cloves garlic, quartered

3 tablespoons olive oil

Olives and caper berries for garnish (optional)

MAKES 8 SERVINGS

Spit-roasting a spice-coated leg of lamb is a grilling tradition throughout North Africa and the Middle East. A whole leg is usually too heavy for most home grills, so this recipe is for a half leg. If you have a bigger spit and are hosting a large party, just double the spice mixture, use a whole leg, and add additional time for grilling. If you have no spit at all, prepare a fire and grill the lamb over indirect heat; the timing should be about the same.

To make the Tunisian spice rub, in a small bowl, stir together the coriander, cumin, 1 teaspoon salt, cinnamon, cloves, and cayenne. Using a small, sharp knife, make 32 tiny slits over the surface of the lamb leg and insert a garlic piece into each slit. Sprinkle the lamb evenly with the spice mixture, patting and rubbing it into all parts of the meat. Brush the lamb with 1$^1/_2$ tablespoons of the oil. Let the lamb stand for at least 20 minutes at room temperature, or cover and refrigerate for up to 24 hours. If refrigerated, remove from the refrigerator 1 hour before grilling.

Prepare a CHARCOAL or GAS grill for ROTISSERIE (spit-) roasting (page 28) or for INDIRECT grilling (page 19 or 23) over MEDIUM HEAT. If using a charcoal grill, place a drip pan in the center of the fire bed.

CHARCOAL: Thread the lamb onto the spit (page 28) and insert the spit into the slots following the manufacturer's directions. Or place the lamb on the grill rack over the drip pan. Cover the grill and cook the lamb, brushing once or twice with the remaining 1$^1/_2$ tablespoons oil, until well browned and cooked to your liking, about 2 hours for medium-rare.

GAS: Thread the lamb onto the spit (page 28) and insert the spit into the slots following the manufacturer's directions. Or place the lamb on the grill rack away from the heat elements. Cover the grill and cook the lamb, brushing once or twice with the remaining 1$^1/_2$ tablespoons oil, until well browned and cooked to your liking, about 2 hours for medium-rare.

To test for doneness, insert an instant-read thermometer into the thickest part of the leg away from the bone; it should register 130°F (54°C). The temperature will rise another 5°–10°F (3°–6°C) while the meat is resting.

Let the lamb rest for 15 minutes before carving. Serve garnished with olives and caper berries, if desired.

Lamb Chops with Anchovies, Garlic, and Lemon

Anchovies and garlic, mashed together with fruity olive oil and aromatic lemon juice and zest, make a lovely bath in which to soak thick, meaty loin lamb chops. The Italian-style marinade complements chicken breasts, tuna steaks, or jumbo shrimp (prawns) as well. For a nice presentation, garnish plates with watercress or arugula (rocket).

To make the anchovy-garlic marinade, select a shallow, nonreactive dish just large enough to hold the lamb in a single layer. Add the lemon juice, olive oil, and the oil from the anchovies to the dish and stir well. Add the anchovies, mashing them well with the back of a spoon. Stir in the green onion, garlic, lemon zest, and 1/2 teaspoon pepper. Transfer 1–2 tablespoons of the marinade to a small bowl and set aside. Add the lamb to the large dish and turn to coat both sides. Let stand at room temperature for 20 minutes, or cover and refrigerate for up to 2 hours, turning occasionally. If refrigerated, remove from the refrigerator 30 minutes before grilling.

Prepare a CHARCOAL or GAS grill for DIRECT grilling over HIGH heat (page 18 or 22). Remove the lamb chops from the marinade and discard the marinade.

CHARCOAL: Grill the meat over the hottest part of the fire, turning once or twice, until nicely charred and cooked to your liking, 10–15 minutes total for medium-rare. About 2 minutes before the lamb is done, brush the lemon slices with the reserved marinade and place at the edges of the grill where the heat is less intense. Grill the lemon until softened and lightly charred, turning once, 30–60 seconds per side.

GAS: Grill the meat directly over the heat elements, turning once or twice, until nicely charred and cooked to your liking, 10–15 minutes total for medium-rare. About 2 minutes before the lamb is done, brush the lemon slices with the reserved marinade and place on an area with lower heat. Grill the lemon until softened and lightly charred, turning once, 30–60 seconds per side.

Serve the lamb chops immediately garnished with the grilled lemon slices.

For the Anchovy-Garlic Marinade

1/4 cup (2 fl oz/60 ml) fresh lemon juice

2 tablespoons extra-virgin olive oil

4 oil-packed anchovy fillets, plus 1 tablespoon oil from tin

1/4 cup (3/4 oz/20 g) finely chopped green (spring) onion, including tender green tops

4 cloves garlic, finely chopped

1 1/4 teaspoons grated lemon zest

Freshly ground coarse pepper

8 loin lamb chops, each about 6 oz (185 g) and 1 1/4 inches (4 cm) thick

1 large lemon, cut into 8 slices

MAKES 4 SERVINGS

Five-Spice Lamb Chops

¹/₃ cup (3 fl oz/80 ml) soy sauce

3 tablespoons rice vinegar

1¹/₂ tablespoons hoisin sauce

1 tablespoon peeled and grated fresh ginger

2 teaspoons Asian chile oil

2 teaspoons vegetable oil

2 teaspoons five-spice powder

8 loin lamb chops, each about 6 oz (185 g) and 1¹/₂ inches (4 cm) thick

MAKES 4 SERVINGS

Select a shallow, nonreactive dish just large enough to hold the lamb in a single layer. Add the soy sauce, vinegar, hoisin sauce, ginger, chile and vegetable oils, and five-spice powder to the dish and mix well. Add the lamb chops and turn to coat both sides. Cover and let stand at room temperature for 20 minutes.

Prepare a CHARCOAL or GAS grill for DIRECT grilling over HIGH heat (page 18 or 22). Remove the chops from the marinade, reserving the marinade.

CHARCOAL: Grill the meat over the hottest part of the fire, turning once or twice and brushing with the marinade during the first 5 minutes of cooking, until nicely charred and cooked to your liking, 10–13 minutes total for medium-rare.

GAS: Grill the meat directly over the heat elements, turning once or twice and brushing often with the marinade during the first 5 minutes of cooking, until nicely charred and cooked to your liking, 10–13 minutes total for medium-rare.

Let the lamb chops rest for about 3 minutes before serving. Serve hot.

Five-spice powder is a popular Chinese seasoning made from fennel seeds, star anise, cinnamon, cloves, Sichuan pepper, and sometimes ginger. The exact proportions and even the ingredients can vary, but the combination of sweet and savory spices is always distinctive. Show off these beautifully grilled lamb chops on a bed of sautéed carrot and red bell pepper (capsicum) strips.

Orange-Rosemary Lamb Chops

This Basque-inspired marinade lends itself to double-rib lamb chops, but if you like more charring on your meat, opt for single-rib chops. Watch them carefully on the grill, however, so that they do not overcook. For some added fire, mix $^{1}/_{4}$ teaspoon red pepper flakes into the marinade. Serve the chops with a simple side dish, such as herbed white beans or soft polenta.

Select a shallow, nonreactive dish just large enough to hold the lamb in a single layer. Add the orange juice, wine, oil, vinegar, orange zest, rosemary, and $^{1}/_{2}$ teaspoon salt to the dish and stir well. Add the lamb and turn to coat both sides with the marinade. Cover and let stand for 30 minutes.

Prepare a CHARCOAL or GAS grill for DIRECT grilling over HIGH heat (page 18 or 22). Oil the grill rack. Remove the lamb from the marinade; discard the marinade.

CHARCOAL: Grill the chops over the hottest part of the fire, turning once, until they are nicely charred and done to your liking, 4–5 minutes per side for medium-rare.

GAS: Grill the chops directly over the heat elements, turning once, until they are nicely charred and done to your liking, 4–5 minutes per side for medium-rare.

Let the lamb chops rest for about 3 minutes before serving. Serve hot.

$^{1}/_{3}$ cup (3 fl oz/80 ml) each fresh orange juice and dry red wine

3 tablespoons olive oil

2 tablespoons sherry vinegar

1 tablespoon each grated orange zest and chopped fresh rosemary

Salt

8 double-rib lamb chops, $2^{1}/_{2}$–3 lb (1.25–1.5 kg) total weight

MAKES 4 SERVINGS

Lamb Chops Two Ways

Rib lamb chops are simply racks of lamb cut into chops, of either double thickness or single thickness. For this recipe, the thinner cut is preferred since it allows more surface for the potent garam masala or gently spiced tahini (sesame paste) to flavor the chops. Since both of the mixtures are easy to make, grill some chops using some of each. Serve the lamb chops with a Middle Eastern or Indian side dish, such as tabbouleh or rice pilaf studded with dried fruits.

To make the garam masala rub, in a small, dry frying pan set over medium heat, combine the peppercorns, coriander seeds, cloves, cumin seeds, cardamom seeds, anise seeds, and cinnamon and toss until fragrant and the spices become a shade darker, 1–2 minutes. Immediately pour the hot spices onto a plate and let cool completely. Grind the spices in a spice grinder or with a mortar and pestle. Stir in the turmeric and ³/₄ teaspoon salt.

To make the tahini paste, in a bowl, stir together the tahini, yogurt, chopped mint, lemon juice, sesame seeds, cumin, coriander, garlic, and salt and pepper to taste.

Brush both sides of half of the lamb chops with the oil, then sprinkle with the garam masala rub, patting it in with your fingers. Add the remaining half of the lamb chops to the tahini paste and turn to coat both sides. Let the lamb stand at room temperature for 20 minutes, or cover and refrigerate for up to 3 hours. If refrigerated, remove from the refrigerator 20 minutes before grilling.

Prepare a CHARCOAL or GAS grill for DIRECT grilling over HIGH heat (page 18 or 22). Oil the grill rack.

CHARCOAL: Grill the meat over the hottest part of the fire, turning once, until nicely charred and cooked to your liking, 3–4 minutes per side for medium-rare.

GAS: Grill the meat directly over the heat elements, turning once, until nicely charred and cooked to your liking, 3–4 minutes per side for medium-rare.

Let the lamb chops rest for 5 minutes before serving. Serve hot.

For the Garam Masala Rub

1 teaspoon peppercorns

1 teaspoon coriander seeds

1 teaspoon whole cloves

³/₄ teaspoon cumin seeds

³/₄ teaspoon cardamom seeds

¹/₂ teaspoon anise seeds

¹/₂ cinnamon stick, broken into pieces

2 teaspoons ground turmeric

Salt

For the Tahini Paste

²/₃ cup (6¹/₂ oz/200 g) tahini

¹/₂ cup (4 oz/125 g) whole-milk or low-fat plain yogurt

¹/₄ cup (¹/₃ oz/10 g) chopped fresh mint

3 tablespoons fresh lemon juice

1 tablespoon sesame seeds

2 teaspoons ground cumin

1¹/₂ teaspoons ground coriander

3 cloves garlic, minced

Salt and freshly ground coarse pepper

16 single-rib lamb chops, 2¹/₂–3 lb (1.25–1.5 kg) total weight

2 tablespoons olive oil

MAKES 4 SERVINGS

Souvlakia

For the Tzatziki

1 cup (8 oz/250 g) whole-milk or low-fat plain yogurt

$1/2$ cup ($2^1/2$ oz/75 g) peeled, seeded, and chopped cucumber

3 tablespoons finely chopped green (spring) onion, including tender green tops

2 tablespoons chopped fresh dill

Salt and freshly ground pepper

$1/3$ cup (3 fl oz/80 ml) fresh lemon juice

3 tablespoons olive oil

$1^1/2$ tablespoons chopped fresh oregano

3 cloves garlic, finely chopped

Salt and freshly ground pepper

$1^1/2$ lb (750 g) boneless lamb from leg

16–20 long bamboo skewers, soaked (page 10), or metal skewers

4 pita breads

1 large tomato, chopped

$1/2$ red onion, chopped

2 cups (4 oz/125 g) chopped romaine (cos) lettuce

MAKES 4 SERVINGS

To make the *tzatziki*, in a bowl, stir together the yogurt, cucumber, green onion, dill, $1/2$ teaspoon salt, and $1/4$ teaspoon pepper. Cover and refrigerate for at least 30 minutes or for up to 6 hours.

Select a shallow, nonreactive dish just large enough to hold the meat in a single layer. Add the lemon juice, oil, oregano, garlic, and $1/2$ teaspoon each salt and pepper to the dish and mix well. Cut the lamb into 1–$1^1/4$ inch (2.5–3 cm) chunks. Add the lamb to the marinade and turn to coat all sides. Cover and refrigerate for at least 1 hour or for up to 4 hours.

Prepare a CHARCOAL or GAS grill for DIRECT grilling over HIGH heat (page 18 or 22). Remove the lamb from the marinade and thread the chunks onto bamboo or metal skewers.

CHARCOAL: Grill the skewered meat over the hottest part of the fire, turning to char all sides, until cooked to your liking, 5–7 minutes total for medium-rare. About 1 minute before the lamb is done, gently warm the pita breads at the edges of the grill where the heat is less intense.

GAS: Grill the skewered meat directly over the heat elements, turning to char all sides, until cooked to your liking, 5–7 minutes total for medium-rare. About 1 minute before the lamb is done, gently warm the pita breads on an area with lower heat.

To serve, place the meat on a platter. Surround it with the pita breads and separate bowls of the tomato, onion, lettuce, and *tzatziki*. Have each guest spoon some of the *tzatziki* into the pocket of a pita bread, and then add the meat, tomato, onion, lettuce, and additional *tzatziki*.

Souvlakia is the big-city street food of Greece, sold by roadside vendors who rely on its smoky aroma to lure customers. The meat is usually rolled into large, soft pita breads and served with *tzatziki*, a simple herbed yogurt sauce. The traditional condiments are chopped tomato, onion, and shredded romaine. Souvlakia makes a great lunch or informal supper for family and friends.

Moroccan-Spiced Lamb Burgers

Throughout North Africa and the Middle East, highly seasoned ground lamb is popular for grilling. Many traditions call for molding the lamb mixture onto metal skewers in an elongated sausage shape. The lamb is grilled and then the "sausage" is slipped off the skewer in a single piece and served with traditional garnishes of pita breads, seasoned chopped tomatoes and onions, and citrus wedges. Here, the lamb is formed into oval burger shapes, grilled, and then inserted into pita pockets for a terrific, informal supper.

In a bowl, combine the lamb, onion, bread crumbs, mint, garlic, cumin, coriander, 3/4 teaspoon salt, and cayenne. Using your hands, mix gently but thoroughly. Form the mixture into 4 oval patties, each about 4 1/2 inches (11.5 cm) long and about 3/4 inch (2 cm) thick.

In a small bowl, stir together the tomato and cilantro. Season to taste with salt. Let the patties and the tomato mixture stand at room temperature for 15 minutes, or cover and refrigerate for up to 2 hours. If refrigerated, remove from the refrigerator 15 minutes before grilling.

Prepare a CHARCOAL or GAS grill for DIRECT grilling over HIGH heat (page 18 or 22).

CHARCOAL: Grill the patties over the hottest part of the fire, turning once, until nicely charred and cooked to your liking, 5–6 minutes per side for medium. About 1 minute before the patties are done, place the pita breads at the edges of the grill where the heat is less intense to warm.

GAS: Grill the patties directly over the heat elements, turning once, until nicely charred and cooked to your liking, 5–6 minutes per side for medium. About 1 minute before the patties are done, place the pita breads on an area with lower heat to warm.

To assemble the sandwiches, coat the pockets of the pita breads lightly with some of the yogurt, then slip a lamb patty into each bread. Add the tomato mixture, sprouts, and remaining yogurt, or serve these condiments on the side.

1 1/2 lb (750 g) ground (minced) lean lamb

1 yellow onion, finely chopped

3/4 cup (1 1/2 oz/45 g) fine fresh bread crumbs

1/4 cup (1/3 oz/10 g) chopped fresh mint

2 cloves garlic, finely chopped

1 teaspoon ground cumin

3/4 teaspoon ground coriander

Salt

1/4 teaspoon ground cayenne pepper

1 large tomato, diced

3 tablespoons chopped fresh cilantro (fresh coriander)

4 whole-wheat (wholemeal) pita breads

1 cup (8 oz/250 g) whole-milk or low-fat plain yogurt

1 cup (2 oz/60 g) alfalfa sprouts

MAKES 4 SERVINGS

Pork

About Pork

Around the world, pork turns up in countless guises on the grill. With an amazing capacity to marry with a wide variety of both bold and delicate flavors, tender, succulent pork absorbs fragrant smoke and spices wonderfully, and cooks well over both direct and indirect heat.

Pork is complemented by a wide variety of seasonings and cooking styles. Because of its versatility and the fact that pigs are easy to domesticate and raise, pork has become a central ingredient of cultures throughout the ages, from ancient China to modern America. Pork is also admired for its tenderness and juiciness.

Pork chops on the grill, whether bone-in or boneless, make a hearty main course. Vary the flavorings however you like, as chops can take on a number of different culinary personalities, from Tuscan to Asian to traditional American. Bone-in chops have more flavor, while boneless chops cook faster and are easier to serve. Equally versatile,

steaks cut from the shoulder section are the ideal centerpiece for quick weeknight suppers, pairing easily with just about any sauce or condiment you desire.

Pork roasts can be fancy—imagine a center-cut loin grill-roasted and accompanied with fresh herbs and vegetables—or down-home—think of satisfying baby back ribs. Pork's split personality can be attributed to its fine-grained meat and just the right amount of fat, making it a perfect candidate for the grill, no matter how you cook it.

Forget the notion that pork is white meat; properly cooked, a pork tenderloin will be lightly pink in the center and wonderfully flavorful and tender. Simple enough for a

weekday dinner, but special enough for company, lean, flavorful tenderloins are good choices to grill anytime.

Spareribs, cut from the pig's belly, are meaty and succulent. Long, slow barbecuing is the only way, in many people's opinion, to cook these popular ribs, although the exact treatments and accompaniments are hotly debated from Kansas City to Chicago to Memphis. For a selection of spareribs and other barbecue recipes, turn to page 262. Baby back ribs are more versatile and can be cooked long and slow or quickly over direct heat, and can be found in both this chapter and the one on true barbecue.

Any type of sausage, fresh or fully cooked, can be grilled. Grill a selection of pork sausages at your next cookout as an alternative to hot dogs. Embellish them in any number of ways—try them strewn over sauerkraut and accompanied with coarse mustard for a new take on *choucroute garnie*.

Working with Pork

SHOPPING FOR PORK

Rib chops have a substantial eye of meat, with the upper part of the rib bone attached. They have a little more fat (and stay juicier) than loin chops, which have a distinct T-bone and, like their beef counterparts, have some of the loin and tenderloin muscles attached. Both types of chops can be found boneless, though bone-in chops tend to be more flavorful.

Pork steaks, cut from the shoulder, can be found bone-in or boneless. A zesty marinade nicely balances their richness. Steaks can be cut from ham, too, and they take well to the charred flavors they pick up on the grill.

The best pork "roasts" for grilling include pork loin and tenderloin. Pork loin can be found bone-in or boneless. The bones help the lean meat stay moist and flavorful. A boneless loin benefits from a soak in a brine to help lock in moisture. Tenderloins are small versions of pork roasts and are quick cooking, perfect for last-minute meals.

Spareribs, from the pig's belly, should have a good amount of meat on them and not be too fatty. Baby back ribs, which are cut from the loin, have less meat on the bones, but it is usually tender and lean. Choose the meatiest ribs you can find.

Pork shoulder, also known as Boston butt, is a popular cut for barbecue devotees. It contains a lot of internal fat that leaves the meat flavorful and juicy after long, slow cooking. Pork shoulder can be found both bone-in and boneless.

Look for pork that is well trimmed—any fat should be white and smooth—with no dark patches or blemishes. If it is bought packaged, look for a minimum of clear (not cloudy) liquid, and smell to detect any off odors. The surface of raw pork should be moist, but not sticky or slimy, and somewhat firm; avoid soft or watery meat. Look for pork that is fine grained and reddish pink, passing up meat that is pale and has a gray cast. If possible, always buy fresh, rather than frozen, pork.

Like with all meat, the best assurance of quality is to purchase it from a reputable butcher. Seek one who deals in high volume to ensure a fresh supply of meat.

PREPARING PORK FOR GRILLING

Cut off any excess exterior fat, which could cause flare-ups. On tenderloins, remove the silver skin (the thin, pearlescent membrane that connects the tenderloin to the loin and covers the length of the tenderloin) with a small, sharp knife (page 293).

Don't be afraid to season pork generously with salt, as it adds to its flavor and juiciness. When using lean cuts, consider using a marinade or dry rub to make up for the flavor that is missing in the absence of fat. If you want to keep things simple, brush the pork with olive oil to keep it from drying out on the grill.

TESTING PORK FOR DONENESS

Many of us grew up with the notion that pork should be cooked until no trace of pink could be seen, thereby killing the trichinosis parasite that was a major health concern in the past. But pork was much fattier then and remained juicy even when thoroughly cooked. Today, pork is leaner, and if we followed the old advice, we would be left with a dry, tasteless piece of meat. Due to changes in the way pigs are raised and processed, trichinosis has been all but eradicated from the United States. To ease concerns further, researchers have determined that trichinae are killed at 137°F (58°C), or medium-rare.

For roasts that are allowed to rest for 5 to 15 minutes before serving, the carryover heat will increase the temperature by 5° to 10°F (3° to 6°C). Be sure to remove the roast from the covered grill at a point that accounts for this increase.

Pork chops, loin roasts, and tenderloins should be cooked to a final temperature of 150° to 155°F (65° to 68°C) after resting. You can cook larger, fattier cuts, such as Boston butt or shoulder, to 155° to 165°F (68° to 74°C) after resting. The fat in these meats will ensure that they stay juicy and flavorful even though cooked to a slightly higher temperature. Ribs should be cooked to 170°F (77°C) for tenderness and flavor.

To judge the doneness of grilled pork visually, cut into the thickest part. The meat should be faintly pink to almost white, depending on how you like it cooked. To be precise, use an instant-read thermometer and compare the results to the chart below.

DONENESS	COLOR	TEMPERATURE °F	TEMPERATURE °C
Medium	Slightly pink	140° to 150°	60° to 65°
Medium-well	No trace of pink	150° to 160°	65° to 71°
Well	Grayish brown	160° and higher	71° and higher

Pork Cuts for Grilling

Butchers in the United States divide the pig into five primary sections: the ham, loin, shoulder, picnic, and belly. The loin is sometimes subdivided into the center loin and the sirloin. Small thin pork cuts, from any section, are suitable for direct-heat cooking, while thick roasts or rib slabs do best when grill-roasted over an indirect-heat fire. Some of the most famous barbecued dishes are made from pork, such as North Carolina pulled pork, which uses the shoulder; and Memphis ribs, which come from the belly. The picnic portion and much of the ham portion of the pig are better suited to other cooking methods, such as braising.

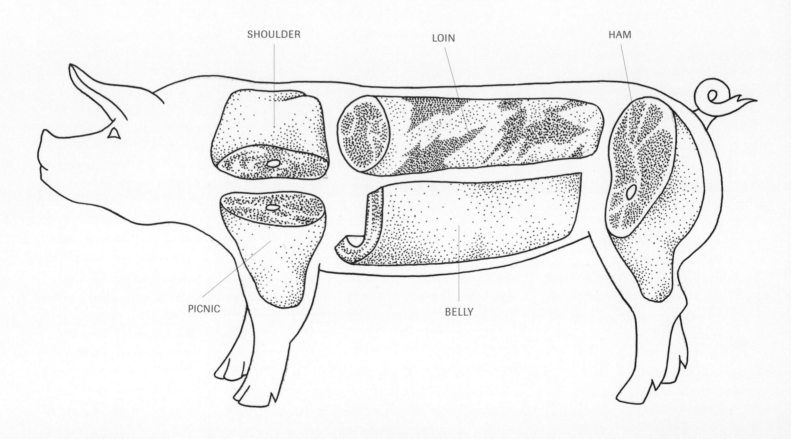

SHOULDER

Shoulder Steak

Shoulder Roast

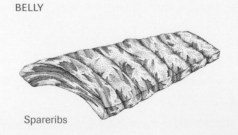

BELLY

Spareribs

LOIN (CENTER LOIN)

Loin Chop

Rib Chop

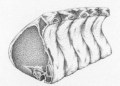

Baby Back Ribs

Boneless Top-loin Roast

Bone-in Top-loin Roast

LOIN
(SIRLOIN)

Tenderloin

PORK CUTS FOR GRILLING

As with most meat, select pork that's freshly cut from the butcher's case rather than pre-packaged cuts. Prepare pork soon after you buy it, as it doesn't freeze well.

Shoulder Steaks

Known as shoulder or blade steaks, these economical cuts taste best when marinated or brushed with an assertive "mopping" sauce. A combination of direct-heat grilling and smoking is a traditional treatment for pork steaks in the Missouri Ozarks.

Shoulder Roast

Shoulder roast goes by many other names, like Boston shoulder roast, Boston butt, and pork butt. Cut from the top of the shoulder, it has sufficient fat and flavor to be slowly roasted over indirect heat into fall-apart shreds and showcases smoke flavors beautifully.

Spareribs

The ribs of choice for Memphis-style barbecue, spareribs must be cooked over a long, slow indirect-heat fire to infuse them with smoke flavor and make them tender.

Bone-in Pork Chops

Whether cut from the loin (with a T-shaped bone) or rib (with a large eye of rib meat and a small rib bone attached), pork chops measuring 3/4 to 1 inch (2 to 2.5 cm) thick are perfect for grilling. Thinner chops may cook too quickly over direct heat and dry out. Chops take well to spice rubs and marinades. Bone-in pork chops are also well suited to stuffing—the bone makes a natural wall for holding the stuffing. Or try brining unstuffed pork chops before grilling for a juicier and more flavorful chop.

Boneless Pork Chops

Boneless pork chops can be handled like their bone-in kin. But also like their kin, they must be of sufficient thickness (3/4 to 1 inch/ 2 to 2.5 cm) to stand up to the heat of a hot, direct fire without drying out.

Baby Back Ribs

Tender enough to grill over a direct-heat fire, baby back ribs are delicious with a thick, sweet-spicy sauce.

Pork Loin

Cooked in an oven, bone-in or boneless loins would be considered roasts, ideal for Sunday family suppers. But grilled by indirect heat, and/or infused with smoke flavor, these same cuts are transformed into company fare.

Tenderloin

A small, cylindrical piece of meat that is quite lean, a tenderloin is a versatile grilling staple. Direct heat is appropriate here, but you can also use a hybrid method, searing it first and then moving it to a cooler spot on the grill to finish. Pork tenderloin soaks up a marinade quickly and is complemented by an array of sweet fruits and glazes or bold spice rubs.

Country-Style Ribs

Country-style ribs are butterflied or split chops from the shoulder end of the loin. Bone-in or boneless, they are usually quite meaty, and can be grilled over direct heat in the manner of a chop or slowly barbecued.

Sausages

Fresh or cooked, sausages taste wonderful grilled. If using fresh sausages, poach them first to make sure they cook through over a direct fire without burning.

Peach-Glazed Pork Chops with Fresh Peach Salsa

Pork and fruit are a natural pairing. Here, pork chops are served with a salsa made from fresh peaches and are basted with a sauce made from peach jam. But other fresh fruits and jams can be used in their place, such as apricots and apricot jam or pineapple and pineapple jam.

To make the sauce, in a small saucepan over medium heat, combine the jam, bourbon, vinegar, and 1/4 teaspoon salt. Bring to a simmer and cook, stirring often, until slightly thickened, 5–8 minutes. Stir in the hot-pepper sauce and remove from the heat. Use the sauce immediately, or let cool, cover, and refrigerate for up to 24 hours. If refrigerated, remove from the refrigerator 30 minutes before using. Measure out 3 tablespoons of the sauce to use as a glaze for the pork and reserve.

Prepare a CHARCOAL or GAS grill for DIRECT grilling over MEDIUM-HIGH heat (page 18 or 22). Oil the grill rack. Brush both sides of each chop with oil and then season with salt and pepper. Finally, brush some of the sauce on both sides of each chop.

CHARCOAL: Grill the chops over the hottest part of the fire, turning once and brushing with additional sauce, until cooked to your liking, 4–5 minutes per side for medium (slightly pink at the center and juicy).

GAS: Grill the chops directly over the heat elements, turning once and brushing with additional sauce, until cooked to your liking, 4–5 minutes per side for medium (slightly pink at the center and juicy).

Brush the finished chops with the reserved peach sauce and let rest for 3 minutes. Serve with the salsa spooned on top or alongside.

For the Sauce

3/4 cup (8 oz/235 g) peach jam or preserves

6 tablespoons (3 fl oz/90 ml) bourbon whiskey or peach nectar

4 tablespoons white wine vinegar

Salt

1/2–3/4 teaspoon hot-pepper sauce, to taste

6 boneless pork chops, each about 6 oz (185 g) and 3/4 inch (2 cm) thick

3 tablespoons olive oil

Salt and freshly ground pepper

Fruit Salsa (page 288), made with peaches

MAKES 4–6 SERVINGS

Pork Chops with Garlic and Herbs

4 bone-in, center-cut loin pork chops, each about $^3/_4$ lb (375 g) and 1 inch (2.5 cm) thick

4 cloves garlic, 2 cut into slivers and 2 chopped

$^2/_3$ cup (5 fl oz/160 ml) dry white wine

2 tablespoons olive oil

$^1/_2$ teaspoon sugar

Salt and freshly ground pepper

2 tablespoons finely chopped fresh sage

2 tablespoons finely chopped fresh rosemary

MAKES 4 SERVINGS

Working with 1 chop at a time, and using a sharp paring knife, cut small slits on both sides of the chop and insert a garlic sliver into each slit. Arrange in a single layer in a nonreactive dish.

In a food processor, combine the wine, oil, sugar, and $^1/_2$ teaspoon each salt and pepper. Process to blend. With the motor running, drop the 2 chopped garlic cloves, the sage, and the rosemary through the feed tube and process until fairly smooth. Pour the wine mixture over the chops, cover, and marinate at room temperature, turning once or twice, for at least 30 minutes or for up to 2 hours. If refrigerated, remove from the refrigerator 30 minutes before grilling.

Prepare a CHARCOAL or GAS grill for DIRECT grilling over MEDIUM heat (page 18 or 22). Remove the chops from the marinade, reserving the marinade.

CHARCOAL: Grill the meat over the hottest part of the fire, turning once and basting with the marinade for up to 5 minutes before the meat is done, until done to your liking, 4–5 minutes per side for medium (slightly pink at the center and juicy).

GAS: Grill the meat directly over the heat elements, turning once and basting with the marinade for up to 5 minutes before the meat is done, until done to your liking, 4–5 minutes per side for medium (slightly pink at the center and juicy).

Serve the chops immediately on warmed individual plates.

This simple and savory marinade transforms plain pork chops into something wonderfully Italian. For a casual dinner party, serve the hot chops with a crisp, cool salad of arugula (rocket) and chopped tomatoes dressed with balsamic vinegar and olive oil. The marinade is also good on boneless chops or pork tenderloins.

DIRECT METHOD • MEDIUM-HIGH HEAT • MARINATE UP TO 2 HOURS

Deviled Pork Chops

To devil a dish is to make it spicy, usually with mustard. Pork lends itself particularly well to deviling, especially since the mustard coating also helps to seal in the juices of today's lean pork. You can use bone-in or boneless chops, or even thinner pork cutlets, depending on your preference. Bone-in chops have more flavor, but boneless chops cook faster and are easier to eat. Serve these chops southern style, with wilted dandelion greens.

1/3 cup (2 1/2 oz/75 g) whole-grain Dijon mustard

2 tablespoons fresh orange juice

2 tablespoons brandy

2 tablespoons Worcestershire sauce

1 tablespoon chopped fresh tarragon

Freshly cracked pepper

6 boneless pork chops, each about 6 oz (185 g) and 3/4 inch (2 cm) thick

MAKES 6 SERVINGS

In a small bowl, stir together the mustard, orange juice, brandy, Worcestershire sauce, tarragon, and 3/4 teaspoon pepper. Smear the mustard mixture over both sides of each pork chop. Let stand for 20 minutes at room temperature, or cover and refrigerate for up to 2 hours. If refrigerated, remove from the refrigerator 30 minutes before grilling.

Prepare a CHARCOAL or GAS grill for DIRECT grilling over MEDIUM-HIGH heat (page 18 or 22). Oil the grill rack.

CHARCOAL: Grill the meat over the hottest part of the fire, turning once, until done to your liking, 4–5 minutes per side for medium (slightly pink at the center and juicy).

GAS: Grill the meat directly over the heat elements, turning once, until done to your liking, 4–5 minutes per side for medium (slightly pink at the center and juicy).

Serve the chops immediately on warmed individual plates.

Pork Adobo

For the Marinade

$1/2$ cup (4 fl oz/125 ml) cider vinegar

$1/3$ cup (3 fl oz/80 ml) soy sauce

2 tablespoons firmly packed golden brown sugar

4 cloves garlic, crushed

2 bay leaves

1 teaspoon dried oregano

Freshly ground pepper

$1^1/2$ lb (750 g) boneless pork chops, about $3/8$ inch (9 mm) thick, trimmed of fat

8–10 flour tortillas, about 7 inches (18 cm) in diameter

Olive oil for brushing

1 tablespoon unsalted butter, at room temperature

1 tablespoon all-purpose (plain) flour

MAKES 4–6 SERVINGS

To make the marinade, in a small bowl, combine the vinegar, soy sauce, sugar, garlic, bay leaves, oregano, and $1/2$ teaspoon pepper and stir the mixture until the sugar dissolves. Place the pork chops in a shallow, nonreactive dish just large enough to hold them and pour the marinade over. Turn the chops to coat on both sides. Cover and refrigerate, turning the chops once or twice, for 2 hours. Remove from the refrigerator 20–30 minutes before grilling and blot the chops dry with paper towels. Wrap the tortillas in aluminum foil.

Prepare a CHARCOAL or GAS grill for DIRECT grilling over HIGH heat (page 18 or 22). Oil the grill rack. Remove the chops from marinade. Pour the marinade into a small saucepan, place over medium-high heat, bring to a boil, reduce the heat to medium-low, and simmer for 5 minutes. Strain the marinade through a fine-mesh sieve into a small bowl, and then return the strained marinade to the saucepan and set aside. Brush the chops on both sides with olive oil.

CHARCOAL: Grill the pork over the hottest part of the fire, turning once, until the meat is nicely charred, about 3 minutes per side.

GAS: Grill the pork directly over the heat elements, turning once, until nicely charred, about 3 minutes per side.

While the chops are finishing cooking, in a small bowl, mix together the butter and flour until a paste forms. Bring the strained marinade back to a boil and whisk in the butter-flour mixture a little at a time, being careful that no lumps form. Cook, stirring, until the marinade thickens to the consistency of heavy (double) cream, 2–3 minutes.

Remove the meat from the grill and set on a board to rest for about 3 minutes. Place the packet of tortillas on a lower-heat area to warm, turning the packet once. Cut each chop into 5 or 6 strips. Place in a warmed serving bowl. Spoon thickened marinade over the meat and toss to coat. Wrap in warm tortillas and serve.

Adobo, pieces of pork or chicken simmered in a mix of vinegar, soy sauce, and garlic, is the national dish of the Philippines. This recipe calls for a marinade that draws on that Southeast Asian tradition, and then quickly grills the marinated pork, slices it, and spoons it into warmed tortillas. Slices of ripe avocado and pieces of mango or orange dressed with a squeeze of lime are a colorful and fresh-tasting accompaniment.

Ozark Pork Steaks

Pork shoulder steaks are a favorite throughout the Midwest, and this grill-smoked and simmered treatment is a classic in Missouri and southern Illinois. Ozark tradition holds that the pork steaks are served with creamy coleslaw and lots of corn bread for sopping up the sauce. Traditionally sauces were applied to grilling pork with a clean, cotton dish mop, hence the name "mopping sauce."

Prepare a CHARCOAL or GAS grill for DIRECT grilling over MEDIUM-HIGH heat (page 18 or 22). Trim the pork of excess fat, then season with salt and pepper. Set aside.

While the grill is heating, make the simmering sauce: In a large saucepan or Dutch oven over medium heat, warm the oil. Add the onion and cook, stirring often, until softened, about 5 minutes. Add the garlic and cook, stirring, for 1 minute until fragrant. Add the barbecue sauce, beer, and chili sauce, stir well, and simmer gently, uncovered, until lightly thickened, about 30 minutes.

To make the mopping sauce, in a shallow roasting pan, combine the ginger ale, water, vinegar, and red pepper flakes and place at the edge of the charcoal grill or on an area with lower heat on the gas grill to heat to a simmer.

CHARCOAL: Sprinkle half of the wood chips on the coals. Grill the pork steaks, a few at a time, over the hottest part of the fire, turning once, for 2 minutes per side. Using tongs, transfer the steaks, one at a time, to the simmering vinegar mop for a few seconds. Sprinkle the remaining wood chips on the coals. Return the steaks to the grill and continue to cook, turning and basting with the mopping sauce, until the pork is very tender, about 20 minutes total.

GAS: Add the wood chips to the grill in a smoker box or perforated foil packet (page 10). Grill the pork steaks, a few at a time, directly over the heat elements, turning once, for 2 minutes per side. Using tongs, transfer the steaks, one a time, to the simmering vinegar mop for a few seconds. Return the steaks to the grill and continue to cook, turning and basting with the mopping sauce, until the pork is very tender, about 20 minutes total.

As the steaks are finished grilling, transfer them to the simmering sauce. Simmer them in the sauce on a cool part of the grill, or on the stove top over medium-low heat, until the meat is nearly falling off the bone, 45–60 minutes. Serve the pork with the sauce.

---

3 lb (1.5 kg) pork shoulder steaks, cut slightly less than ¹/₂ inch (12 mm) thick

Salt and freshly ground pepper

For the Simmering Sauce

1 tablespoon vegetable oil

1 large yellow onion, thinly sliced

4 cloves garlic, finely chopped

6 cups (48 fl oz/1.5 l) bottled barbecue sauce, regular or hickory flavored

1¹/₂ cups (12 fl oz/375 ml) beer or ginger ale

¹/₂ cup (4 fl oz/125 ml) bottled chili sauce

For the Mopping Sauce

1 bottle (32 fl oz/1 l) ginger ale

4 cups (32 fl oz/1 l) water

¹/₄ cup (2 fl oz/60 ml) cider vinegar

¹/₂ teaspoon red pepper flakes

3 or 4 handfuls hickory chips, soaked if using charcoal (page 13)

MAKES 6 SERVINGS

Pork Medallions with Pomegranate Molasses Glaze

These flavorful pork medallions, cut from tender pork tenderloins, are grilled quickly and then brushed with a pomegranate molasses glaze. Pomegranate molasses, which is made cooking down pomegranate juice to a thick syrup, has a sweet-tart flavor that perks up glazes and marinades for grilled meats or chicken. Look for it in the international food section of well-stocked food stores or in markets specializing in Middle Eastern products.

Prepare a CHARCOAL or GAS grill for DIRECT grilling over MEDIUM-HIGH heat (page 18 or 22). Oil the grill rack.

To make the glaze, whisk together the pomegranate molasses, mustard, oil, Worcestershire sauce, sugar, ginger, $1/4$ teaspoon salt, $1/4$ teaspoon pepper, and hot-pepper sauce until the sugar dissolves and all the ingredients are well mixed.

Cut the pork tenderloins crosswise into medallions 1 inch (2.5 cm) thick. Using the heel of your hand, lightly flatten each medallion to about $1/2$ inch (12 mm) thick. Brush each pork medallion on both sides with olive oil and season with salt and pepper.

CHARCOAL: Grill the meat over the hottest part of the fire, turning once, until nicely charred and cooked to your liking, about 4 minutes per side for medium (slightly pink at the center and juicy) When you turn the medallions, brush the tops with some of the glaze.

GAS: Grill the meat directly over the heat elements, turning once, until nicely charred and cooked to your liking, about 4 minutes per side for medium (slightly pink at the center and juicy). When you turn the medallions, brush the tops with some of the glaze.

Remove the medallions from the grill, brush both sides with some of the glaze, and let rest for about 3 minutes. Serve the pork at once. Pass the remaining glaze at the table.

For the Glaze

2 tablespoons pomegranate molasses

1 tablespoon Dijon mustard

1 tablespoon extra-virgin olive oil

2 teaspoons Worcestershire sauce

1 teaspoon firmly packed golden brown sugar

1 teaspoon peeled and grated fresh ginger

Salt and freshly ground pepper

3 or 4 drops hot-pepper sauce

2 pork tenderloins, about 1 lb (500 g) each, trimmed of fat and silver skin

Extra-virgin olive oil for brushing

Salt and freshly ground pepper

MAKES 4–6 SERVINGS

Fennel-Crusted Pork Tenderloin

1 tablespoon fennel seeds, coarsely ground

2 teaspoons peppercorns, coarsely ground

Grated zest of 1 orange or lemon

1 tablespoon extra-virgin olive oil

3 tablespoons Dijon mustard

2 pork tenderloins, about 2 lb (1 kg) total weight, trimmed

MAKES 4–6 SERVINGS

Prepare a CHARCOAL or GAS grill for DIRECT grilling over MEDIUM-LOW heat (page 18 or 22). Oil the grill rack.

In a small bowl, stir together the fennel seeds, peppercorns, zest, and oil. Set aside.

Place the tenderloins on a platter or baking sheet and spread a light coat of the mustard over the entire surface of each tenderloin. Pat the fennel mixture evenly over the coat of mustard.

CHARCOAL: Place the meat on the grill rack over the hottest part of the fire. Cover the grill and cook, turning every 4–5 minutes, until cooked to your liking, about 20 minutes total for medium (slightly pink at the center and juicy).

GAS: Place the meat on the grill rack over the hottest part of the fire. Cover the grill and cook the loin, turning every 4–5 minutes, until cooked to your liking, about 20 minutes total for medium (slightly pink at the center and juicy).

To test for doneness, insert an instant-read thermometer into the thickest part of the tenderloins; it should register 150°F (65°C). The temperature will rise another 5°–10°F (3°–6°C) while the meat is resting.

Let the tenderloins rest for 5 minutes. Carve into thin slices, cutting across the grain and at an angle to the cutting board. Serve the pork hot, warm, or at room temperature.

A mixture of coarsely ground fennel seeds, pepper, and lemon or orange zest spread over a coating of mustard results in a zesty crust for these tenderloins. Grilled Fennel and Orange Salad (page 250), which echoes the flavors of the pork, makes a refreshing accompaniment. To shape each tenderloin into a compact cylinder that will cook more evenly, fold the thin tail end under and secure it in place with a small metal skewer.

Pork Loin with Grilled Onions

For the Thyme-Balsamic
Marinade

**²/₃ cup (5 fl oz/160 ml)
balsamic vinegar**

**¹/₂ cup (4 fl oz/125 ml)
fruity olive oil**

**4 large cloves garlic, finely
chopped**

**3 tablespoons chopped fresh
thyme**

**1¹/₂ tablespoons Dijon
mustard**

1 teaspoon fennel seeds

**Salt and freshly ground
coarse pepper**

**1 center-cut, boneless pork
loin, about 3 lb (1.5 kg), tied**

**1 large sweet onion such as
Vidalia, sliced about ¹/₄ inch
(6 mm) thick**

**Fresh thyme sprigs for
garnish**

MAKES 6–8 SERVINGS

To make the thyme-balsamic marinade, select a shallow, nonreactive dish just large enough to hold the pork. Add the vinegar, oil, garlic, thyme, mustard, fennel seeds, 1 teaspoon salt, and ³/₄ teaspoon pepper to the dish and mix well. Remove and reserve ¹/₃ cup (3 fl oz/80 ml) of the marinade. Add the pork to the dish and turn to coat all sides. Cover and refrigerate for at least 2 hours or for up to 24 hours. Remove from the refrigerator 30 minutes before grilling.

Prepare a CHARCOAL or GAS grill for INDIRECT grilling over MEDIUM heat (page 19 or 23). Oil the grill rack. If using a charcoal grill, place a drip pan on the center of the fire bed. Remove the pork from the marinade, reserving the marinade.

CHARCOAL: Grill the meat over the hottest part of the fire, turning to sear and lightly char on all sides, about 20 minutes total. Then move the meat over the drip pan, cover the grill, and continue to cook, turning occasionally and brushing with the marinade left in the dish for up to 5 minutes before the meat is done, until done to your liking, 45–60 minutes more for medium (slightly pink at the center and juicy). Shortly before the meat is done, brush the onion slices with all but about 1 tablespoon of the reserved marinade. Grill over the hottest part of the fire, turning once or twice, until softened and lightly charred, about 5 minutes total.

GAS: Grill the meat directly over the heat elements, turning to sear and lightly char on all sides, about 20 minutes total. Then move the meat away from the heat elements, cover the grill, and continue to cook, turning occasionally and brushing with the any marinade left in the dish for up to 5 minutes before the meat is done, until done to your liking, 45–60 minutes more for medium (slightly pink at the center and juicy). Shortly before the meat is done, brush the onion slices with all but about 1 tablespoon of the reserved marinade. Grill directly over the heat elements, turning once or twice, until softened and lightly charred, about 5 minutes total.

To test for doneness, insert an instant-read thermometer into the thickest part of the loin; it should register 150°F (65°C). The temperature will rise another 5°–10°F (3°–6°C) while the meat is resting.

Place the pork on a platter and surround with the onion slices and thyme sprigs. Let rest for 5–10 minutes, then slice about ³/₄ inch (2 cm) thick.

Pork loin is easy to "roast" on the grill, especially if it is boned and tied into a nice, neat shape, which the butcher can do for you. Because today's pork is lean, it is important to marinate it in an oil-based bath for at least a couple of hours before grilling, then cook it slowly over an indirect-heat fire.

Mango Jerk Pork Tenderloins

Jerk—Jamaican barbecue—derives much of its uniquely fiery flavor from a seasoning paste that traditionally includes allspice, thyme, and ultrahot habanero chiles, among other ingredients, many of them included at the discretion of the cook. Ripe, juicy mangoes, which give the jerk a welcome touch of tropical fruitiness, are just one of those possible additions.

To make the jerk paste, place 1 mango on a cutting board, resting it on one of its narrow edges. Using a sharp knife, cut lengthwise slightly off center, cutting off all the flesh from one side of the pit. Repeat on the other side. Peel away the skin from the pulp and chop the pulp. Repeat with the second mango, if using. You should have 1 cup (6 oz/185 g) pulp. Add the mango pulp to a food processor along with the onion, lime juice, soy sauce, ginger, sugar, garlic, chile, allspice, thyme, and $1/2$ teaspoon pepper. Process until fairly smooth.

Place the tenderloins in a shallow, nonreactive dish just large enough to hold them and pour the jerk paste over them. Cover and let stand at room temperature, turning the pork occasionally, for up to 30 minutes, or refrigerate for up to 2 hours. If refrigerated, remove the dish from the refrigerator about 30 minutes before grilling.

Prepare a CHARCOAL or GAS grill for DIRECT grilling over MEDIUM-HIGH heat (page 18 or 22). Oil the grill rack. Remove the pork from the marinade, reserving the marinade.

CHARCOAL: Place the meat over the hottest part of the fire and cover the grill. Cook, turning the meat every 4–5 minutes and brushing with the marinade left in the dish for up to 5 minutes before the meat is done, until the tenderloins are cooked to your liking, 16–18 minutes total for medium (slightly pink at the center and juicy).

GAS: Place the meat directly over the heat elements and cover the grill. Cook, turning every 4–5 minutes and brushing with the marinade left in the dish for up to 5 minutes before the meat is done, until the pork is cooked to your liking, 16–18 minutes total for medium (slightly pink at the center and juicy).

To test for doneness, insert an instant-read thermometer into the thickest part of the loin; it should register 150°F (65°C). The temperature will rise another 5°–10°F (3°–6°C) while the meat is resting.

Let the tenderloins rest for 5 minutes. Carve into thin slices, cutting across the grain and at an angle to the cutting board. Season to taste with salt. Serve hot, warm, or at room temperature.

For the Jerk Paste

2 small mangoes or 1 large

1 small yellow onion, coarsely chopped

$1/4$ cup (2 fl oz/60 ml) fresh lime juice

$1/4$ cup (2 fl oz/60 ml) soy sauce

2 tablespoons peeled and grated fresh ginger with juice

2 tablespoons firmly packed dark brown sugar

2 cloves garlic, chopped

1 habanero chile, chopped

1 teaspoon ground allspice

$3/4$ teaspoon dried thyme

Freshly ground pepper

2 pork tenderloins, about $2^1/2$ lb (1.25 kg) total weight, trimmed

Salt

MAKES 4–6 SERVINGS

Pork Kabobs with Pancetta, Sage, and Red Onion

For the Marinade

¹/₄ cup (2 fl oz/60 ml) extra-virgin olive oil

1 teaspoon chopped fresh sage

1 large clove garlic, minced

¹/₄ teaspoon salt

¹/₄ teaspoon freshly ground pepper

1¹/₄–1¹/₂ lb (625–750 g) boneless pork loin or tenderloin, trimmed and cut into 1¹/₂-inch (4-cm) cubes

8–10 thin slices pancetta

16–20 fresh sage leaves

4 long metal skewers or soaked bamboo skewers (page 10)

1 large red onion, layers separated and cut into 1¹/₂-inch (4-cm) squares

MAKES 4–6 SERVINGS

To make the marinade, choose a shallow, nonreactive dish just large enough to hold the meat. Combine the oil, sage, garlic, and salt and pepper in the dish and mix well. Add the meat and turn to coat on all sides. Cover and refrigerate for 2 hours. Remove from the refrigerator 20–30 minutes before grilling.

Prepare a CHARCOAL or GAS grill for DIRECT grilling over MEDIUM-HIGH heat (page 18 or 22). Oil the grill rack. Remove the meat from the marinade; discard the marinade. Unfurl the pancetta slices and cut each slice in half crosswise. To assemble the skewers, place 1 fresh sage leaf on top of a pork cube and wrap 1 piece of pancetta around the cube to secure the sage leaf. Thread the wrapped pork cubes onto a skewer, passing the skewer through the side not covered by the pancetta. Follow the pork cube with a square of onion. Repeat to load the skewer with one-fourth of the pork and onion, then assemble 3 additional skewers the same way.

CHARCOAL: Grill the skewers over the hottest part of the fire, turning once or twice, until the pancetta is crisp and the meat is cooked to your liking, 9–10 minutes total for medium (slightly pink at the center and juicy).

GAS: Grill the skewers directly over the heat elements, turning once or twice, until the pancetta is crisp and the meat is cooked to your liking, 9–10 minutes total for medium (slightly pink at the center and juicy).

Slide the pork and onion from the skewers onto warmed individual plates and serve at once.

Here, chunks of pork are marinated for flavor and moisture and then wrapped with pancetta before being skewered alternately with onion and grilled. The crisp browned pancetta and sweet red onion pieces add flavor and texture contrast to the pork. Thin bacon slices can be used in place of the pancetta, and red bell pepper can be substituted for the onion. Serve with a dry rosé for a summer supper.

Cuban Pork Loin Stuffed with Rum-Soaked Prunes

Prunes, of course, are simply dried plums, and nowadays shoppers often find them labeled that way. *Mojo,* the all-purpose barbecue sauce favored by Cuban cooks, is based on the juice of sour oranges, a flavor that can be approximated by a combination of orange and lime juices. Here, pork, prunes, and a Caribbean-style *mojo* come together in a festive Cuban-inspired main course. For the pork, buy a boneless rolled loin, unroll to add the stuffing, and roll and tie again before grilling.

Combine the prunes, lemon juice, and rum and let plump at room temperature for at least 30 minutes or for up to 1 hour. Drain the prunes, reserving any liquid.

If the pork is rolled and tied, cut the string and lay the meat out flat. Season the entire surface of the pork with salt and pepper. Arrange the prunes evenly over the surface. Roll up the loin and, using kitchen string, secure the roll at 2-inch (5-cm) intervals along its length. (If you have an unrolled pork loin, you can use a small, sharp knife to make a large horizontal pocket in the roast, cutting almost to the other side and to the ends but taking care not to cut all the way through. Season and stuff this pocket, then tie.) Set aside while making the marinade.

To make the marinade, select a shallow, nonreactive dish just large enough to hold the pork. Combine the orange and lime juices, vinegar, oil, oregano, thyme, cumin, $1/2$ teaspoon each salt and pepper, orange and lime zests, parsley, garlic, and any rum reserved from the prunes in the dish. Place the pork in the marinade and turn to coat all sides. Cover and refrigerate, turning occasionally, for at least 3 hours or for up to 12 hours. Remove from the refrigerator 30 minutes before grilling.

Prepare a CHARCOAL or GAS grill for INDIRECT grilling over MEDIUM heat (page 19 or 23). Oil the grill rack. Remove the pork from and reserve the marinade.

CHARCOAL: Place a drip pan half full of water on the center of the fire bed. Place the pork on the grill rack over the drip pan. Cover the grill and cook, turning occasionally and brushing with the marinade left in the dish for up to 5 minutes before the meat is done, until cooked to your liking, $1 1/4$–$1 3/4$ hours for medium.

GAS: Place a shallow pan half full of water at the edge of the grill rack. Place the pork on the rack away from the heat elements. Cover the grill and cook, turning occasionally and brushing with the marinade left in the dish for up to 5 minutes before the meat is done, until cooked to your liking, $1 1/4$–$1 3/4$ hours for medium.

To test for doneness, insert an instant-read thermometer into the thickest part of the meat; it should register 150°F (65°C). The temperature will rise another 5°–10°F (3°–6°C) while the meat is resting.

Let the pork rest for 10 minutes. Remove the strings and slice crosswise to serve.

1 cup (6 oz/185 g) pitted prunes, coarsely diced

2 tablespoons fresh lemon or orange juice

$1/3$ cup (3 fl oz/80 ml) rum

1 boneless center-cut pork loin, $2 1/2$–3 lb (1.25–1.5 kg), preferably rolled

Salt and freshly ground pepper

For the Mojo Marinade

$1/3$ cup (3 fl oz/80 ml) fresh orange juice

$1/3$ cup (3 fl oz/80 ml) fresh lime juice

$1/4$ cup (2 fl oz/60 ml) red wine vinegar

3 tablespoons olive oil

1 tablespoon chopped oregano

1 tablespoon chopped thyme

1 teaspoon ground cumin

Salt and ground pepper

1 teaspoon grated orange zest

1 teaspoon grated lime zest

$1/4$ cup ($1/3$ oz/10 g) chopped fresh flat-leaf (Italian) parsley

5 cloves garlic, minced

MAKES 6 SERVINGS

Marinated Pork Tenderloins

For the Balsamic-Rosemary
Marinade

**^{2}/$_3$ cup (5 fl oz/160 ml)
balsamic vinegar**

**^{1}/$_3$ cup (3 fl oz/80 ml)
olive oil**

2 tablespoons soy sauce

**4^1/$_2$ teaspoons firmly packed
golden brown sugar**

Freshly ground pepper

**^{1}/$_2$ cup (^{1}/$_3$ oz/10 g) finely
chopped fresh rosemary**

5 cloves garlic, chopped

**2 pork tenderloins, about
2^1/$_2$ lb (1.25 kg) total weight,
trimmed**

Salt

MAKES 4–6 SERVINGS

To make the balsamic-rosemary marinade, in a food processor, combine the vinegar, oil, soy sauce, brown sugar, and ^{3}/$_4$ teaspoon pepper. Pulse until blended. With the motor running, drop the rosemary and garlic through the feed tube. Continue to process until fairly smooth. Place the tenderloins in a nonreactive dish and pour the marinade over them. Cover and let stand at room temperature, turning occasionally, for up to 2 hours.

Prepare a CHARCOAL or GAS grill for DIRECT grilling over MEDIUM-HIGH heat (page 18 or 22). Remove the tenderloins from the marinade, reserving the marinade.

CHARCOAL: Grill the meat over the hottest part of the fire, turning every 4–5 minutes and basting with the marinade for up to 5 minutes before the meat is done, until done to your liking, about 20 minutes total for medium (slightly pink at the center and juicy).

GAS: Grill the meat directly over the heat elements turning every 4–5 minutes and basting with the marinade for up to 5 minutes before the meat is done, until done to your liking, about 20 minutes total for medium (slightly pink at the center and juicy).

To test for doneness, insert an instant-read thermometer into the thickest part of the tenderloins; it should register 150°F (65°C). The temperature will rise another 5°–10°F (3°–6°C) while the meat is resting.

Let the tenderloins rest for 5 minutes. Carve into thin slices, across the grain and at an angle to the cutting board. Season to taste with salt. Serve the tenderloins hot, warm, or at room temperature.

Here, an easy marinade complements lean pork tenderloins beautifully. The dish is simple enough for a weekday supper but tasty enough for company. Consider grilling an extra tenderloin or two, as they are also terrific sliced and served cold the next day.

Sesame-Hoisin Baby Back Ribs

Baby back ribs, true to their name, are smaller than their sparerib cousins. Cut from the top end of the loin, they are also more tender and take about half as long to cook. This sesame-hoisin coating is excellent on pork tenderloin as well. Thick and rich, it gives maximum flavor to the meat and protects this delicate cut from the heat of the grill.

To make the sesame-hoisin sauce, in a small bowl, stir together the soy sauce, hoisin sauce, vinegar, peanut butter, ginger, sesame oil, chile-garlic sauce, lime juice, and garlic. Place the ribs in a shallow, nonreactive dish, and brush a thin coating of the sauce evenly over them. Cover and refrigerate for at least 1 hour or for up to 3 hours. Cover and refrigerate the remaining sauce; bring it to room temperature before grilling.

Prepare a CHARCOAL or GAS grill for INDIRECT grilling over MEDIUM heat (page 19 or 23). If using a charcoal grill, place a drip pan in the center of the fire bed. Oil the grill rack.

CHARCOAL: Place the ribs on the grill rack over the drip pan. Cover the grill and cook, turning once or twice and brushing with the sauce, for 30 minutes total. Using tongs, transfer the ribs to a plate. Add some hot coals to the fire, then return the ribs to the grill directly over the fire. Grill over direct heat, turning 2 or 3 times and brushing with the sauce, until the ribs are fork-tender and crisply browned on the outside, about 30 minutes longer.

GAS: Place the ribs on the grill rack away from the heat elements. Cover the grill and cook, turning once or twice and brushing with the sauce, for 30 minutes total. Adjust the grill for direct grilling over medium heat. Grill the ribs over directly over the heat elements, turning 2 or 3 times and brushing with the sauce, until the ribs are fork-tender and crisply browned on the outside, about 30 minutes longer.

Cut the rib slabs into 2- or 3-rib portions and serve hot.

For the Sesame-Hoisin Sauce

2 tablespoons soy sauce

1^1/$_2$ tablespoons hoisin sauce

1^1/$_2$ tablespoons rice vinegar

1^1/$_2$ tablespoons creamy peanut butter

1 tablespoon peeled and chopped fresh ginger

1 tablespoon Asian sesame oil

1 tablespoon Asian chile-garlic sauce

2 teaspoons fresh lime juice

3 cloves garlic, finely chopped

4 lb (2 kg) baby back pork ribs, in slabs

MAKES 4 MAIN-COURSE SERVINGS OR 8 APPETIZER SERVINGS

Sausages, Smoked Pork, and Apples with Sauerkraut

6 bratwursts or other similarly seasoned fresh link sausages

2 cups (16 fl oz/500 ml) dry white wine

3 tablespoons whole-grain Dijon mustard

6 boneless center-cut pork chops, about 1 lb (500 g) total weight and 1/2 inch (12 mm) thick

Salt and freshly ground pepper

1 yellow onion, sliced crosswise about 1/4 inch (6 mm) thick

1 tart apple, cored and sliced crosswise about 1/4 inch (6 mm) thick

2 cups (8 oz/250 g) drained fresh sauerkraut

1 teaspoon caraway seeds

MAKES 6 SERVINGS

In a large, deep frying pan over medium heat, combine the sausages and wine, bring to a simmer, and cook, turning occasionally, until nearly cooked through, about 5 minutes. Remove the sausages from the pan and reserve. Raise the heat to high, bring the wine to a boil, then simmer until reduced by about one-third, about 5 minutes. Stir in the mustard and remove from the heat. Reserve the sauce in the pan. Season the pork chops with salt and pepper.

Prepare a CHARCOAL or GAS grill for DIRECT grilling over MEDIUM-HIGH heat (page 18 or 22). Oil the grill rack.

CHARCOAL: Grill the sausages and pork chops over the hottest part of the fire, turning once or twice, until the sausages are no longer pink and the pork chops are barely pink at the center, 6–9 minutes total, or until done to your liking. Brush the onion and apple slices with about 2 tablespoons of the wine sauce. Place them at the edges of the grill rack and cook, turning once or twice, until softened and lightly charred, about 5 minutes total.

GAS: Grill the sausages and pork chops directly over the heat elements, turning once or twice, until the sausages are no longer pink and the pork chops are barely pink at the center, 6–9 minutes total, or until done to your liking. Brush the onion and apple slices with about 2 tablespoons of the wine sauce. Place them on an area with lower heat and cook, turning once or twice, until softened and lightly charred, about 5 minutes total.

Stir the sauerkraut, caraway seeds, and 1/2 teaspoon pepper into the wine sauce in the frying pan. Cut the grilled onion and apple slices into chunks and stir them into the sauerkraut. Add the sausages and pork chops, pushing them into the sauerkraut. Simmer on the grill rack over medium heat or on the stove top over medium-low heat until heated through, 5–7 minutes.

Serve directly from the pan, or spoon onto a platter for serving.

Choucroute garnie, an Alsatian specialty, features sauerkraut and a mixture of smoked pork and sausages or other meats braised in the oven or on the stove top. In this contemporary grilled adaptation, the sausages are bratwurst and the pork is thin, boneless, center-cut pork chops. Heat the sauerkraut and meats on the stove top, or place the frying pan right on the grill.

Poultry

About Poultry

The aroma of chicken cooking over hot coals is universally appealing. All over the world, people grill this popular bird, pairing it with everything from garlic and herbs to fruits. But any fowl, from a tiny poussin to a hefty turkey, benefits from exposure to the smoke and heat of a grill.

Whole birds, from chicken to turkey, cook with little fuss—and great success—over an indirect-heat fire. Duck is a bit more challenging to grill, because it is rich in flavorful fat that can cause flare-ups. It's well worth the effort, however, as duck's sweet, succulent meat tastes delicious when tinged with a bit of grill smoke. If you have a grill with a rotisserie attachment, there's perhaps no better way to present a perfectly cooked bird: gilded and crisp on the outside and wonderfully juicy on the inside.

Brining, a recently repopularized method for ensuring moist meat, is especially suited to some of the traditionally leaner birds such as turkey. For example, your next holiday turkey, brined and grill-roasted over indirect heat, will be evenly succulent throughout. Even the typically drier breasts will be moist and flavorful.

Butterflying poultry helps to put more of the bird into contact with the hot fire. Halved, flattened, and attentively grilled, the birds come off the rack with juicy meat and plenty of crisp, golden skin to satisfy even the fussiest diners. Borrow a trick from the Italians, who weight down butterflied birds with a foil-covered brick or cast-iron frying pan. This technique holds the flattened poultry uniformly against the grill so it cooks evenly.

Grilled chicken parts, common fare at backyard barbecues, are always popular with guests, but you don't need to limit yourself to the familiar barbecue sauces. Add interest to your outdoor feasts by mixing up sauces from global traditions for brushing on chicken and serving at the table. The secret to perfect barbecued chicken is to brush the pieces with sauce only during the last few minutes of cooking. Doing so earlier will cause the sugars in the sauce to burn, creating an undesirable charred flavor on the exterior of the chicken.

The ubiquitous chicken breast, bone-in with skin or boneless and skinless, is quickly done on a grill and can be flavored in any number of ways. Consider, too, the rich, dark meat of duck breasts, which is an even better foil to the grill's smoky flavors and takes on exotic flavorings beautifully.

Lean ground turkey is the perfect base for making into burgers. The flavorful meat can be complemented by almost any seasoning.

Working with Poultry

SHOPPING FOR POULTRY

If possible, buy fresh chicken, which can be labeled as such only if it has never been held at temperatures below 26°F (-3°C). If chicken has been frozen and then thawed for sale, the label will say "previously frozen."

The terms *natural*, *free range*, *organic*, and *kosher* are used to indicate a higher-quality chicken that also costs more in most cases.

Natural is the broadest of these terms and means that the chicken contains no artificial ingredients and was minimally processed. It gives no indication of how or where the chicken was raised and may be only a limited indication of quality. *Free range* is used for a chicken that was allowed access to the outdoors, which is believed to develop lean, meaty muscles. Some free-range poultry is better than others; it is important to judge for yourself rather than rely solely on the label. *Organic* means that the chicken producer has undergone a lengthy certification process to prove that his or her chickens have been raised in free-range conditions, without hormones or antibiotics, and on exclusively organic feed. *Kosher* chickens, increasingly available in specialty food stores and well-stocked supermarkets, are raised naturally in a strict, impeccably clean environment based on Jewish Kosher laws. These chickens are raised on natural, preservative-free feed and are not injected with hormones.

If possible, choose a fresh turkey (frozen turkeys tend to have drier meat) that was raised free range and fed organic grain. Although they are more expensive, these turkeys have more flavor than those raised on factory farms. If they are not regularly stocked in your local market, you can special order

them from a butcher. In rural areas, look for a turkey farm and buy straight from the source.

Most likely the duck you buy at the supermarket or from a butcher will be frozen; it should be solidly frozen with no signs of thawing. If it is fresh, look for smooth skin without discoloration.

All poultry should have even coloring, from white to pale yellow to ivory. Look for plump birds with well-defined breasts and legs. Pressed gently, the meat should feel firm and resilient. Any visible fat should be white to light yellow. The skin should be unbroken, clean, and appear dry. If the poultry is packaged, be sure to buy it before the sell-by date and smell to detect any off odors.

PREPARING POULTRY FOR GRILLING

Remove external fat from poultry, or it will melt and drip into the fire, causing flare-ups. Some cooks remove the skin from chicken before grilling to cut down on fat, but the skin protects the delicate meat, keeping it from drying out, and adds flavor during cooking. It's better to keep the skin on during grilling and remove it afterward, if desired.

Recent research has discovered a link between the poultry industry and bacterial contamination, especially from salmonella. While not all poultry is contaminated, it is best to assume that it is in order to avoid potentially serious illness.

When working with chicken, be careful to keep raw chicken juices from coming in contact with foods that are to be eaten raw, such as salads and sauces. With the exception of duck breasts, cook poultry to a minimum of 160°F (71°C) to kill bacteria. Clean hands, cutting boards, knives, and countertops thoroughly with hot, soapy water after working with poultry to guarantee that bacteria will not contaminate other foods.

TESTING POULTRY FOR DONENESS

Cook chicken until the meat is no longer pink at the bone, the juices run clear when a thigh is pierced with a knife, or the breast meat is opaque throughout. To test whole birds for doneness, insert an instant-read thermometer into the thickest part of the thigh, without touching the bone. To test bone-in poultry cuts for doneness, make an incision near the bone; the meat, except duck breasts, should look opaque with no sign of pink. Duck breasts will be reddish pink. To test boneless cuts for doneness, press on the center of the cut. Perfectly cooked poultry should feel firm and spring back to the touch.

PART TESTED	APPEARANCE	TEMPERATURE °F	TEMPERATURE °C
Chicken breasts	Opaque; white	150° to 160°	65° to 71°
Chicken thighs	Opaque; brownish	165° to 170°	74° to 77°
Turkey breasts	Opaque; white	150° to 160°	65° to 71°
Turkey thighs	Opaque; brownish	165° to 170°	74° to 77°
Duck breasts	Pink to reddish pink	150° to 160°	65° to 71°

Poultry Types for Grilling

From poussins to ducks to chickens to turkeys, birds cook wonderfully on the grill. Whole birds do well cooked over indirect-heat or spit-roasted on a rotisserie, which keeps them moist and tender. Butterflied poultry and cut-up poultry parts can be direct-heat grilled, where they gain crisp, grill-marked skin and juicy, smoky meat. Smoking is another fine way of cooking poultry on a grill. Poultry flesh, from mild chicken and turkey to full-bodied duck, soaks up smoke flavors deliciously.

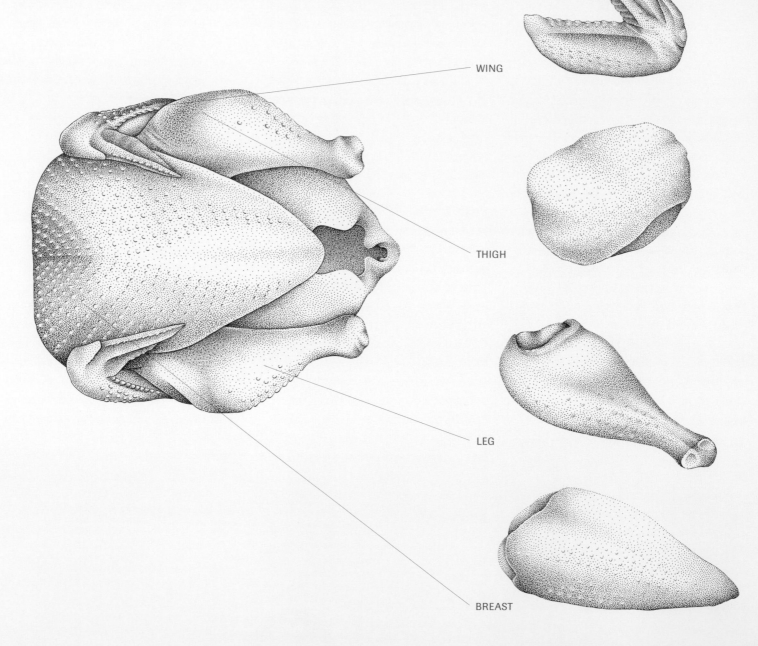

WING

THIGH

LEG

BREAST

POULTRY TYPES FOR GRILLING

For best results, seek out fresh poultry and purchase it whole. If you want to serve parts, cut them from the whole chicken and use the remaining parts for another recipe or for soup.

Whole Turkeys

Whole turkeys are wonderful grilled over indirect heat or smoked. A 12- to 14-pound (6- to 7-kg) turkey is the ideal size and will feed 10 to 12 people. A brine contributes moisture and flavor to the bird, especially to the breasts, which have a reputation for being dry. Make sure your grill is large enough to accommodate the bird with the cover in place.

Whole Chickens

Cook whole chickens over indirect heat, for crisp, deep golden skin and succulent meat. Or, thread them onto a rotisserie spit where it can slowly turn, basting itself with its own juices as it cooks. Trussing chickens (page 290) helps them hold a nice shape while cooking. Flavor whole chickens with seasoned butters, citrus juice, or fresh herbs.

Whole Ducks

Grilling a whole duck can be tricky, as it has a lot of fat that can cause flare-ups. But done correctly over indirect heat or on a rotisserie spit, whole duck will have ultracrisp skin and slightly smoky meat. Marry duck with Chinese sauces or fruit relishes.

Whole Poussins

Young chickens weighing about 1 pound (500 g), poussins are tender and sweet tasting. Grill them whole over an indirect fire or on a spit, or butterfly them (page 290) for cooking over a direct fire.

BUTTERFLIED CHICKENS Butterflying a chicken (page 290) creates meat of even thickness, which helps all the flesh cook at the same rate. Butterflied chickens are cooked over direct-heat fires and often brushed with spicy mixtures of chiles and herbs.

CHICKEN BREASTS Grilling chicken breasts with the skin and bones intact keeps them moist, while using boneless chicken breasts, whole or in chunks threaded on skewers, makes quick work of dinner. Flavor these lean pieces of poultry with simple embellishments such as a bold marinade or an assertive spice rub.

MIXED CHICKEN PARTS Sear chicken parts over a direct-heat fire to create crisp skin, then finish cooking them over a cooler part of the grill. Sweet sauces and glazes are ideal for chicken parts, but they should be brushed on only toward the end of grilling

TURKEY BREASTS AND TENDERLOINS When a whole turkey is too large for your dinner crowd, grilling a bone-in turkey breast is a good option. Treat it as you would a whole bird. The tenderloin, a strip of meat from the bottom of the breast, ranges in size from that of a large chicken breast to that of a large steak and can be treated in much the same way in flavoring and cooking on the grill.

TURKEY BURGERS Consider low-fat and low-cholesterol turkey burgers as an alternative to hamburgers. They stand up to the same bold condiments as their beef burger cousins. Grill turkey burgers over a direct-heat fire.

DUCK BREASTS Quickly grill rich, meaty duck breasts over direct heat. Choose an exotic spice blend or sweet fruit glaze as their partner.

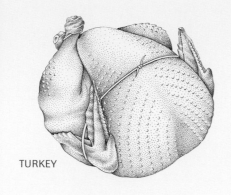

TURKEY

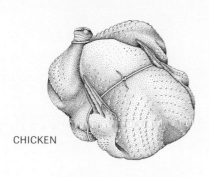

CHICKEN

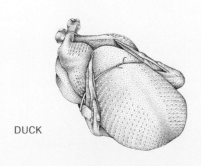

DUCK

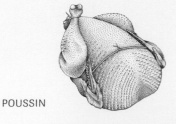

POUSSIN

Grill-Roasted Chicken

A whole chicken is arguably the single best food to roast in the dry heat of an indirect fire in a covered grill: it is small enough to cook through in about the same amount of time that it takes the skin, which automatically bastes the bird during roasting, to become crisp and turn golden brown. Grill-roasting also adds subtle smoky flavor and makes cleanup easy. If you have a big family or have company coming, grill-roast two chickens, rather than one huge bird.

Rinse the chicken, inside and out, and pat dry with paper towels. Cut the lemon in half, then cut one-half into wedges. Set the remaining lemon half aside. Stuff the chicken cavity with the lemon wedges and half of the chopped herbs. Using your fingers and starting at the tail cavity, carefully loosen the skin of the chicken. Insert the remaining herbs under the skin, spreading them as evenly as possible. Truss the chicken (page 290).

In a large, deep, nonreactive bowl, combine the wine, oil, lemon juice, $1/2$ teaspoon salt, and 1 teaspoon pepper. Mix well. Remove 1 tablespoon marinade and set the reserved marinade aside. Place the chicken in the bowl and turn to coat evenly. Cover and refrigerate, turning the chicken occasionally, for at least 3 hours or for up to 12 hours. Remove from the refrigerator 30 minutes before grilling.

Prepare a CHARCOAL or GAS grill for INDIRECT grilling over MEDIUM HEAT (page 19 or 23). If using a charcoal grill, place a drip pan half full of water in the center of the fire bed. Oil the grill rack. Remove the chicken from the marinade, discarding the marinade.

CHARCOAL: Place the chicken, breast side up, on the grill rack over the drip pan. Cover the grill and cook, adding more coals about halfway through the grilling, until the juices run clear when the thigh joint is pierced with a knife tip, $1^1/2$–$1^3/4$ hours. Brush the chicken with the reserved marinade 2 or 3 times during grilling, and toss a few herb sprigs, if using, onto the coals near the end of grilling time.

GAS: Place the chicken, breast side up, on the grill rack away from the heat elements. Cover the grill and cook until the juices run clear when the thigh joint is pierced with a knife tip, $1^1/2$–$1^3/4$ hours. Brush the chicken with the reserved marinade 2 or 3 times during grilling, and toss a few herb sprigs, if using, onto the heat elements near the end of grilling time.

To test for doneness, insert an instant-read thermometer into the thickest part of the thigh away from the bone; it should register 170°F (77°C). The temperature will rise another 5°–10°F (3°–6°C) while the chicken is resting.

Transfer the chicken to a cutting board and let rest for 10 minutes before carving.

1 roasting chicken, about 4 lb (2 kg), neck and giblets removed

1 large lemon

$1/4$ cup ($1/3$ oz/10 g) chopped mixed fresh herbs such as sage, thyme, and/or flat-leaf (Italian) parsley, plus a small handful of mixed herb sprigs for grilling (optional)

$1/2$ cup (4 fl oz/125 ml) dry white wine

3 tablespoons olive oil

3 tablespoons fresh lemon juice

Salt and freshly ground coarse pepper

MAKES 4 SERVINGS

Hickory Grill-Smoked Chicken

1 roasting chicken, about 4 lb (2 kg), neck and giblets removed

Coarse sea or kosher salt and freshly ground coarse pepper

2 teaspoons sweet paprika

2 teaspoons dried thyme

2 teaspoons dried oregano

1/4 teaspoon ground cayenne pepper

4–6 handfuls hickory or other wood chips, soaked if using charcoal (page 13)

MAKES 4 SERVINGS

Rinse the chicken, inside and out, and pat dry with paper towels. Season the inside of the chicken with 1/4 teaspoon salt and 1/4 teaspoon black pepper. Truss the chicken (page 290). In a small bowl, combine 3/4 teaspoon salt, 1/2 teaspoon black pepper, the paprika, thyme, oregano, and cayenne. Using your fingers, and starting at the tail cavity, carefully loosen the skin of the chicken over the breast and thighs. Insert about half of the spice mixture under the skin, and rub it on as evenly as possible. Rub the remaining spice mixture over the skin of the chicken. Let the chicken stand for 30 minutes at room temperature.

Prepare a CHARCOAL or GAS grill for INDIRECT grilling over MEDIUM heat (page 19 or 23). Oil the grill rack.

CHARCOAL: Place a drip pan half full of water in the center of the fire bed. Sprinkle about one-third of the wood chips on the coals. Place the chicken, breast side up, on the grill rack over the drip pan. Cover the grill and cook, adding more coals about halfway through grilling to maintain the temperature, until the juices run clear when the thigh joint is pierced with a knife tip, about 2 hours. Add the remaining wood chips in 2 additions, and add additional water to the drip pan as needed.

GAS: Place a shallow pan half full of water at the edge of the grill rack. Add the wood chips to the grill in a smoker box or a perforated foil packet (page 10). Place the chicken, breast side up, on the grill rack away from the heat elements. Cover the grill and smoke the chicken until the juices run clear when the thigh joint is pierced with a knife tip, about 2 hours. Add additional water to the pan as needed.

To test for doneness, insert an instant-read thermometer into the thickest part of the thigh away from the bone; it should register 170°F (77°C). The temperature will rise another 5°–10°F (3°–6°C) while the chicken is resting.

Transfer the chicken to a cutting board and let rest for 10 minutes before carving.

Grill-smoking a chicken is similar to grill-roasting it, but with the addition of wood chunks or chips to the fire and a drip pan with water to promote smoke. Choose the wood according to the degree and kind of smoky flavor desired. Hickory is the most potent, and this peppery rub is bold enough to hold its own with the aromatic wood. Serve the chicken for any occasion, with grilled vegetables for a dinner party, or with corn bread and coleslaw for a backyard picnic.

Spit-Roasted Piri-Piri Chicken

Piri-piri, which means "pepper-pepper" in Swahili, is a fiery sauce common to the Portuguese-speaking world, from Brazil to Mozambique to Portugal itself. If you live near Portuguese or Hispanic markets, you will probably find vinegar-based *piri-piri* sauce on the shelves, but you may also substitute Tabasco or any other favorite hot-pepper sauce. In the absence of a rotisserie, this can be cooked on the grill rack.

Rinse the chicken, inside and out, and pat dry with paper towels. Truss the chicken (page 290). In a large, deep, nonreactive bowl, combine the oil, lemon and orange juices, vinegar, *piri-piri* sauce to taste, paprika, cumin, and ¹/₂ teaspoon each salt and pepper. Stir in the parsley, ginger, thyme, and garlic. Spoon out and reserve ¹/₄ cup (2 fl oz/60 ml) of the marinade for basting. Place the chicken in the bowl, and turn the chicken to coat evenly. Cover and refrigerate the chicken and reserved sauce, turning the chicken occasionally, for at least 2 hours or for up to 12 hours. Remove from the refrigerator 30 minutes before grilling.

Prepare a CHARCOAL or GAS grill for ROTISSERIE (spit-) roasting (page 28) or for INDIRECT grilling over MEDIUM heat (page 19 or 23). If using a charcoal grill, place a drip pan half full of water on the center of the fire bed. Remove the chicken from the marinade. Truss the chicken (page 290).

CHARCOAL: If using the wood chips, sprinkle about one-third of them on the coals. Secure the chicken onto the spit (page 28), or according to the manufacturer's instructions. Or place the chicken, breast side up, on the rack over the drip pan. Cover the grill and cook the chicken, basting occasionally with the reserved marinade, until the juices run clear when the thigh joint is pierced with a knife tip, about 1¹/₂ hours. Add more coals as needed and the remaining wood chips, in 2 batches.

GAS: If using the wood chips, add them to the grill in a smoker box or perforated foil packet (page 10). Secure the chicken on the spit (page 28), or according to the manufacturer's instructions. Or place the chicken, breast side up, on the grill rack away from the heat elements. Cover the grill and cook, basting occasionally with the reserved marinade, until the juices run clear when the thigh joint is pierced with a knife tip, about 1¹/₂ hours.

To test for doneness, insert an instant-read thermometer into the thickest part of the thigh away from the bone; it should register 170°F (77°C). The temperature will rise another 5°–10°F (3°–6°C) while the chicken is resting.

Transfer the chicken to a cutting board and let rest for 10 minutes before carving.

1 roasting chicken, about 4 lb (2 kg), neck and giblets removed

¹/₂ cup (4 fl oz/125 ml) olive oil

¹/₄ cup (2 fl oz/60 ml) fresh lemon juice

¹/₄ cup (2 fl oz/60 ml) fresh orange juice

¹/₄ cup (2 fl oz/60 ml) red wine vinegar

2–3 tablespoons *piri-piri* sauce or other hot-pepper sauce

2 teaspoons paprika

¹/₂ teaspoon ground cumin

Salt and freshly ground pepper

2 tablespoons chopped fresh flat-leaf (Italian) parsley

2 teaspoons peeled and finely chopped fresh ginger

2 teaspoons chopped fresh thyme

4 cloves garlic, finely chopped

1 or 2 handfuls mesquite wood chips, soaked if using charcoal (page 13) (optional)

MAKES 4 SERVINGS

Chicken Under a Brick

1 large fryer chicken, about 3¹/₂ lb (1.75 kg), neck and giblets removed, butterflied (page 290)

Salt and freshly ground pepper

6 tablespoons (3 fl oz/90 ml) fresh lemon juice

3 tablespoons olive oil

2 teaspoons grated lemon zest

¹/₄ teaspoon red pepper flakes

3 cloves garlic, finely chopped

1 heavy cast-iron skillet, or 1 or 2 bricks wrapped in aluminum foil

MAKES 4 SERVINGS

Rinse the chicken and pat dry with paper towels. Season the chicken all over with salt and pepper. In a shallow, nonreactive dish just large enough to hold the chicken, combine the lemon juice, oil, lemon zest, red pepper flakes, and garlic. Add the chicken and turn to coat. Cover and refrigerate, turning occasionally, for at least 30 minutes or for up to 3 hours. If refrigerated, remove from the refrigerator 30 minutes before grilling.

Prepare a CHARCOAL or GAS grill for DIRECT grilling over MEDIUM heat (page 18 or 22). Oil the grill rack.

CHARCOAL: Place the chicken, skin side down, over the hottest part of the fire. Place the pan or brick(s) on top of the chicken and cook for 15 minutes. Turn the chicken over, replace the pan or brick(s), and cook until the juices run clear when the thigh joint is pierced with a knife tip, 15–20 minutes longer.

GAS: Place the chicken, skin side down, directly over the heat elements. Place the pan or brick(s) on top of the chicken and cook for 15 minutes. Turn the chicken over, replace the pan or brick(s), and cook until the juices run clear when the thigh joint is pierced with a knife tip, 15–20 minutes longer.

Transfer the chicken to a cutting board and let rest for 5 minutes before carving.

Grilling chicken under a brick is a classic method in Italy. Instead of a brick, you can weight the chicken with a cast-iron skillet. Either weighs down the chicken so that it cooks evenly and with the maximum amount of browned and crisped skin. You can also cook boneless breasts or thighs this way, a method that produces beautiful grill marks.

Classic Barbecued Chicken

Purists take issue with calling America's favorite backyard grill real barbecue. True barbecue calls for cooking food over a slow indirect-heat wood fire. For devotees, this leisurely—though technically demanding—cooking method becomes a way of life. But what most of us think of as classic backyard "barbecued" chicken is cooked over direct heat and brushed with a tangy, tomato-based sauce near the end of cooking. Any part of the chicken can be grilled, but serving an assortment of parts is economical and provides something to suit every taste.

To make the quick barbecue sauce, in a large saucepan over medium heat, warm the oil. Add the onion and sauté until just softened, about 4 minutes. Add the garlic and sauté for 1 minute, until fragrant. Stir in the chili powder, mustard, paprika, and cayenne. Add the chili sauce, ketchup, beer, molasses, Worcestershire sauce, and vinegar. Simmer, stirring often, until the sauce is lightly thickened, 20–25 minutes. Use the sauce immediately or cover and refrigerate for up to 1 week. You should have 3–3$^1/_2$ cups (24–28 fl oz/750–875 ml). Reheat the sauce before using.

Prepare a CHARCOAL or GAS grill for DIRECT grilling over MEDIUM heat (page 18 or 22). Oil the grill rack. If using chicken breasts and they are large, cut them in half crosswise before grilling. Season the chicken with salt and pepper. Have ready about 1 cup (8 fl oz/250 ml) of the barbecue sauce, reserving the remainder to serve separately or for other uses.

CHARCOAL: Grill the chicken thighs, skin side down, and drumsticks over the hottest part of the fire for 5 minutes, then add the breasts and wings. Grill, turning once or twice, for 10 minutes. Brush the chicken with some of the sauce and continue to grill, turning occasionally and brushing with more sauce, until the juices run clear when a thigh or breast is pierced with a knife tip, about 10 minutes.

GAS: Grill the chicken thighs, skin side down, and drumsticks directly over the heat elements for 5 minutes, then add the breasts and wings. Grill, turning once or twice, for 10 minutes. Brush the chicken with some of the sauce and continue to grill, turning occasionally and brushing with more sauce, until the juices run clear when a thigh or breast is pierced with a knife tip, about 10 minutes.

Serve the chicken hot with the reserved barbecue sauce, if desired.

For the Quick Barbecue Sauce

2 tablespoons vegetable oil

1 yellow onion, chopped

2 cloves garlic, finely chopped

2 teaspoons chili powder

2 teaspoons dry mustard

1 teaspoon sweet paprika

$^1/_4$ teaspoon ground cayenne pepper

1 cup (8 fl oz/250 ml) bottled chili sauce

1 cup (8 fl oz/250 ml) tomato ketchup

1 cup (8 fl oz/250 ml) beer or ginger ale

$^1/_4$ cup (3 oz/90 g) molasses

3 tablespoons Worcestershire sauce

3 tablespoons cider vinegar

2$^1/_2$ lb (1.25 kg) mixed chicken parts such as breasts, thighs, drumsticks, and wings

Salt and freshly ground pepper

Mahogany Chicken

For the Mahogany Glaze

¹/₄ cup (3 oz/90 g) molasses

¹/₄ cup (2 fl oz/60 ml) cider vinegar

1 tablespoon vegetable oil

1 tablespoon Worcestershire sauce

1 tablespoon whole-grain Dijon mustard

1 tablespoon fresh orange juice

1 teaspoon grated orange zest

Freshly ground pepper

2¹/₂ lb (1.25 kg) mixed chicken parts such as breasts, thighs, drumsticks, and wings

2 handfuls wood chips such as hickory or mesquite, soaked if using charcoal (page 13) (optional)

MAKES 4 SERVINGS

To make the mahogany glaze, in a small saucepan, combine the molasses, vinegar, oil, Worcestershire sauce, mustard, orange juice and zest, and ¹/₂ teaspoon pepper. Place over medium heat and bring to a simmer, stirring often. Simmer for 2 minutes to blend the flavors, stirring often. Use the glaze immediately, or cover and refrigerate for up to 2 days.

Prepare a CHARCOAL or GAS grill for INDIRECT grilling over MEDIUM heat (page 19 or 23). If using a charcoal grill, place a drip pan half full of water on the center of the fire bed. Oil the grill rack. Brush the chicken parts with some of the glaze.

CHARCOAL: Sprinkle half of the wood chips on the coals, if using. Grill the chicken, skin side down, over the drip pan for 10 minutes. Turn the chicken, brush with more glaze, and grill for 10 minutes. Sprinkle the remaining wood chips on the coals. Continue to grill, turning and brushing the chicken 2 more times, until the juices run clear when a thigh or breast is pierced with a knife tip, about 20 minutes longer.

GAS: Add the wood chips to the grill in a smoker box or perforated foil packet (page 10). Grill the chicken, skin side down, away from the heat elements for 10 minutes. Turn the chicken, brush with more glaze, and grill for 10 minutes. Continue to grill, turning and brushing the chicken 2 more times, until the juices run clear when a thigh or breast is pierced with a knife tip, about 20 minutes longer.

Serve the chicken hot or at room temperature, letting diners choose the portions they prefer.

This molasses-rich glaze is brushed on during the relatively long, slow cooking over an indirect fire, resulting in a deeply browned bird. Wood chips, especially mesquite, further contribute to the mahogany color and sweet, smoky flavor. You can use any chicken parts, but this is an especially good treatment for drumsticks or thighs. Try it also with turkey drumsticks, an underused and highly flavorful turkey part. A tangy cucumber and tomato salad is a nice counterpoint to the sweetness of the glaze.

Garlic Butter Chicken Breasts

These chicken breasts are basted from both the inside and the outside. Some of the garlic butter is inserted under the skin, then the remaining butter is melted and thinned with a little wine to become a brushing sauce. The result is incredibly moist and tender chicken pieces. The technique is especially well suited to delicate chicken breasts, which tend to dry out if conventionally grilled. The idea translates nicely to chicken thighs or halved Cornish hens, too. Serve with grilled radicchio for a striking presentation.

To make the garlic butter, in a saucepan, using a fork, mash together the butter, garlic, chives, and $^1/_2$ teaspoon each salt and pepper. Using your fingers, carefully loosen the skin on each chicken breast and insert about $1^1/_2$ teaspoons of the garlic butter under the skin, spreading it as evenly as possible. Add the white wine to the remaining butter mixture and place over low heat until melted. Set aside.

Prepare a CHARCOAL or GAS grill for a DIRECT grilling over MEDIUM heat (page 18 or 22). Oil the grill rack.

CHARCOAL: Grill the chicken, skin side down, over the hottest part of the fire, turning once or twice, for 10 minutes. Brush the chicken with some of the melted butter mixture. Continue to grill, turning occasionally and brushing with more of the butter mixture, until the juices run clear when the thickest part of the breast, away from the bone, is pierced with a knife tip, about 10 minutes longer.

GAS: Grill the chicken, skin side down, directly over the heat elements, turning once or twice, for 10 minutes. Brush the chicken with some of the melted butter mixture. Continue to grill, turning occasionally and brushing with more of the butter mixture, until the juices run clear when the thickest part of a breast, away from the bone, is pierced with a knife tip, about 10 minutes longer.

Serve the chicken breasts hot, either whole or carved off the bone.

For the Garlic Butter

$^1/_4$ cup (2 oz/60 g) unsalted butter, at room temperature

4 large cloves garlic, finely chopped

2 tablespoons snipped fresh chives

Salt and freshly ground pepper

4 bone-in chicken breast halves

2 tablespoons dry white wine

MAKES 4 SERVINGS

Citrus-and-Honey Chicken Breasts

For the Citrus-Honey Marinade

1 orange

1 lemon

1 lime

3 tablespoons snipped fresh chives or finely chopped green (spring) onion

1 tablespoon chopped fresh mint

2 tablespoons olive oil

2 tablespoons wildflower honey

6 boneless, skinless chicken breast halves

Salt and freshly ground pepper

1 orange, cut crosswise into slices $1/4$ inch (6 mm) thick

1 lemon, cut crosswise into slices $1/4$ inch (6 mm) thick

1 lime, cut crosswise into slices $1/4$ inch (6 mm) thick

4 fresh mint sprigs

MAKES 6 SERVINGS

To make the citrus-honey marinade, finely shred the zest from the orange, lemon, and lime, then squeeze the juice from each fruit. In a shallow, nonreactive dish just large enough to hold the chicken in a single layer, stir together the orange, lemon, and lime juices and zest; chives; chopped mint; oil; and honey. Pour off about 2 tablespoons of the marinade and set aside.

Use the palm of your hand to flatten each chicken breast to an even thickness of about $3/4$ inch (2 cm). Season the chicken on both sides with salt and pepper. Add the chicken to the dish and turn to coat both sides with the marinade. Cover and refrigerate, turning occasionally, for at least 1 hour or for up to 4 hours. Remove from the refrigerator 30 minutes before grilling. Add the orange, lemon, and lime slices to the marinade during the last 15 minutes.

Prepare a CHARCOAL or GAS grill for DIRECT grilling over MEDIUM-HIGH heat (page 18 or 22). Oil the grill rack. Remove the chicken and the citrus slices from the marinade and discard the marinade.

CHARCOAL: Grill the chicken over the hottest part of the fire, turning once or twice and brushing with the reserved marinade, until firm to the touch and opaque throughout, 4–6 minutes per side. A few minutes before the chicken is done, arrange the citrus slices at the edges of the grill where the heat is less intense. Grill, turning once, until softened and grill marks appear, about 1 minute per side.

GAS: Grill the chicken directly over the heat elements, turning once or twice and brushing with the reserved marinade, until firm to the touch and opaque throughout, 4–6 minutes per side. A few minutes before the chicken is done, place the citrus slices on an area with lower heat. Grill, turning once, until softened and grill marks appear, about 1 minute per side.

Serve the chicken immediately, garnished with the grilled citrus slices.

This marinade has a delicate flavor, making it perfect for boneless chicken breasts, although it is also ideal for shrimp (prawns), meaty fish, or scallops. Wildflower honey has been used here, but many wonderful honeys are available today, so choose one that has a fragrance that appeals to you. When grating the zest from the citrus fruits, be sure to remove only the colored part, leaving the bitter white pith behind. A simple green vegetable, such as baby broccoli or broccoli rabe, is a nice accompaniment.

Chipotle-Maple Chicken

2 tablespoons maple syrup

2 tablespoons fresh lemon juice

1 tablespoon chopped fresh cilantro (fresh coriander), plus sprigs for garnish

2 canned chipotle chiles in adobo sauce, plus 1 tablespoon adobo sauce

8 boneless, skinless chicken thighs, trimmed of excess fat

Salt

MAKES 4 SERVINGS

Prepare a CHARCOAL or GAS grill for DIRECT grilling over MEDIUM HEAT (page 18 or 22). Oil the grill rack. Stir together the maple syrup, lemon juice, chopped cilantro, and adobo sauce to make a glaze. Split open each chipotle, scrape out the seeds, and cut each into 8–10 pieces. Lay the thighs, boned surface up, on a work surface, season with salt, and brush with glaze. Sprinkle with the chipotles and roll up each thigh into a compact package, securing with a toothpick. Brush the other side with glaze. Let stand at room temperature for 30 minutes.

CHARCOAL: Grill the rolled thighs over the hottest part of the fire, turning occasionally, until the meat is firm and the juices run clear when the meat is pierced at the thickest point with a knife tip, 20 minutes.

GAS: Grill the thighs directly over the heat elements, turning occasionally, until the meat is firm and the juices run clear when the meat is pierced at the thickest point with a knife tip, about 20 minutes.

Serve the chicken immediately, garnished with the cilantro sprigs.

Chipotles, which are smoke-dried jalapeño chiles, are available in cans and jars in a spicy adobo sauce. Maple syrup also has a natural smoky sweetness. Combine the two, and the result is an irresistible glaze that perfectly flavors slowly grilled chicken. The chipotles are chopped and rolled up in the chicken for a surprise kick. Serve this dish to guests with adventurous palates.

Hoisin-Lime Chicken Thighs

Chicken thighs are a terrific choice for grilling because they stay moist and juicy over the fire. These are marinated in an Asian-style blend of hoisin sauce and lime juice, accented with a little piquant Sriracha sauce or other hot-pepper sauce.

Whisk together the hoisin, lime juice, oil, soy sauce, Sriracha, ginger, and garlic to make a marinade. Pour over the chicken and turn to coat well. Cover and refrigerate, turning the pieces occasionally, for 2–3 hours. Remove the bowl from the refrigerator about 30 minutes before grilling.

Prepare a CHARCOAL or GAS grill for DIRECT grilling over MEDIUM-LOW heat (page 18 or 22). Oil the grill rack.

CHARCOAL: Grill the chicken over the hottest part of the fire, turning several times, until the juices run clear when a thigh is pierced, 30–35 minutes. If the chicken is browning too fast, move it to a cooler edge of the grill.

GAS: Grill the chicken directly over the heat elements, turning several times, until the juices run clear when a thigh is pierced, 30–35 minutes. If the chicken is browning too fast, move it to an area with lower heat.

Serve the chicken immediately.

½ cup (4 fl oz/125 ml) hoisin sauce

3 tablespoons fresh lime juice

2 tablespoons vegetable oil

1 tablespoon soy sauce

1 tablespoon Sriracha sauce

1 teaspoon grated fresh ginger

2 cloves garlic, finely chopped

12 skinless, bone-in chicken thighs, excess fat trimmed

MAKES 6 SERVINGS

Asian Chicken Salad

4 boneless, skinless chicken breast halves

^{2}/$_3$ cup (2 oz/60 g) thinly sliced green (spring) onions

^{1}/$_2$ cup (4 fl oz/125 ml) canola oil

^{1}/$_4$ cup (2 fl oz/60 ml) fresh lime juice

^{1}/$_4$ cup (^{1}/$_3$ oz/10 g) slivered fresh Thai basil or regular sweet basil

^{1}/$_4$ cup (^{1}/$_3$ oz/10 g) slivered fresh mint

2 tablespoons Asian fish sauce

2 teaspoons peeled and chopped fresh ginger

^{1}/$_4$ teaspoon red pepper flakes

2 cloves garlic, finely chopped

1 small green bell pepper (capsicum), seeded and quartered lengthwise

1 small yellow bell pepper (capsicum), seeded and quartered lengthwise

^{3}/$_4$ lb (375 g) soba or somen noodles or Italian vermicelli

^{1}/$_4$ cup (1 oz/30 g) sliced radishes

MAKES 4 SERVINGS

Use the palm of your hand to flatten each chicken breast to an even thickness of about ^{3}/$_4$ inch (2 cm). Set aside.

In a bowl, stir together ^{1}/$_3$ cup (1 oz/30 g) of the green onion, the oil, lime juice, basil, mint, fish sauce, ginger, red pepper flakes, and garlic. Pour about one-third of the marinade into a shallow, nonreactive dish just large enough to hold the chicken; reserve the remaining marinade to use as the salad dressing. Add the chicken to the dish and turn to coat both sides. Cover and refrigerate, turning once or twice, for at least 30 minutes or for up to 3 hours. If refrigerated, remove from the refrigerator about 30 minutes before grilling. Add the green and yellow bell peppers to the marinade during the last 15 minutes.

Prepare a CHARCOAL or GAS grill for DIRECT grilling over MEDIUM-HIGH heat (page 18 or 22). Oil the grill rack. Remove the chicken from the marinade and discard the marinade.

CHARCOAL: Grill the chicken over the hottest part of the fire, turning once or twice, until firm to the touch and opaque throughout, 8–10 minutes total. About halfway through the grilling time, place the bell peppers along the edges of the grill where the heat is less intense. Grill, turning once or twice, until softened and lightly charred, 4–6 minutes total.

GAS: Grill the chicken directly over the heat elements, turning once or twice, until firm to the touch and opaque throughout, 8–10 minutes total. About halfway through the grilling time, place the bell peppers on an area with lower heat. Grill, turning once or twice, until they are softened and lightly charred, 4–6 minutes total.

While the chicken and peppers are grilling, or after they are done, bring a large saucepan three-fourths full of salted water to a boil. Add the noodles and boil until al dente, about 8 minutes, or according to package directions. Drain well. Transfer to a bowl, add the reserved marinade, and toss well.

Cut the bell peppers lengthwise into narrow strips, and cut the chicken against the grain into thin strips. If you are serving the salad immediately, add the chicken, bell peppers, the remaining ^{1}/$_3$ cup (1 oz/30 g) green onion, and the radishes to the noodles, toss well, and serve.

Variations on this salad are served all over Southeast Asia, but especially in Vietnam and Thailand, where fish sauce is a pantry staple. Peppery, lemony Thai basil is increasingly available, but if you can't locate it, use regular European basil. You can also use Italian vermicelli in place of the thin Asian soba (buckwheat) or somen (wheat) noodles. Cook the noodles while the chicken is grilling or even afterward, since the salad is as good at room temperature as it is warm.

Beer-Barbecued Turkey Tenderloin

A turkey tenderloin is cut from the breast and, depending on its size, looks like a large chicken breast or a thick steak. Indeed, it can be treated like a steak, marinated and sauced. The marinade here is a simple beer base that, with the addition of a homemade or good-quality bottled barbecue sauce, becomes the basting sauce, too. Turn to page 169 for a basic barbecue sauce recipe, or purchase one to save time. Nowadays, many fine barbecue sauces are available in specialty stores or by mail order, so experiment a bit to find which ones you like best.

To make the marinade, select a shallow, nonreactive dish just big enough to hold the turkey. Combine 1 1/2 cups (12 fl oz/375 ml) of the beer, 1/4 cup (2 fl oz/60 ml) of the vinegar, 1 of the onions, 2 of the garlic cloves, and 1 teaspoon of the hot-pepper sauce in the dish and mix well. Add the turkey tenderloin(s) and turn to coat both sides. Cover and refrigerate, turning often, for at least 1 hour or for up to 4 hours. Remove from the refrigerator about 30 minutes before grilling.

To make the sauce, in a saucepan over medium heat, combine the remaining 1 1/2 cups (12 fl oz/375 ml) beer, 1/4 cup (2 fl oz/60 ml) vinegar, 1 onion, 2 garlic cloves, and 1 teaspoon hot-pepper sauce and all of the chili sauce, barbecue sauce, and Worcestershire sauce. Bring to a simmer and cook, stirring from time to time, until slightly thickened, about 15 minutes. Remove from the heat and measure out 1 cup (8 fl oz/250 ml) of the sauce to use for basting the turkey on the grill. Reserve the remaining sauce for passing at the table.

Prepare a CHARCOAL or GAS grill for DIRECT grilling over MEDIUM-HIGH heat (page 18 or 22). Oil the grill rack. Remove the turkey from the marinade and discard the marinade. Season the turkey on both sides with salt and pepper and then brush on both sides with the oil.

CHARCOAL: Grill the turkey over the hottest part of the fire, turning once or twice, until opaque throughout, 12–20 minutes total, depending on the size of the tenderloin(s). When turning the turkey, brush it with the sauce reserved for basting.

GAS: Grill the turkey directly over the heat elements, turning once or twice, until opaque throughout, 12–20 minutes total, depending on the size of the tenderloin(s). When turning the turkey, brush it with the sauce reserved for basting.

Let the turkey tenderloin(s) rest for 5–10 minutes, depending on size, before slicing across the grain to serve. Reheat the reserved sauce and pass it at the table.

3 cups (24 fl oz/750 ml) beer

1/2 cup (4 fl oz/125 ml) cider vinegar

2 yellow onions, chopped

4 cloves garlic, finely chopped

2 teaspoons hot-pepper sauce

1 1/2 lb (625 g) turkey breast tenderloin(s), about 3/4 inch (2 cm) thick

1 cup (8 fl oz/250 ml) bottled chili sauce

1 cup (8 fl oz/250 ml) barbecue sauce

3 tablespoons Worcestershire sauce

Salt and freshly ground pepper

1 tablespoon vegetable oil

MAKES 4 SERVINGS

Cajun-Brined Smoked Turkey Breast

For the Cajun Rub

2 tablespoons chili powder

1 tablespoon sweet paprika

2 teaspoons dried thyme

2 teaspoons dried oregano

2 teaspoons dried onion flakes

1 teaspoon dried garlic flakes

1 teaspoon sugar

$^1/_2$ teaspoon ground cayenne pepper

For the Cajun Brine

Cajun rub

$^1/_4$ cup (2 oz/60 g) coarse sea or kosher salt

4 cups (32 fl oz/1 l) water

1 skin-on, bone-in turkey breast, 4–5 lb (2–2.5 kg), halved

2 tablespoons vegetable oil

2 handfuls wood chips such as hickory or mesquite, soaked if using charcoal (page 13)

MAKES 6–8 SERVINGS

To make the Cajun rub, in a small dish, stir together the chili powder, paprika, thyme, oregano, onion and garlic flakes, sugar, and cayenne. The rub can be made up to 2 weeks ahead and stored, tightly covered, at cool room temperature.

To make the Cajun brine, in a saucepan, combine 3 tablespoons of the Cajun rub, the salt, and the water. Bring to a boil over medium-high heat, stirring to dissolve the salt. Remove from the heat and let cool completely, then transfer to a large, deep, nonreactive container that will hold the turkey breast. Rinse the turkey breast halves, add them to the brine, then add enough water to cover the breast halves completely. Cover and refrigerate for at least 8 hours or for up to 24 hours. Remove from the refrigerator 30 minutes before grilling.

Prepare a CHARCOAL or GAS grill for INDIRECT grilling over MEDIUM heat (page 19 or 23). Oil the grill rack. Remove the turkey breast halves from the brine and pat them dry. Discard the brine. Rub the turkey breast halves with the remaining Cajun rub, then brush them with oil.

CHARCOAL: Place a drip pan half filled with water in the center of the fire bed. Sprinkle half of the wood chips on the coals. Place the turkey breast halves on the grill rack over the drip pan. Cover the grill and cook the turkey breast halves until they are a rich golden brown and cooked through, 1–1$^1/_2$ hours. Add the remaining wood chips halfway through the grilling process, and add more water to the pan and hot coals as needed.

GAS: Place a shallow pan half full of water at the edge of the grill rack away from the heat elements. Add the wood chips to the grill in a smoker box or a perforated foil packet (page 10). Place the turkey breast halves on the grill rack away from the heat elements. Cover the grill and cook the turkey breast halves, adding more water to the pan as needed, until they are a rich golden brown and cooked through, 1–1$^1/_2$ hours.

To test for doneness, insert an instant-read thermometer into the thickest part of the breast halves, away from the bone; it should register 160°F (71°C). The temperature will rise another 5°–10°F (3°–6°C) while the turkey is resting.

Transfer the turkey breast halves to a cutting board, tent loosely with aluminum foil, and let rest for at least 20 minutes before carving.

It's easier to grill turkey breast halves than the whole breast, which sits awkwardly on the grill rack. Turkey, by its nature, has dry meat, and the breast meat is particularly lean. This makes soaking the turkey in a brine especially important. Then, for added protection against dry meat, put some water in a pan to create extra moisture. An accurate thermometer is also a good tool for guarding against overcooking.

Echo the Louisiana roots of this dish by serving it with red beans and rice.

Grill-Roasted Turkey with Orange and Fennel Pan Gravy

For the Orange Brine

4 large oranges

6 cups (48 fl oz/1.5 l) orange juice

$^1/_2$ cup (4 oz/125 g) coarse sea or kosher salt

10 whole cloves

3 tablespoons fennel seeds

2 cinnamon sticks, broken in half

1 turkey, 12–14 lb (6–7 kg)

Freshly ground coarse pepper

2 fennel bulbs, trimmed and coarsely diced

1 large orange

2 tablespoons olive oil

4–6 cups (32–48 fl oz/1–1.5 l) chicken broth

Salt and freshly ground pepper

MAKES 10–12 SERVINGS

To make the orange brine, using a small, sharp knife, remove the zest from the oranges, being careful to cut away only the colored part. Place the zest in a large saucepan. Squeeze the juice from the oranges, and add to the saucepan along with the 6 cups orange juice, the salt, cloves, fennel seeds, and cinnamon sticks. Bring to a boil over medium-high heat, stirring to dissolve the salt. Remove from the heat and let cool completely, then transfer to a deep, nonreactive 5-gal (20-l) container. Remove the neck and giblets from the turkey cavity and discard or reserve for another use. Rinse the turkey, add it to the brine, and then add enough water so that the turkey is completely submerged. Cover and refrigerate for at least 12 hours or for up to 24 hours. Remove from the refrigerator 1 hour before grilling.

Prepare a CHARCOAL or GAS grill for INDIRECT grilling over MEDIUM heat (page 19 or 23). Remove the turkey from the brine and pat it dry.

Discard the brine. Season the bird inside and out with the coarse pepper, then stuff half of the fennel into the cavity. Using a small, sharp knife, remove the zest from the orange, being careful to cut away only the colored part. Put half of the zest into the cavity of the turkey. With your fingers, pull off most of the white pith from the orange, then cut it into sections. Place half of the sections in the cavity. Truss the turkey (page 290). Brush the turkey all over with the oil.

Place the remaining fennel and orange zest and sections in a heavy-duty, aluminum foil pan large enough to hold the turkey. Place the turkey, breast side up, on the fennel and orange sections. Pour 1 cup (8 fl oz/250 ml) of the broth into the pan.

CHARCOAL: Place the turkey in the pan on the grill rack away from the fire. Cover the grill and grill-roast the turkey, adding more coals as needed, until the skin is a rich golden brown, $2^1/_2$–3 hours. Baste with the drippings or broth every 30 minutes and add additional broth to the pan as needed to prevent the drippings from burning.

GAS: Place the turkey in the pan on the grill rack away from the heat elements. Cover the grill and grill-roast the turkey until it is a rich golden brown, $2^1/_2$–3 hours. Baste with the drippings or broth every 30 minutes and add additional broth to the pan as needed to prevent the drippings from burning.

Grill-roasting is the easiest and most foolproof way to grill a whole turkey. Aromatic vegetables, in this case fennel, can be added to the pan, which increases the smoke. Additionally, you can make gravy from the drippings in the pan.

Although it is possible to grill any-sized turkey, you'll have the best results with a small bird, 12 to 14 pounds (6 to 7 kilograms), which roasts in about 3 hours. The turkey will have a nice bronze skin, and the meat will remain moist and juicy due both to the cooking time and to the brining, which improves any turkey cooked indoors or out.

If the turkey wings begin to burn during cooking, tent them with aluminum foil. To test for doneness, insert an instant-read thermometer into the thickest part of the thigh away from the bone; it should register 170°F (77°C). The temperature will rise another 5°–10°F (3°–6°C) while the turkey is resting.

Transfer the turkey to a cutting board, tent loosely with aluminum foil, and let rest for at least 20 minutes while making the gravy.

Skim excess fat from the pan drippings, leaving about 2 tablespoons in the pan. Place the foil pan back on the grill rack directly over the coals or heat elements. Add 3 cups (24 fl oz/750 ml) broth to the pan and bring to a simmer, scraping up the browned bits on the bottom of the pan. Simmer, stirring the fennel into the broth and mashing it with the back of a large spoon to thicken the liquid slightly, until the liquid reduces to a light gravy consistency, about 10 minutes. Season to taste with salt and pepper. If desired, stir some of the fennel, orange zest, and orange sections from the turkey cavity into the gravy.

Carve the turkey and serve with the gravy.

Apple-Brined Smoked Turkey

The difference between grill-roasting and smoking a turkey is that for the latter the bird is put directly on the grill rack, rather than in an aluminum pan, and wood chips are added to the grill. The cooking time is about the same, but the result is a bird with firmer meat and a smokier flavor. Choose the wood chips according to how strong you want the smoky taste to be: hickory is most pronounced, fruitwood is mellow, and mesquite lends a robust aroma.

Lady apples, small fruits with lovely green and red skins, are nice for garnishing the platter of the carved smoked turkey.

To make the apple brine, in a large saucepan, combine the apple juice; $1/2$ bunch each of the sage, summer savory, and thyme; the bay leaves; and the salt and pepper. Place over medium-high heat and bring to a boil, stirring to dissolve the salt. Remove from the heat and let cool completely, then transfer to a 5-gallon (20-l) container deep enough to hold the turkey. Remove the neck and giblets from the turkey cavity and discard or reserve for another use. Rinse the turkey, add it to the brine, then add enough water to completely submerge the bird. Cover the container and refrigerate for at least 12 hours or up to 24 hours.

Prepare a CHARCOAL or GAS grill for INDIRECT grilling over MEDIUM heat (page 19 or 23). Oil the grill rack.

Remove the turkey from the brine and pat it dry. Discard the brine. Season the bird inside and out with the coarse pepper, then stuff the cavity with the remaining $1/2$ bunch each sage, summer savory, and thyme, reserving a few sprigs for garnish. Truss the turkey (page 292), then brush it all over with the oil.

CHARCOAL: Place a drip pan half full of water on the center of the fire bed. Sprinkle 2 handfuls of the wood chips on the coals. Place the turkey, breast side up, on the grill rack over the drip pan. Cover the grill and cook the turkey, adding more coals as needed to maintain the temperature, until it is a rich, golden brown and cooked through, $2^{1}/2$–3 hours. Add the remaining wood chips in 2 additions, and add more water to the drip pan as needed.

GAS: Place a shallow pan half full of water at the edge of the grill rack. Add the wood chips to the grill in a smoker box or a perforated foil packet (page 10). Place the turkey, breast side up, on the grill rack away from the heat elements. Cover the grill and cook the turkey until it is a rich golden brown and cooked through, $2^{1}/2$–3 hours.

If the turkey wings begin to burn, tent them with aluminum foil. To test for doneness, insert an instant-read thermometer into the thickest part of the thigh away from the bone; it should register 170°F (77°C). The temperature will rise another 5°–10°F (3°–6°C) while the turkey is resting.

Transfer the turkey to a cutting board, tent loosely with aluminum foil, and let rest for at least 20 minutes before carving. Serve the turkey garnished with the reserved herb sprigs.

For the Apple Brine

8 cups (64 fl oz/2 l) apple juice or sweet apple cider

1 bunch fresh sage

1 bunch fresh summer savory or marjoram

1 bunch fresh thyme

6 bay leaves

$1/2$ cup (4 oz/125 g) coarse sea or kosher salt

2 tablespoons freshly cracked pepper

1 turkey, 12–14 lb (6–7 kg)

Freshly ground coarse pepper

2 tablespoons vegetable oil

4 handfuls wood chips such as hickory, fruitwood, or mesquite, soaked if using charcoal (page 13)

MAKES 10–12 SERVINGS

Turkey Burgers with Cranberry Relish

For the Cranberry Relish

1 cup (10 oz/315 g) whole-berry cranberry sauce

2 tablespoons freshly grated or prepared horseradish

2 teaspoons fresh lemon juice

Pinch of ground cinnamon

Pinch of ground cloves

Salt and freshly ground pepper

1 tablespoon unsalted butter

$1/2$ cup ($2^1/2$ oz/75 g) finely chopped celery

$1/2$ cup ($2^1/2$ oz/75 g) finely chopped yellow onion

$1^1/2$ lb (750 g) ground (minced) turkey (see note)

1 cup (4 oz/125 g) day-old small corn bread cubes

2 tablespoons chopped fresh flat-leaf (Italian) parsley

1 tablespoon chopped fresh sage

1 tablespoon chopped fresh thyme

1 teaspoon poultry seasoning

Salt and freshly ground pepper

1 egg

4 sandwich rolls, preferably freshly baked

MAKES 6 SERVINGS

To make the cranberry relish, in a small bowl, stir together the cranberry sauce, horseradish, lemon juice, cinnamon, and cloves. Season to taste with salt and pepper. Let the mixture stand for at least 15 minutes at room temperature before using, or cover and refrigerate for up to 24 hours. Return the relish to room temperature before using.

In a small frying pan over medium heat, melt the butter. Add the celery and onion and cook, stirring often, until softened, about 4 minutes. Remove from the heat and let cool completely. In a large bowl, combine the turkey, corn bread, parsley, sage, thyme, poultry seasoning, 1 teaspoon salt, $1/2$ teaspoon pepper, the egg, and the onion mixture. Using your hands, mix together the ingredients until evenly distributed. Divide the mixture into 4 equal portions and form each into a patty 4–$4^1/2$ inches (10–11.5 cm) in diameter and about $3/4$ inch (2 cm) thick. Take care not to handle the meat more than necessary or to compact the patties too much.

Prepare a CHARCOAL or GAS grill for DIRECT grilling over MEDIUM-HIGH heat (page 18 or 22). Oil the grill rack.

CHARCOAL: Grill the burgers over the hottest part of the fire, turning once, until opaque throughout, 6–7 minutes per side. About 1 minute before the burgers are done, place the rolls, cut sides down, along the edges of the grill where the heat is less intense and grill until lightly toasted.

GAS: Grill the burgers directly over the heat elements, turning once, until opaque throughout, 6–7 minutes per side. About 1 minute before the burgers are done, place the rolls, cut sides down, on an area with lower heat and grill until lightly toasted.

Serve the burgers in the buns with the cranberry relish.

This is Thanksgiving in July: all the right flavors in a summer burger on the grill. Use regular ground turkey, which is a mix of white and dark meat, as ground turkey breast is too lean and bland for good grilling. For the relish, use prepared cranberry sauce from the deli, or use canned whole-berry sauce. Serve with grilled sweet potato fries.

Orange-Glazed Duck Breasts

This is a distinctly different view of the French classic duck à l'orange, but distinctly delicious nonetheless. Chicken breasts or thighs make good substitutes for the duck breasts if you wish. Use a high-quality, not excessively sweet orange marmalade, such as Seville orange. Wild rice pilaf is a traditional accompaniment for duck.

Using a zester, remove 1 tablespoon zest from 1 or 2 of the oranges, then squeeze enough juice from 2 of the oranges to measure 6 tablespoons (3 fl oz/90 ml). Cut the remaining orange into 6 crosswise slices. Remove 1 teaspoon zest from the lemons, then squeeze enough juice from the lemons to measure 3 tablespoons.

In a shallow, nonreactive dish just large enough to hold the duck in a single layer, stir together the orange and lemon zest and juices, the oil, tarragon, and pepper flakes. Transfer half of the mixture to a small saucepan and stir in the marmalade; set aside. Place the duck in the dish and turn to coat both sides. Cover the marmalade mixture and the duck and refrigerate for at least 1 hour or for up to 4 hours.

Prepare a CHARCOAL or GAS grill for DIRECT grilling over MEDIUM-HIGH heat (page 18 or 22). Oil the grill rack. Set the saucepan with the orange mixture over medium-low heat on the stove top or on the grill to simmer for 2 minutes. Keep the sauce warm. Season the duck breasts with salt and pepper.

CHARCOAL: Place the duck breasts on the grill rack over the hottest part of the fire and cook, turning once or twice and brushing with the warm sauce, until lightly charred and cooked to your liking, 8–10 minutes total for medium (pink in the middle and juicy). A few minutes before the duck is done, brush the orange slices with the sauce and place at the edges of the grill where the heat is less intense. Grill the orange slices, turning once, until softened and grill marks appear, 1–2 minutes per side.

GAS: Place the duck breasts directly over the heat elements and cook, turning once or twice and brushing with the warm sauce, until lightly charred and cooked to your liking, 8–10 minutes total for medium (pink in the middle and juicy). A few minutes before the duck is done, brush the orange slices with the sauce and place on an area with lower heat. Grill the orange slices, turning once, until softened and grill marks appear, 1–2 minutes per side.

Serve the duck garnished with the orange slices.

3 oranges

2 lemons

3 tablespoons olive oil

1$^1/_2$ tablespoons chopped fresh tarragon

$^1/_4$ teaspoon red pepper flakes

6 tablespoons (3 oz/90 g) orange marmalade

6 boneless, skinless duck breasts

Salt and freshly ground pepper

MAKES 6 SERVINGS

Tea-Smoked Duck Breasts

For the Tea Paste

$1/3$ cup (1 oz/30 g) loose tea leaves

5 whole cloves

3 whole star anise

$1^1/2$ tablespoons grated orange zest

$1/4$ cup (2 fl oz/60 ml) thawed, frozen orange juice concentrate

1 tablespoon soy sauce

1 tablespoon rice vinegar

Salt

$1/4$ teaspoon red pepper flakes

$1/4$ teaspoon ground cinnamon

6 bone-in, skin-on duck breast halves

For the Tea Smoking Mixture

2 handfuls wood chips such as fruitwood or mesquite

$1/3$ cup (1 oz/30 g) loose tea leaves

1 cinnamon stick, broken in half

3 whole star anise

3 whole cloves

MAKES 6 SERVINGS

To make the tea paste, in a spice grinder or with a mortar and pestle, grind together the tea leaves, cloves, star anise, and orange zest. Transfer to a small bowl. Add the orange juice concentrate, soy sauce, vinegar, $1/2$ teaspoon salt, red pepper flakes, and cinnamon and mix well. Let the mixture stand for 15 minutes at room temperature, or cover and refrigerate for up to 2 hours before using.

Smear the tea paste over the duck breasts. Let the duck breasts stand for 20 minutes at room temperature, or cover and refrigerate for up to 2 hours. If refrigerated, remove from the refrigerator 20 minutes before grilling.

To make the tea smoking mixture, in a container, combine the wood chips, tea leaves, cinnamon stick, star anise, and cloves. Add water just to cover and let soak for at least 30 minutes (page 13). Drain, reserving the soaking water.

Prepare a CHARCOAL or GAS grill for INDIRECT grilling over MEDIUM heat (page 19 or 23). Oil the grill rack.

CHARCOAL: Pour the water from the smoking mixture to a depth of $3/4$ inch (2 cm) into a drip pan, and place the pan in the center of the fire bed. Sprinkle about half of the smoking mixture on the coals. Place the duck breasts on the grill rack over the drip pan. Cover the grill and smoke the duck breasts until richly browned and cooked through, about 45 minutes. Add the remaining smoke mixture to the coals about halfway through the smoking.

GAS: Add the drained smoking mixture to the grill in a smoker box or a perforated foil packet (page 10). Place the soaking water in a shallow pan at the edge of the grill rack. Place the duck breasts on the grill rack away from the heat elements. Cover the grill and smoke the duck breasts until richly browned and cooked through, about 45 minutes.

To check for doneness, insert an instant-read thermometer into the thickest part of the breast, away from the bone; it should register 150°–160°F (65°–71°C). The temperature will rise another 5°–10°F (3°–6°C) while the duck is resting.

Serve hot or at room temperature, cut into serving sections if you like.

Look for bone-in, skin-on duck breasts for smoking. During the long, slow cooking, the bone adds flavor while the skin protects the meat from drying out and burning. Here, the duck receives a double infusion of tea, in a paste smeared onto the breasts, and mixed in with the wood chips. Choose the tea according to your preference, but be sure it is of good quality and has a distinctive flavor. Prepare some simply cooked carrots and bok choy to complement the aromatic duck.

Poussins with Summer Herbs

Grilled poussins, young chickens with sweet, tender meat, make a lovely presentation and can enliven an ordinary meal. Serve them in the style of Provence with green beans, grilled tomato and potato slices, and a baguette. Don't worry if you can't find poussins. Cornish hens are a good substitute.

Cut the poussins in half and remove the backbones. Rinse the poussins and pat dry. In a small bowl, toss together the chopped savory, chives, mint, and parsley. Using your fingers, and starting at the tail end, carefully loosen the skin over the breast and thigh of each poussin half. Using about half of the mixed herbs and dividing them evenly among the poussin halves, insert them under the skin of each bird half, spreading them as evenly as possible.

Add the oil, lemon juice, garlic, and $^1/_2$ teaspoon each salt and pepper to the herbs remaining in the bowl. Mix well. Brush the oil mixture evenly over the poussin halves, reserving a little of it for basting on the grill. Let the birds stand for 15 minutes at room temperature, or cover and refrigerate for up to 4 hours. If refrigerated, remove from the refrigerator 30 minutes before grilling.

Prepare a CHARCOAL or GAS grill for DIRECT grilling over MEDIUM-HIGH heat (page 18 or 22). Oil the grill rack.

CHARCOAL: Grill the poussins, skin side down, over the hottest part of the fire for 15 minutes. Turn and brush with the reserved herb-oil mixture. Continue to grill, turning once or twice, until richly browned, about 30 minutes longer.

GAS: Grill the poussins, skin side down, directly over the heat elements for 15 minutes. Turn and brush with the reserved herb-oil mixture. Continue to grill, turning once or twice, until richly browned, about 30 minutes longer.

To test for doneness, insert an instant-read thermometer into the thickest part of a thigh away from the bone; it should register 170°F (77°C). The temperature will rise another 5°–10°F (3°–6°C) while the birds are resting.

Serve the poussins immediately.

2 poussins or large Cornish hens

$^1/_4$ cup ($^1/_3$ oz/10 g) chopped fresh summer savory

$^1/_4$ cup ($^1/_3$ oz/10 g) chopped fresh chives

$^1/_4$ cup ($^1/_3$ oz/10 g) chopped fresh mint

$^1/_4$ cup ($^1/_3$ oz/10 g) chopped fresh flat-leaf (Italian) parsley

2 tablespoons olive oil

2 tablespoons fresh lemon juice

2 cloves garlic, finely chopped

Salt and coarsely ground pepper

MAKES 4 SERVINGS

Seafood

About Seafood

Fish's delicate flesh becomes deliciously smoky and charred on a hot grill, transforming it into the perfect companion for a vast array of sauces, relishes, and garnishes. Shellfish are excellent for the grill, too. Nearly every type of shellfish can be grilled and is easy to prepare.

Firm-fleshed fish, thickly cut, cook best on the grill. Choose tuna, salmon, swordfish, halibut, grouper, or sea bass for the starring role at your dinner party. Grilled vegetables and crisp salads are nice, light accompaniments. Delicate fish such as sole can also be grilled, although they may need a little extra care. Grill delicate fish fillets in a hinged basket or on a bed of sliced citrus fruit to prevent the fish from sticking to the grill rack.

A whole fish stuffed with herbs, citrus slices, or other aromatics before grilling makes a dramatic presentation. Trout and other small fish are a treat served on individual plates and sauced with a tangy vinaigrette or fresh salsa. Larger whole fish look attractive when arranged on a bed of fresh vegetables and presented on a decorative platter.

The oil-rich flesh of salmon is ideal for smoking. Impress your friends with a platter of home-smoked salmon, fresh bagels, and the traditional accompaniments for Sunday brunch. Or, grill the salmon on a cedar plank, an old technique that's newly in vogue. The flavors of the wood plank seep into the flesh during grilling, lending an intriguing, smoky flavor to the fish.

Salmon, tuna, and other types of oily fish are ideal for sandwich ingredients, whether the flesh is ground (minced) and formed into a burger, or grilled and served as a fish steak sandwich.

Kabobs cut from such meaty fish as swordfish can be threaded on skewers, with or without vegetable chunks. They cook quickly and, served with a savory dipping sauce, are a popular appetizer or main course for party guests.

Lobster, shrimp (prawns), and scallops all boast sweet, slightly salty flesh that benefits from a light charring on a grill and mild or intense sauces at the table. Briny oysters and succulent mussels are also complemented by fragrant grill smoke, making a summertime shellfish roast, accompanied with grilled corn and fresh air, a feast to remember.

Before you purchase any fish or shellfish, check with a reliable source to make sure it is not in danger of extinction due to overfishing or another cause. Your fishmonger will likely have the answer, or you can research the information on the Internet from such groups as the Audubon Society or by calling your regional fish and game regulatory agency.

Working with Seafood

SHOPPING FOR SEAFOOD

Always buy fish fresh from a reputable supplier and cook it the day you buy it. Fish fillets and steaks should look moist and bright and have a fresh, clean scent. Whole fish, in general, should look almost alive, with clear eyes; bright, intact scales and skin; and red, moist gills.

Choose firm, sweet-smelling fresh shrimp that are still in the shell when possible, although most "fresh" shrimp sold today have been previously frozen and thawed. Pass over shrimp with yellowing or black-spotted shells, an off odor, or a gritty feel.

The best scallops are sold as "dry," meaning they have not been treated with a solution to help them absorb more water. Look for scallops with a mild scent that are creamy white or slightly pink. Although shucked scallops will always have some odor, choose those with the mildest scent.

Purchase live lobsters, the feistier the better. Any that are sluggish and apathetic have been in the tank too long. Male lobsters will have slightly larger claws, while females have slightly bigger tails.

Mollusks, such as oysters and mussels, should have a mild, sweet smell, and their shells should be closed tightly and feel heavy with water. Do not buy any oysters or mussels that remain open when touched. It is especially important that your fishmonger can vouch that the shellfish come from unpolluted waters.

Refrigerate fish and shellfish the moment you get home. It is best to remove shellfish from any plastic packaging and store it directly on ice set in a bowl or on a sheet pan. As the ice melts, make sure that the seafood doesn't become submerged in water.

PREPARING SEAFOOD FOR GRILLING

Trim off excess skin from fish fillets or steaks and remove any small bones remaining in fillets or steaks with needle-nose pliers.

Whole fish bought from a fishmonger should be gutted, cleaned, and scaled before they are placed in the display case. If using fish that you caught yourself, consult a book specifically devoted to fish for instructions on gutting, cleaning, and scaling.

To refresh frozen shrimp before cooking, soak in salted water for 10 to 15 minutes, then rinse well.

To shell shrimp, pull or cut off the heads, if present. Carefully pull off the legs on the inside curve of the shrimp. Beginning at the head end of the shrimp, peel off the shell, pulling off the tail segments as well unless the recipe calls for them to be left attached.

To devein shrimp after shelling, cut a shallow groove along the back of the shrimp with a small knife. With the tip of the knife, gently lift and scrape away the dark vein, if present, then rinse the shrimp under running cold water. Drain the shrimp on paper towels before proceeding with the recipe.

Rinse scallops and, if present, remove the small tendon attached to the side.

Cut lobsters in half lengthwise, exposing the tail meat, and remove the grain sac and white intestinal veins.

Before shucking oysters, scrub them with a stiff brush and rinse well. To shuck oysters, use a folded cloth to hold the oyster in one hand with the flat top shell facing up. Holding an oyster knife in your other hand, insert its tip into the oyster's hinge. Twist the knife sharply to break the hinge. Run the knife carefully along the inside surface of the top shell, severing the muscle that grips it. Take care not to cut the oyster or to spill its liquor. Discard the top shell. Carefully cut the muscle under the oyster to loosen it from the shell.

Scrub the grit off the shells of fresh mussels with a stiff-bristled brush, then remove the beards, if needed, by pulling or cutting them off just before cooking. Discard any mussels that feel light, as they are likely dead, or any that are heavy with sand.

All fish and shellfish should be kept very cold, preferably on a bed of ice set over a perforated pan, right up until the time they are put on the hot grill.

TESTING FISH FOR DONENESS

Fish is done when the tip of a small, sharp knife can easily separate the flesh into broad flakes. Or cut into the fish at its thickest point and look at it. Unless you are deliberately cooking to rare or medium-rare, as with tuna, the fish should be still moist at its center and the flesh should be just opaque and easy to flake. If it is already flaking without being prodded, the fish is overdone.

TESTING SHELLFISH FOR DONENESS

Shrimp is done when the color of the shell just turns bright and the flesh is just opaque. When overcooked, shrimp become dry and rubbery.

Scallops should feel slightly firm when lightly pressed with your fingers. Or cut into one with the tip of a small knife. The flesh should be moist and just opaque.

Lobsters are done when their shells turn bright red and the flesh becomes creamy white with no trace of translucence.

Oysters and mussels are done as soon as the shells pop open; discard any that fail to open.

Seafood Types for Grilling

Both round fish (fish with a rounded body) and flat fish (fish with a flat, narrow body) can be grilled with success. Many types of round fish can be grilled whole after being cleaned, scaled, and gutted. Meaty, oily varieties of round fish can be cut into steaks, fillets, or fillet portions for grilling. Fillets from flat fish such as sole are delicate and need extra care when grilling.

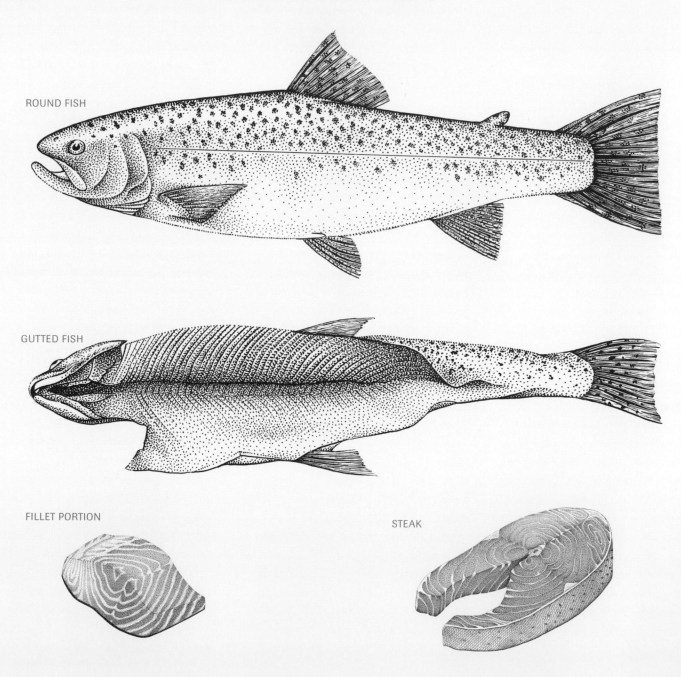

ROUND FISH

GUTTED FISH

FILLET PORTION

STEAK

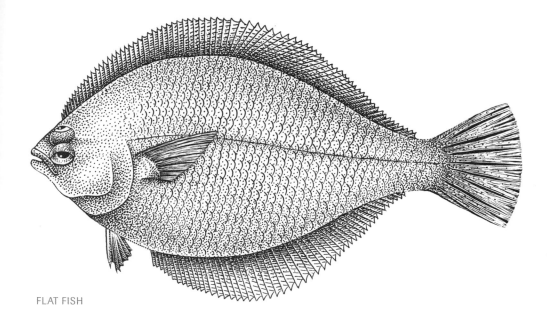

FLAT FISH

FISH FOR GRILLING

Grilling is one of the best ways to cook fish. The high heat of the grill sears the surface and cooks the fish quickly so that its natural juices do not have a chance to escape.

Whole Fish

Cook round fish such as trout and striped bass over direct or indirect heat. You can add wood chips, grapevine cuttings, or other aromatic ingredients to lend deep flavor to the fish flesh. A fish basket is useful when grilling one large fish or several small fish to ease turning and ensure that each fish cooks at the same rate.

Meaty Fish Fillets and Steaks

Salmon, tuna, swordfish, and other types of meaty round fish are often strongly flavored, so make sure your accompaniments complement the character of the fish. Meaty fillets and steaks cook quickly over a direct-heat fire.

Thin Fish Fillets

Sole, flounder, and other types of delicate, flaky flat fish need a moderately hot direct fire. A fish-grilling basket is useful to keep the fillets intact on the grill. You can also grill these fragile fillets on a bed of citrus slices, which will shield the fish from the harsh heat of the grill while subtly flavoring the flesh. Pair their subtly flavored flesh with simple sauces.

Fish Burgers

Another wonderful twist on hamburgers, fish burgers—whether featuring ground (minced) fish patties or whole fish steaks—should be cooked over direct heat. In either case, make sure that the burger accompaniments complement the flavors of the fish.

Fish Kabobs

Cut into cubes and threaded onto skewers, meaty fish, such as swordfish, tuna, or salmon, can be grilled over a direct fire to infuse them with smoky flavor. Pair with zesty marinades, strong spice rubs, or robust dipping sauces.

SHELLFISH FOR GRILLING

Shellfish are at their best when grilled quickly over a hot fire. Take care to not overcook these delicate foods. If possible, grill shellfish in its shells, which protects it from the heat and keeps it from drying out.

Shrimp

Shrimp needs a hot direct-heat fire to make sure that its delicate flesh is quickly cooked through without turning rubbery. Large and jumbo shrimp can be cooked directly on the grill rack. Use a grill screen or grill basket (page 10) to grill smaller shrimp, which could fall through the grill grate into the fire. Shrimp pairs well with both mild and intense sauces.

Scallops

You may want to use a grill screen or grill basket (page 10) to grill scallops to prevent them from falling into the fire. Or thread them on skewers to make grilling and turning easy. Pair grilled scallops with a spicy dry rub or zesty finishing sauce.

Lobster

A direct-heat fire infuses the sweet flesh of lobster with smoky flavor, while retaining its delicate texture. Lobsters need little more than a drizzle of melted herbed butter.

Oysters and Mussels

These mollusks can be grilled in their shells over a direct-heat grill, and snatched from the flames as soon as the shells pop open. Or, use a combination cooking method: put the mollusks in a cast-iron pan directly on the grill grate and cover the grill to steam the shells open in the smoky air of the covered grill. Pair with your favorite shellfish sauce or herbed butter.

Halibut with Two Sauces

For the Saffron Mayonnaise

Large pinch of saffron threads, crushed

2 tablespoons hot water

1 cup (8 fl oz/250 ml) mayonnaise

2 oil-packed sun-dried tomatoes, minced

1/8 teaspoon dried oregano

1 tablespoon minced fresh flat-leaf (Italian) parsley

For the Parsley-Mustard Vinaigrette

1/2 cup (4 fl oz/125 ml) extra-virgin olive oil

1/4 cup (2 fl oz/60 ml) red wine vinegar or balsamic vinegar

1 clove garlic, minced

1 teaspoon whole-grain mustard

1/4 cup (1/3 oz/10 g) minced fresh flat-leaf (Italian) parsley

Salt and freshly ground pepper

6 halibut fillets, each 5–6 oz (155–185 g) and 1/2–3/4 inch (12 mm–2 cm) thick

Extra-virgin olive oil for brushing

Sea salt and freshly ground pepper

MAKES 6 SERVINGS

Prepare one or both sauces, as desired. To make the saffron mayonnaise, in a small bowl, combine the saffron with the hot water and allow to steep for 2 minutes. In a bowl, mix the saffron and its liquid into the mayonnaise. Add the tomatoes, oregano, and parsley and mix well. Cover and refrigerate until serving. Stir again just before serving. To make the parsley-mustard vinaigrette, in a small bowl, whisk together the oil, vinegar, garlic, and mustard. Add the parsley and salt and pepper to taste and mix well. Cover and refrigerate until serving. Bring to room temperature and whisk again just before serving.

Prepare a CHARCOAL or GAS grill for DIRECT grilling over MEDIUM-HIGH heat (page 18 or 22). Generously oil the grill rack or a fish-grilling basket. Brush the fillets on both sides with oil. Sprinkle on both sides with salt and pepper.

CHARCOAL: Arrange the fish fillets on the rack or in the basket over the hottest part of the fire. Cook the fish, turning once, until it is opaque throughout and flakes when prodded with a fork, 3–5 minutes per side.

GAS: Arrange the fish fillets on the rack or in the basket directly over the heat elements. Cook the fish, turning once, until it is opaque throughout and flakes when prodded with a fork, 3–5 minutes per side.

Transfer the fillets to warmed individual plates and serve immediately, accompanied with the sauce(s).

This master recipe is designed to make the art of grilling fish easy. Select firm-fleshed halibut fillets, brush them with extra-virgin olive oil or melted unsalted butter, and then grill them briefly. You can substitute grouper, mahimahi, or swordfish for the halibut.

Sicilian-Style Swordfish

Swordfish has firm flesh and a distinctive flavor, making it ideal for grilling. It also marries well with a robust sauce, marinade, or dry rub. If the market has no swordfish, use grouper or cod in its place. Hot cooked pasta is a nice accompaniment to the Italian-style fish.

To make the tomato-olive salsa, in a small bowl, combine the tomatoes, onion, celery, olives and liquid, and parsley and toss to mix. Season with a little pepper, then taste and adjust the seasoning. Cover and refrigerate until serving. Stir lightly just before serving.

Prepare a CHARCOAL or GAS grill for DIRECT grilling over MEDIUM-HIGH heat (page 18 or 22). Generously oil the grill rack. Brush the fish fillets on both sides with the oil and vinegar. Sprinkle on both sides with salt and pepper.

CHARCOAL: Grill the fish over the hottest part of the fire, turning once, until it is opaque throughout and flakes when prodded with a fork, 4–5 minutes per side.

GAS: Grill the fish directly over the heat elements, turning once, until it is opaque throughout and flakes when prodded with a fork, 4–5 minutes per side.

Transfer the fillets to warmed individual plates. Spoon the salsa evenly on top and serve immediately.

For the Tomato-Olive Salsa

2 tomatoes, seeded and chopped

1 small yellow onion, chopped

2 celery stalks, chopped

2 tablespoons pitted, chopped green olives, plus 1 tablespoon brine

$1/4$ cup ($1/3$ oz/10 g) chopped fresh flat-leaf (Italian) parsley

Freshly ground pepper

6 swordfish fillets, each 5–6 oz (155–185 g) and $3/4$–1 inch (2–2.5 cm) thick

Olive oil for brushing

Balsamic vinegar for brushing

Sea salt and freshly ground pepper

MAKES 6 SERVINGS

Sea Bass with Miso Glaze

For the Miso Glaze

3 tablespoons firmly packed dark brown sugar

2 tablespoons mayonnaise

2 tablespoons *mirin*

¹/₄ cup (2 oz/60 g) light miso

1 green (spring) onion, white part only, minced

6 sea bass or grouper fillets, each 5–6 oz (155–185 g) and ¹/₂–³/₄ inch (12 mm–2 cm) thick

Minced green (spring) onion for garnish

MAKES 6 SERVINGS

To make the miso glaze, in a saucepan over medium heat, stir together the brown sugar, mayonnaise, *mirin*, miso, and green onion. Bring to a simmer and simmer for 2 minutes to blend the flavors. Remove from the heat and let cool slightly.

Prepare a CHARCOAL or GAS grill for DIRECT grilling over MEDIUM-HIGH heat (page 18 or 22). Oil the grill rack or a grill screen. Brush the fillets on both sides with some of the glaze.

CHARCOAL: Arrange the fish on the rack or screen over the hottest part of the fire. Cook the fish, turning once and brushing with the remaining glaze, until it is opaque throughout and flakes when prodded with a fork, 3–5 minutes per side.

GAS: Place the fish on the rack or screen directly over the heat elements. Cook the fish, turning once and brushing with the remaining glaze, until it is opaque throughout and flakes when prodded with a fork, 3–5 minutes per side.

Transfer the fish to warmed individual plates, sprinkle with the green onion, and serve immediately.

Miso, fermented soybean paste rich in protein, is a staple of the Japanese kitchen. It comes in various colors, flavors, and textures, but the pale yellow, mild-flavored type should be used here. *Mirin*, a sweet, low-alcohol rice wine for cooking, is another popular Japanese ingredient. Look for both products in Japanese markets and in many large food stores. Serve the fish with grilled eggplant (aubergine) and steamed rice.

Tuna with Wasabi Cream

For the Sake Marinade

⅓ cup (3 fl oz/80 ml) soy sauce

⅓ cup (3 fl oz/80 ml) sake or dry sherry

1 teaspoon Asian sesame oil

1 teaspoon Asian chile oil

1 teaspoon sesame seeds

6 sashimi-grade ahi tuna steaks, each 5–6 oz (155–185 g) and ¾–1 inch (2–2.5 cm) thick

For the Wasabi Cream

1 cup (8 fl oz/250 ml) crème fraîche

2 teaspoons wasabi powder, or to taste

Sesame seeds for garnish

2–4 whole fresh chives

MAKES 6 SERVINGS

To make the sake marinade, select a shallow, nonreactive dish large enough to accommodate the tuna in a single layer. Add the soy sauce, sake, sesame oil, chile oil, and sesame seeds to the dish and mix well. Add the tuna in a single layer and turn to coat both sides. Cover and refrigerate for 2 hours.

To make the wasabi cream, in a small bowl, stir together the crème fraîche and wasabi powder. Cover and refrigerate until ready to serve. Reserve the sesame seeds and chives to add just before serving.

Prepare a CHARCOAL or GAS grill for DIRECT grilling over MEDIUM-HIGH heat (page 18 or 22). Oil the grill rack. Remove the tuna steaks from the marinade. Discard the marinade.

CHARCOAL: Grill the fish over the hottest part of the fire, turning once, until it is seared on the outside and rare in the center when tested with a knife, 3–5 minutes per side. If you prefer your tuna cooked through, leave it on the grill for a minute or two longer on each side.

GAS: Grill the fish directly over the heat elements, turning once, until it is seared on the outside and rare in the center when tested with a knife, 3–5 minutes per side. If you prefer your tuna cooked through, leave it on the grill for a minute or two longer on each side.

Transfer the tuna steaks to warmed individual plates. Garnish the wasabi cream with the sesame seeds and chives, and pass it at the table.

This Japanese-inspired tuna recipe calls for wasabi, which is sometimes compared to Western horseradish because it has a similar biting, hot taste. The two are not related botanically, however. Wasabi is sold as a powder and a paste in Japanese markets and some well-stocked food stores. Here, the fiery condiment accompanies grilled rare tuna. Always use tuna from a highly reputable market when grilling it rare, asking for sashimi grade and serving it the same day you purchase it.

Salmon Burgers
with Vegetable Slaw

Salmon is among the most prized of all fish, found wild in both the Atlantic and Pacific Oceans and in many lakes, and now farmed as well. To grind it for this recipe, cut it into chunks and pulse it in a food processor until ground, taking care not to overprocess. Or ask your fishmonger to grind it for you.

To make the vegetable slaw, in a large bowl, toss together the cabbage, carrots, bell pepper, and green onions. In a small bowl, stir together the mayonnaise, vinegar, sugar, garlic, and mustard to make a dressing. Add the dressing to the cabbage mixture and mix well. Season with salt and pepper. Cover and refrigerate for up to 3 hours. Just before serving, toast the pine nuts, add them to the salad, and toss again lightly.

In a bowl, combine the salmon, bread crumbs, cucumber, shallots, and parsley and mix lightly but thoroughly. Divide into 6 equal portions and shape each portion into a patty 3 inches (7.5 cm) in diameter and $^3/_4$–1 inch (2–2.5 cm) thick. Place on a plate, cover, and refrigerate until ready to grill.

Prepare a CHARCOAL or GAS grill for DIRECT grilling over MEDIUM-HIGH heat (page 18 or 22). Oil the grill rack or a fish-grilling basket.

CHARCOAL: Arrange the salmon patties on the rack or in the basket over the hottest part of the fire. Cook the patties, turning once, until cooked through when tested with a knife, 5–6 minutes per side. About 1 minute before the burgers are ready, place the onion roll halves, cut sides down, at the edges of the grill where the heat is less intense and toast lightly.

GAS: Arrange the salmon patties on the rack or in the basket directly over the heat elements. Cook the patties, turning once, until cooked through when tested with a knife, 5–6 minutes per side. About 1 minute before the burgers are ready, place the onion roll halves, cut sides down, on an area with lower heat and toast lightly.

Place the bottoms of the onion rolls on individual plates. Top with the burgers and the tops of the rolls. Spoon the slaw on the side. Serve immediately.

For the Vegetable Slaw

6 cups (18 oz/560 g) finely shredded mixed green and red cabbage

2 carrots, shredded

1 red bell pepper (capsicum), seeded and chopped

3 green (spring) onions, including tender green tops, chopped

1 cup (8 fl oz/250 ml) mayonnaise

$^1/_4$ cup (2 fl oz/60 ml) cider vinegar

2 tablespoons sugar

2 cloves garlic, minced

1 teaspoon whole-grain mustard

Salt and freshly ground pepper

$^1/_2$ cup (2 oz/60 g) pine nuts

$1^1/_2$–2 lb (750 g–1 kg) salmon fillet, ground (minced) (see note)

1 cup (4 oz/125 g) fine dried bread crumbs

1 small cucumber, peeled, seeded, and chopped

4 large shallots, chopped

$^1/_2$ cup ($^3/_4$ oz/20 g) chopped fresh flat-leaf (Italian) parsley

6 onion rolls

MAKES 6 SERVINGS

Niçoise Salad with Salmon

1/3 cup (3 fl oz/80 ml) fresh
lemon juice

1 clove garlic, crushed

1 1/2 teaspoons Dijon mustard

1 teaspoon *herbes de
Provence*

1/2 teaspoon sugar

Sea salt and freshly
ground pepper

1/3 cup (3 fl oz/80 ml)
extra-virgin olive oil

12 small new potatoes

1 lb (500 g) *haricots verts*,
trimmed

1 head butter (Boston)
lettuce, leaves separated

3 large tomatoes, cut into
wedges

3 hard-boiled eggs, peeled
and quartered lengthwise

1 cup (5 oz/155 g)
Niçoise olives

1 red onion, sliced

2 tins (2 oz/60 g each)
anchovy fillets packed in
olive oil, drained

1 center-cut salmon fillet,
1 3/4 lb (875 g) and 3/4–1 inch
(2–2.5 cm) thick

Pure olive oil for brushing

MAKES 6 SERVINGS

In a small bowl, whisk together the lemon juice, garlic, mustard, *herbes de Provence*, sugar, 1/2 teaspoon salt, and 1/4 teaspoon pepper. Whisk in the extra-virgin olive oil. Set aside.

Bring a saucepan three-fourths full of salted water to a boil. Add the potatoes and boil until tender, 12–15 minutes. Drain and let cool completely; set aside. At the same time, bring another saucepan three-fourths full of salted water to a boil. Add the *haricots verts* and boil until tender, 3–5 minutes. Drain and immerse in cold water to halt the cooking and set the color. Drain again and set aside.

Prepare a CHARCOAL or GAS grill for DIRECT grilling over MEDIUM-HIGH heat (page 18 or 22).

Arrange the lettuce leaves on a platter. Place piles of the tomato wedges, *haricots verts*, potatoes, egg quarters, olives, onion slices, and anchovies on the platter, arranging all the elements attractively and leaving room for the salmon.

Oil the grill rack. Brush the salmon fillet on both sides with the pure olive oil. Sprinkle on both sides with salt and pepper.

CHARCOAL: Grill the fish over the hottest part of the fire, turning once, until it is opaque throughout and flakes when prodded with a fork, 3–5 minutes per side.

GAS: Grill the fish directly over the heat elements, turning once, until it is opaque throughout and flakes when prodded with a fork, 3–5 minutes per side.

Transfer the salmon fillets to a plate and break into irregular chunks with a fork. Arrange the pieces on the salad platter. Whisk the vinaigrette. Drizzle the salad elements with the vinaigrette and serve.

The southern French city of Nice and the area surrounding have long been celebrated for the bright flavors and colors of the local dishes. Ingredients such as garlic, anchovies, black olives, tomatoes, and a rich variety of herbs play important roles in the cuisine. Among the favorite vegetables of the region are *haricots verts*, slim, tender green beans that are part of every *salade niçoise*. Usually featuring tuna, this version uses fresh salmon. Set out a crusty baguette to accompany the salad.

Plank-Grilled Salmon with Dill Sauce

For the Dill Sauce

1/4 lb (125 g) fresh goat cheese

1 cup (8 fl oz/250 ml) sour cream

1/4 cup (1/3 oz/10 g) chopped fresh dill

1 clove garlic, minced

Salt and white pepper, preferably freshly ground

For the Bourbon-Maple Glaze

1/2 cup (5 1/2 oz/170 g) maple syrup

2 tablespoons bourbon

White pepper, preferably freshly ground

1 skin-on salmon fillet, about 3 lb (1.5 kg), small bones removed

1 untreated cedar plank or shingle, soaked in water to cover for 4 hours or up to overnight and drained

Lemon wedges

MAKES 6–8 SERVINGS

To make the dill sauce, in a small bowl, combine the goat cheese, sour cream, dill, garlic, and salt and white pepper to taste and mix well. Cover and refrigerate until serving.

To make the bourbon-maple glaze, in a bowl, stir together the maple syrup, bourbon, and white pepper to taste.

Prepare a CHARCOAL or GAS grill for DIRECT grilling over MEDIUM-HIGH heat (page 18 or 22). Brush the salmon thickly on both sides with the glaze. Center the salmon, skin side down, on the plank, trimming it to fit if necessary.

CHARCOAL: Set the plank with the salmon over the hottest part of the fire. Cover the grill and cook until the fish is opaque throughout and flakes when prodded with a fork, 8–12 minutes total. The plank will char slightly. If the coals seem too hot and the plank begins to char rapidly, set the plank off to the side.

GAS: Set the plank with the salmon directly over the heat elements. Cover the grill and cook until the fish is opaque throughout and flakes when prodded with a fork, 8–12 minutes total. The plank will char slightly. If the heat seems too high and the plank begins to char rapidly, set the plank off to the side.

Using heavy-duty pot holders, remove the salmon, still on the plank, from the grill and set it on a serving platter. Serve the salmon hot or warm. To serve, cut the salmon through the flesh into individual portions. Pass the dill sauce and lemon wedges at the table.

This grilling technique is adapted from a Native American tradition. Here, the salmon is laid on a cedar plank (available at specialty-food stores) or cedar shingle (available at hardware stores), which is placed directly on the grill rack. As the fish cooks, it absorbs a little flavor from the wood. Make sure the plank has not been treated with any preservatives and is about the same size as the salmon.

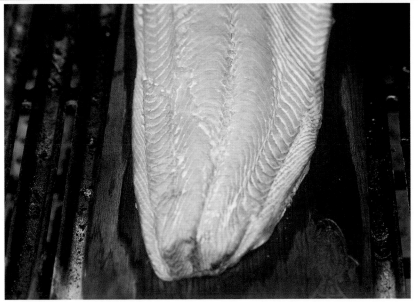

Grill-Smoked Salmon with Horseradish Sauce

The rich, oily flesh of salmon takes well to smoking. Brining the fish first helps balance the flavors and keep it moist during the cooking process. Serve this salmon hot as a main course, or offer it chilled on the brunch table or as an interesting appetizer.

To make the brown sugar brine, select a baking pan or dish large enough to hold the salmon comfortably. Add the water, salt, brown sugar, and bay leaves to the pan or dish and stir to dissolve the sugar and salt. Add the salmon; it should be completely submerged. If it is not, add water as needed. Cover lightly and refrigerate for at least 8 hours or for up to 12 hours.

Prepare a CHARCOAL or GAS grill for INDIRECT grilling over MEDIUM-HIGH heat (page 19 or 23). Remove the salmon from the brine, drain well, and pat dry with paper towels. Discard the brine. Brush the salmon with the oil.

CHARCOAL: Place a drip pan half full of water in the center of the fire bed. Sprinkle the wood chips on the coals. Place the salmon, skin side down, on the rack over the drip pan. Cover the grill and smoke the fish until cooked through and infused with smoke flavor, about 1 1/2 hours. Add water to the drip pan as needed, and add more coals as needed to maintain the temperature.

GAS: Place a shallow pan half full of water at the edge of the grill rack. Add the wood chips to the grill in a smoker box or a perforated foil packet (page 10). Place the salmon, skin side down, on the grill rack away from the heat elements. Cover the grill and smoke the fish until cooked through and infused with smoke flavor, about 1 1/2 hours. Add water to the pan as needed.

To test for doneness, insert an instant-read thermometer into the thickest part of the salmon; it should register 140°F (60°C).

While the fish is smoking, make the horseradish sauce: With an electric mixer, whip the cream until stiff peaks form. Fold in the horseradish, vinegar, and granulated sugar, mixing carefully but thoroughly. Spoon into a serving bowl and chill until serving time.

Using 2 spatulas, transfer the smoked salmon to a large serving platter. Pull off and discard the skin. Garnish the salmon with the lemon slices. Serve the salmon hot or cold with the horseradish sauce.

For the Brown Sugar Brine

8 cups (64 fl oz/2 l) water

1/2 cup (4 oz/125 g) sea salt

1 1/2 cups (10 1/2 oz/330 g) firmly packed brown sugar

4 large bay leaves

1 skin-on salmon fillet, 2 1/2–3 lb (1.25–1.5 kg), small bones removed

Olive oil for brushing

3 handfuls wood chips such as apple, maple, hickory, alder, or pecan, soaked if using charcoal (page 13)

For the Horseradish Sauce

1 cup (8 fl oz/250 ml) chilled heavy (double) cream

1/2 cup (2 1/2 oz/75 g) finely grated fresh horseradish

2 tablespoons cider vinegar

1 tablespoon granulated sugar

Lemon slices for garnish

MAKES 6–8 SERVINGS

Swordfish Kabobs
with Romesco Sauce

Romesco is a classic sauce of southern Spain, where it is often served to accompany grilled meats and seafood. Smoked paprika, or *pimentón de La Vera*, a specialty of southwestern Spain, is made from red peppers (capsicums) that have been smoke-dried over oak. Although hard to find in some areas, this smoked paprika is worth seeking out for its distinctive flavor. Grilled pineapple or papaya slices are excellent alongside these colorful kabobs. Simply brush the fruit slices with melted butter and grill over the hottest part of the grill, turning once, just until they begin to color, about 2 minutes on each side.

To make the *romesco* sauce, in a food processor or blender, process the almonds until finely ground. Add the tomato, roasted pepper, garlic, vinegar, and sherry. Process until smooth. With the motor running, slowly drizzle in the oil, processing until thickened. Season to taste with salt and paprika. Pour into a bowl, cover, and set aside.

In a bowl, stir together the oil, lemon juice, garlic, and salt and pepper to taste. Generously brush the swordfish pieces on all sides with the oil mixture.

Prepare a CHARCOAL or GAS grill for DIRECT grilling over MEDIUM-HIGH heat (page 18 or 22). Oil the grill rack. Thread the swordfish cubes alternately with the red bell pepper squares onto bamboo or metal skewers.

CHARCOAL: Grill the skewers over the hottest part of the fire, turning once, until the swordfish is opaque throughout but still moist at the center when tested with a knife, 3–5 minutes per side. The peppers should be tender and lightly charred.

GAS: Grill the skewers directly over the heat elements, turning once, until the swordfish is opaque throughout but still moist at the center when tested with a knife, 3–5 minutes per side. The peppers should be tender and lightly charred.

Place the kabobs on warmed individual plates and serve hot, accompanied with the *romesco* sauce.

For the Romesco Sauce

¼ cup (1 oz/30 g) sliced (flaked) almonds, toasted

1 tomato, peeled and chopped

1 large red bell pepper (capsicum), roasted, peeled, and seeded (page 78)

2 cloves garlic, crushed

¼ cup (2 fl oz/60 ml) sherry vinegar

1 tablespoon dry sherry

⅓ cup (3 fl oz/80 ml) extra-virgin olive oil

Salt

Smoked paprika

½ cup (4 fl oz/125 ml) extra-virgin olive oil

2 tablespoons fresh lemon juice

2 cloves garlic, minced

Sea salt and freshly ground pepper

2 lb (1 kg) swordfish fillets, cut into 1–1½-inch (2.5–4-cm) cubes

2 large red bell peppers (capsicums), seeded and cut into 1½-inch (4-cm) squares

6 bamboo skewers, soaked (page 10), or metal skewers

MAKES 6 SERVINGS

Fish Tacos with Tomatillo Salsa

For the Tomatillo Salsa

¹/₂ lb (250 g) tomatillos, husks removed, rinsed, and chopped

1 jalapeño chile, seeded and chopped

³/₄ cup (1 oz/30 g) chopped fresh cilantro (fresh coriander)

2 tablespoons fresh lime juice

1 teaspoon sugar

2 tablespoons extra-virgin olive oil

Salt

¹/₂ small head green cabbage, cut into slices ¹/₂ inch (12 mm) thick

1¹/₂ lb (750 g) red snapper fillets, cut into strips 1 inch (2.5 cm) wide

Vegetable oil for brushing

8 large corn tortillas

1 large avocado, halved, pitted, peeled, and sliced, and then slices brushed with fresh lemon juice

8 large radishes, grated

MAKES 6 SERVINGS

About 2 hours before grilling, make the salsa. In a bowl, stir together the tomatillos, chile, cilantro, lime juice, sugar, and olive oil until the sugar is dissolved and the ingredients are well mixed. Cover and refrigerate until ready to use. Liquid will accumulate in the bowl while the sauce is standing. Drain it away before serving, and season to taste with salt.

Prepare a CHARCOAL or GAS grill for DIRECT grilling over MEDIUM-HIGH heat. Oil the rack or a grill screen. Brush the cabbage slices and fish strips on both sides with vegetable oil. Wrap the tortillas in aluminum foil.

CHARCOAL: Arrange the cabbage slices and fish strips on the rack or screen over the hottest part of the fire. Cover the grill and cook, turning both the fish and the cabbage once. The fish is ready when it is opaque throughout and flakes when prodded with a fork, 6–8 minutes, and the cabbage is ready when it is fork-tender, 10–12 minutes.

GAS: Arrange the cabbage slices and fish strips on the grill rack or screen directly over the heat elements. Cover the grill and cook, turning both the fish and the cabbage once. The fish is ready when it is opaque throughout and flakes when prodded with a fork, 6–8 minutes, and the cabbage is ready when it is fork-tender, 10–12 minutes.

Working quickly, remove the food from the grill. Place the packet of tortillas on a lower-heat area to warm, turning the packet once. Chop the cabbage, then fill each tortilla with about ¹/₃ cup (1 oz/30 g) of the chopped cabbage and an equal amount of the fish strips, avocado slices, radishes, and tomatillo salsa. Serve at once. Pass the extra chopped cabbage and any remaining salsa at the table.

In Mexico, anglers regularly reel in red snapper from gulf waters, a fish with medium-firm flesh and a mild, sweet flavor. Here, it is used as a filling for tacos that are dressed up with a spicy tomatillo salsa. Native to Mexico, firm, green tomatillos are covered with papery brown husks and have a tart, citrusy flavor that mellows with cooking. After your remove their husks, rinse tomatillos under cold running water to wash away the sticky residue.

Trout with Warm Citrus Vinaigrette

These small fish are best cooked in a hinged grill basket, as the basket makes turning them easy. For extra flavor, tuck some parsley sprigs or other fresh herbs between the spokes of the basket and the fish. If desired, make a quick pineapple or orange salsa to accompany the trout by substituting chopped pineapple or orange sections for the tomatoes in your favorite tomato salsa recipe.

To make the warm citrus vinaigrette, using a sharp knife, cut a slice off both ends of the orange to reveal the flesh. Place the orange upright on the cutting board and, using the knife, cut downward to remove the peel, following the contour of the orange. Holding the orange in one hand, cut along either side of each segment to release it from the membrane, catching the segments in a bowl. Set aside.

In a small, nonreactive saucepan over medium heat, combine the orange juice, tangerine juice, and lime juice and bring to a boil. Reduce the heat to low and simmer until the mixture reduces slightly, 5–8 minutes. Remove from the heat and stir in the orange segments, vinegar, and olive oil. Set aside for up to 2 hours.

Prepare a CHARCOAL or GAS grill for DIRECT grilling over MEDIUM-HIGH heat (page 18 or 22). Oil 1 large or 2 small hinged fish-grilling baskets to hold the trout in a single layer. Season the fish with salt.

CHARCOAL: Arrange the fish in the grill basket(s) and place over the hottest part of the fire. Cook, turning once, until opaque throughout but still moist when tested with a knife, 4–5 minutes per side.

GAS: Arrange the fish in the grill basket(s) and place directly over the heat elements. Cook, turning once, until opaque throughout but still moist when tested with a knife, 4–5 minutes per side.

Return the saucepan holding the vinaigrette to the heat and heat until it is just below the boiling point. Remove from the heat.

Make a bed of watercress on a platter or on individual plates. Top with a trout and then drizzle with the warm vinaigrette. Serve immediately.

For the Warm Citrus Vinaigrette

1 orange

1 cup (8 fl oz/250 ml) fresh orange juice

$^1/_2$ cup (4 fl oz/125 ml) fresh tangerine juice

$^1/_4$ cup (2 fl oz/60 ml) fresh lime juice

2$^1/_2$ tablespoons raspberry vinegar

2 tablespoons extra-virgin olive oil

4 rainbow trout, 8–10 oz (250–315 g) each, cleaned

Vegetable oil for brushing

Sea salt

2 bunches watercress, tough stems removed

MAKES 4 SERVINGS

Grilled Whole Striped Bass

1 striped bass, 2–2¹/₂ lb (1–1.25 kg), cleaned

Olive oil for brushing

1 tablespoon ground oregano

Sea salt and freshly ground pepper

Fronds from 3 fennel bulbs

2 lemons, sliced

6 pieces dried grapevine cuttings, each about 8 inches (20 cm) long, soaked if using charcoal (page 13)

MAKES 4 SERVINGS

Prepare a CHARCOAL or GAS grill for DIRECT grilling over MEDIUM-HIGH heat (page 18 or 22). Oil the grill rack. Make deep slits 2¹/₂ inches (6 cm) long in the thick part of both sides of the fish. Brush the fish generously with oil on both sides, then sprinkle with the oregano, salt, and pepper. Place the fennel fronds and lemon slices in the cavity of the fish.

CHARCOAL: Spread the grapevine cuttings evenly over the coals. Grill the fish over the hottest part of the fire, turning it once, until opaque throughout but still moist when tested with a knife, 10–12 minutes per side.

GAS: Place the grapevine cuttings in a smoker box or perforated foil packet (page 10). Grill the fish directly over the heat elements, turning it once, until opaque throughout but still moist when tested with a knife, 10–12 minutes per side.

Transfer the fish to a platter and serve at once.

Striped bass is a popular fish for grilling, as its flesh is firm and slightly oily and has a sweet, mild taste. The addition of grapevine cuttings to the coals lends a smoky, French-wine-country accent to the fish. Look for grapevine cuttings where grilling fuels and flavoring materials are sold. Serve the fish on a bed of steamed or sautéed green beans or with grilled fennel slices.

Southern-Style Barbecued Shrimp

Grilling shrimp in the shell and brushing them with barbecue sauce keep them particularly moist in the intense heat of a covered grill. This old-fashioned dish is a favorite on the menus of backyard barbecues in the American South. Serve with lime juice squeezed over and/or hot pepper flakes, if desired.

Stir together the cumin, brown sugar, chili powder, and paprika to make a rub. Brush the shrimp with the oil and rub with the rub. Let stand for 30 minutes.

Prepare a CHARCOAL or GAS grill for DIRECT grilling over MEDIUM heat (page 18 or 22). Oil a grill screen. Brush the shrimp lightly with barbecue sauce.

CHARCOAL: Arrange the shrimp on the screen over the hottest part of the fire. Cover the grill and cook, turning once, just until opaque throughout, 4–6 minutes. Do not overcook the shrimp, or they will become rubbery.

GAS: Arrange the shrimp on the screen directly over the heat elements. Cover the grill and cook, turning once, just until opaque throughout, 4–6 minutes. Do not overcook the shrimp, or they will become rubbery.

Bring the remaining barbecue sauce to a boil. Arrange the shrimp on individual plates and drizzle with the warm barbecue sauce. Serve hot or warm.

2 tablespoons ground cumin

1/4 cup (2 oz/60 g) packed golden brown sugar

2 tablespoons chili powder

1 tablespoon hot paprika

3 lb (1.5 g) extra-large shrimp (prawns) in the shell

Vegetable oil for brushing

1 cup (8 fl oz/250 ml) bottled barbecue sauce

MAKES 6 SERVINGS

DIRECT METHOD · MEDIUM-HIGH HEAT · MARINATE 1 HOUR

Cilantro Pesto Shrimp

36 jumbo shrimp (prawns), about 2 lb (1 kg), peeled, with tails intact

¹/₄ cup (2 fl oz/60 ml) fresh lime or lemon juice

¹/₄ cup (2 fl oz/60 ml) olive oil

Cilantro Pesto (page 289)

MAKES 6 SERVINGS

Using a small, sharp knife, cut along the length of the back of the shrimp, but do not cut all the way through. Pull out and discard the dark intestinal vein. Flatten the shrimp slightly. Place the shrimp in a nonreactive bowl, add the lime juice and oil, and toss to coat evenly. Cover and refrigerate for about 1 hour.

Prepare a CHARCOAL or GAS grill for DIRECT grilling over MEDIUM-HIGH heat (page 18 or 22). Oil the grill rack, or a fish or vegetable grilling basket. Remove the shrimp from the marinade, draining well. Discard the marinade.

CHARCOAL: Grill the shrimp over the hottest part of the fire, turning once, until opaque throughout, 2¹/₂–3 minutes per side. Do not overcook the shrimp.

GAS: Grill the shrimp directly over the heat elements, turning once, until opaque throughout, 2¹/₂–3 minutes per side. Do not overcook the shrimp.

Brush the shrimp lightly with the pesto and serve at once. Pass the remaining pesto.

For easier and quicker handling of the shrimp on the grill, arrange them in one or two well-oiled fish-grilling baskets, which makes turning them a snap. Serve the shrimp with a bowl of hot pasta or some grilled vegetables.

Shrimp and Scallop Skewers

At the end of the growing season, look for sturdy rosemary branches, strip off their leaves, shape one end of each branch to a point with a small knife, and use the branches as skewers. The rosemary imparts a woodsy flavor to food and makes a pretty presentation. If you can't find rosemary skewers, use metal skewers or soaked bamboo skewers.

Prepare a CHARCOAL or GAS grill for DIRECT grilling over MEDIUM-HIGH heat (page 18 or 22). Oil the grill rack.

Wrap each shrimp in a strip of pancetta. Carefully thread the wrapped shrimp and the scallops onto the skewers, dividing evenly.

CHARCOAL: Grill the skewers over the hottest part of the fire, turning once, until the pancetta begins to brown and the shrimp and scallops are opaque throughout but still moist at the center when tested with a knife, 3–5 minutes per side.

GAS: Grill the skewers directly over the heat elements. Cook, turning once, until the pancetta begins to brown and the shrimp and scallops are opaque throughout but still moist at the center when tested with a knife, 3–5 minutes per side.

Arrange the skewers on a platter and serve at once.

18 jumbo shrimp (prawns), about 1 1/4 lb (625 g) total weight, peeled and deveined (page 199) with tails intact

3–6 slices pancetta, cut into 18 strips each 3 inches (7.5 cm) long

18 large sea scallops, about 1 1/2 lb (750 g) total weight

18 rosemary skewers soaked for 30 minutes and drained (see note) or other skewers

MAKES 6 SERVINGS

Lobster Halves with Tarragon-Lime Butter

Lobsters, plentiful in the summer months, make the perfect centerpiece for an alfresco dinner from the grill. Drawn butter, the traditional companion, is spiked here with fresh tarragon and lime juice.

If you prefer not to work with live lobsters, buy them just before you plan to grill them and have the fishmonger cut and clean them for you. Using this method, you can skip the recipe's boiling step, but plan on adding a minute or two to the grilling time. You can keep the lobsters refrigerated for up to 2 hours, but no longer, before grilling.

Prepare a CHARCOAL or GAS grill for DIRECT grilling over MEDIUM-HIGH heat (page 18 or 22).

Just before grilling, bring a large pot three-fourths full of water to a rolling boil over high heat. Plunge the live lobsters into the boiling water and leave for a minute or two. Drain well. Lay the lobsters, top side up, on a sturdy cutting board. Using a cleaver or large, heavy knife, cut the lobsters in half lengthwise. Remove and discard the white intestinal veins and the grain sacs from the heads. Brush the cut side of each lobster half with the melted butter.

CHARCOAL: Place the lobster halves, cut sides up, over the hottest part of the fire. Cover the grill and cook the lobsters until the meat is opaque throughout but still moist when tested with a knife, 10–12 minutes. The shells may char on the bottom

GAS: Place the lobster halves, cut sides up, directly over the heat elements. Cover the grill and cook the lobsters until the meat is opaque throughout but still moist when tested with a knife, 10–12 minutes. The shells may char on the bottom,

While the lobsters are grilling, make the tarragon-lime butter: In a small saucepan over low heat, melt the butter. Remove from the heat and stir in the tarragon and lime juice.

Place a lobster half on each of 4 plates and drizzle with some of the tarragon-lime butter. Serve at once. Pass the remaining butter at the table.

2 live lobsters, about 2 lb (1 kg) each

Melted unsalted butter for brushing

For the Tarragon-Lime Butter

1 cup (8 oz/250 g) unsalted butter

¹/₄ cup (¹/₃ oz/10 g) minced fresh tarragon

2 tablespoons fresh lime juice

MAKES 4 SERVINGS

Barbecued Oysters

¹/₂ cup (4 oz/125 g) unsalted butter, at room temperature

2 tablespoons chili powder

1 tablespoon ground cumin

Ground cayenne pepper

3–4 lb (1.5–2 kg) rock salt

24 bluepoint oysters, shucked and on the half shell

MAKES 4–6 SERVINGS

In a small bowl, mix together the butter, chili powder, and cumin until well blended. Season to taste with cayenne. Cover and refrigerate. Bring to room temperature before serving.

Prepare a CHARCOAL or GAS grill for DIRECT grilling over MEDIUM-HIGH heat (page 18 or 22). Pour rock salt to a depth of ³/₄–1 inch (2–2.5 cm) into 2 heavy cast-iron frying pans. Nest the oysters in their shells securely in the salt.

CHARCOAL: Place the pans over the hottest part of the fire. Cover the grill and cook the oysters until the edges begin to curl, 2–4 minutes.

GAS: Place the pans directly over the heat elements. Cover the grill and cook the oysters until the edges begin to curl, 2–4 minutes.

Spoon the flavored butter over the oysters, dividing evenly. Serve at once.

You will need two heavy cast-iron frying pans for grilling the oysters. If desired, grill slices of coarse country bread on the grill at the same time and serve alongside the oysters for dipping into the flavorful, smoke-tinged oyster juices.

Grill-Roasted Mussels

A new take on classic *moules marinières* (a French dish of mussels steamed in white wine with herbs and garlic), this preparation utilizes the smoke flavors from the grill to provide a nice counterpoint to the creamy texture of the mussel flesh. Vary the herbs and wine to change the flavor of the dish. Serve the mussels with grilled rustic bread to soak up the juices.

Prepare a CHARCOAL or GAS grill for DIRECT grilling over HIGH heat (page 18 or 22).

Divide the mussels between 2 large, heavy cast-iron frying pans, discarding any that fail to close to the touch.

CHARCOAL: Place the pans over the hottest part of the fire. Cover the grill and cook the mussels until they open, 3–5 minutes, stirring the mussels occasionally with tongs.

GAS: Place the pans directly over the heat elements. Cover the grill and cook the mussels until they open, 3–5 minutes, stirring the mussels occasionally with tongs.

Transfer the mussels to warmed individual bowls, discarding any mussels that failed to open. In a small flameproof saucepan, combine the wine, butter, and garlic. Place the pan on the grill rack and swirl until the butter is melted. Stir in the parsley. Pour the wine mixture over the mussels, dividing evenly. Set out a couple of empty bowls for spent shells.

6 lb (3 kg) mussels, well scrubbed and debearded

1 cup (8 fl oz/250 ml) dry white wine

1/4 cup (2 oz/60 g) unsalted butter

2 cloves garlic, minced

Leaves from 1 bunch fresh flat-leaf (Italian) parsley, chopped

MAKES 6 SERVINGS

Vegetables

About Vegetables

The high heat of the fire brings out the natural sugars in vegetables while infusing smoke flavor into their flesh, making for delicious eating. Grilling vegetables also keeps their flavors fresh and preserves their vitamins and minerals, which can be lost when vegetables are cooked in water.

From asparagus to corn, radicchio to sweet potatoes, vegetables are right at home over a bed of hot coals. The best way to prepare vegetables is to select the freshest ones available and to cook them briefly and simply to conserve their distinctive flavors and nutrients. Grilling is the ideal method for doing just that, as you can watch them cooking, test them for doneness with a sharp knife or skewer (better yet, taste a piece!), and take them off the grill at the moment they are done.

The first thing to remember whenever you're dealing with vegetables is to follow the seasons. Without fail, any vegetable that has been locally grown in a suitable environment and allowed to ripen naturally will be markedly more flavorful than an underripe vegetable that has been flown in from afar. Local farmers' markets or roadside farmstands are ideal places to find vegetables in season. Second best is a specialty foods market that purchases their products from local growers. Better yet, grow your own vegetables in a garden plot in the backyard and harvest them just before you plan to cook them.

When choosing vegetables, seek out the freshest ones you can find. As they sit on the market's display, they will lose moisture and vitamins, and their flavor will begin to dissipate. Fresh vegetables should look plump, moist, and unwrinkled. At a farmers' market or roadside stand, ask the farmer when the vegetables were picked, or ask him or her for a sample.

The key to grilling vegetables successfully is to get the grill nice and hot, and then to coat both the grill rack and the vegetables with oil to prevent sticking and add flavor. A vegetable-grilling basket or grill screen is handy for cooking small vegetables that may fall through the spaces in the rack. As with meat and poultry, the heat of the grill seals in the juices and heightens the natural flavors. Caramelization, which occurs when vegetables' natural sugars come in contact with heat, adds another dimension of flavor.

Grilled vegetables can be eaten as is, or seasoned simply with salt, pepper, and fresh herbs, or perhaps a little citrus juice or minced garlic. They can be added to pastas, salads, sauces, and soups, and are terrific accompaniments to other grilled foods as part of an all-grilled meal.

Working with Vegetables

SHOPPING FOR VEGETABLES

Remember to look for vegetables in season and grown close to home for the best results. Following are some examples of what to look for when buying produce.

Asparagus

Medium-sized and fat stalks grill better than very thin spears, which can be bitter. Peeling the bottom third of the spears with a vegetable peeler will help them cook evenly. Season: February through June.

Bitter Greens

Select heads of Belgian endive (chicory/witloof) and radicchio that are firm, fat, and crisp, with tight, unblemished leaves. Season: year-round; best in winter.

Carrots, Parsnips, and Turnips

Choose smooth, firm, crackfree vegetables with good color and a sweet smell. Small, mature vegetables have the best flavor. Season: year-round; best in winter.

Corn

Look for firm ears with plump kernels and a lot of creamy colored silk; avoid ears with heavily soiled or slimy fringe. The husks should be bright green and appear moist, not dried out. Season: May through September.

Eggplants

Look for evenly colored eggplants (aubergines) with shiny skin. Cut globe eggplants into slices for the grill; cook Asian (slender) eggplants whole or halved. Season: year-round; peak in late summer.

Fennel

Choose fresh bulbs that are smooth and tightly layered with no cracks or bruises. White and pale green, rounded bulbs tend to be more succulent than yellow or thin ones. Grocers sometimes incorrectly label fennel as sweet anise. Season: year-round; peak from late fall through winter.

Mushrooms

Look for mushrooms with relatively clean, firm caps. For portobellos, choose those that are evenly sized and have dry-looking gills below. Season: year-round; best in late summer and early fall.

Onions

Look for onions that are firm and have smooth, dry skins. Avoid any with soft spots, particularly at the stem end; green shoots; moldy areas; or moist, wrinkled skins. In the spring, seek out sweet onions such as Maui, Vidalia, or Walla Walla. Season: year-round; sweet varieties in spring and late summer.

Peppers

Look for peppers (capsicums) and chiles with smooth skin, as they will be easier to char on the grill than gnarled or grooved ones. Thin-skinned varieties need a gentler touch so that they don't develop holes from too-high heat. Season: year-round; best late summer through fall.

Potatoes and Sweet Potatoes

Look for firm tubers that are not blemished, wrinkled, tinged with green, or cracked. Avoid potatoes that have sprouted buds.

Season: year-round; new potatoes best in spring; sweet potatoes best in fall and winter.

Summer Squashes

Select zucchini (courgettes), yellow crooknecks pattypans, and other summer squashes that are mature enough to have full flavor yet small enough to be tender and free of large seeds. Season: year-round; best June through September.

Tomatoes

Select tomatoes only in season, and make sure they are firm but ripe. Heirloom varieties are particularly flavorful. Never store tomatoes in the refrigerator or they will become mealy. Season: June through September.

Winter Squashes

Look for firm, unblemished squashes that feel heavy for their size. Season: some varieties available year-round; widest selection in fall and winter.

TESTING VEGETABLES FOR DONENESS

Piercing a vegetable with a skewer or the tip of a knife will give you some idea of whether or not they are done. However, the best way to test a vegetable for doneness it to cut off a piece and eat it. Some vegetables, such as asparagus and fennel, are most satisfying when tender-crisp—that is, tender when you first bite into them and crunchy at the center. Other vegetables, such as eggplants (aubergines) and mushrooms, should be cooked until soft throughout. Follow the doneness clues in the recipes, or cook until they are done to your liking.

Mixed Grill of Summer Vegetables

Juice of $1/2$ lemon

4 artichokes

12 spears asparagus

$3/4$ **cup (6 fl oz/180 ml) fresh orange juice**

$1/2$ **cup (4 fl oz/125 ml) olive oil**

2 teaspoons chopped fresh thyme

Sea salt and freshly cracked pepper

2 small yellow squashes, halved lengthwise

6 green (spring) onions, including 4 inches (10 cm) of tender green tops, trimmed

1 globe eggplant (aubergine), about 1 lb (500 g), peeled and cut crosswise into slices $1/2$ **inch (12 mm) thick**

1 red bell pepper (capsicum), seeded and cut crosswise into slices $1/2$ **inch (12 mm) thick**

MAKES 6–8 SERVINGS

Have ready a large bowl of cold water to which you have added the lemon juice. Working with 1 artichoke at a time, snap off a few of the tough outer leaves until you reach the pale green inner leaves. Cut off a small piece from the stem end, and trim off the thorny leaf tops with a serrated knife. Cut the artichokes in half lengthwise. With a small spoon, scoop out the fuzzy choke. As each artichoke is trimmed, drop it into the lemon water to prevent discoloration.

Bring a saucepan three-fourths full of water to a boil. Add the artichokes and boil for about 5 minutes. Drain and set aside.

Snap or trim off the tough ends of the asparagus, then, if desired, peel the bottom third of each spear with a vegetable peeler or paring knife.

In a large, nonreactive bowl, whisk together the orange juice, oil, thyme, and salt and pepper to taste. Add the artichokes, asparagus, squashes, green onions, eggplant, and bell pepper and toss to coat evenly. Let stand at room temperature for 2 hours. Drain just before grilling.

Prepare a CHARCOAL or GAS grill for DIRECT grilling over MEDIUM-HIGH heat (page 18 or 22). Oil the grill rack.

CHARCOAL: Arrange the vegetables over the hottest part of the fire, adding and removing them according to the length of cooking time. Start with the artichokes and eggplant (about 10 minutes), followed by the pepper and squashes (5–6 minutes). Finally add the onions (4–5 minutes) and the asparagus (2–4 minutes). To ensure even cooking, turn the vegetables once or twice during grilling, and cook them until tender or tender-crisp, depending on the type of vegetable.

GAS: Arrange the vegetables directly over the heat elements, adding and removing them according to the length of cooking time. Start with the artichokes and eggplant (about 10 minutes), followed by the pepper and squashes (5–6 minutes). Finally add the onions (4–5 minutes) and the asparagus (2–4 minutes). To ensure even cooking, turn the vegetables once or twice during grilling, and cook them until tender or tender-crisp, depending on the type of vegetable.

Arrange all the vegetables decoratively on a platter and serve them hot or at room temperature.

Here, smoky grilled summer vegetables are enlivened with a fresh citrus and herb marinade. If you like, change the assortment of vegetables according to what looks best at the market or what you prefer. You can also make a finishing sauce: Reduce 1 cup (8 fl oz/250 ml) of balsamic vinegar by half over medium-high heat, then swirl in 2 tablespoons unsalted butter. Drizzle the sauce over the vegetables before serving.

Mixed Grill of Winter Vegetables with Aioli

Winter vegetables are usually dense, making it necessary to steam or parboil some of them before putting them on the grill. Grilling brings out the natural sweetness of these cold-weather staples. A lemony aioli provides a satisfying counterpoint.

To make the aioli, in a food processor, combine the egg yolks, lemon juice, garlic, $1/4$ teaspoon salt, and $1/8$ teaspoon white pepper and process until blended. With the motor running, add the oil in a slow, steady stream until the mixture thickens to the consistency of mayonnaise. Cover and refrigerate until serving time.

Fill a large pot three-fourths full of salted water and bring to a rapid boil. Add the carrots, parsnips, rutabagas, and butternut squash and cook until just tender when pierced, 7–10 minutes. Using a slotted spoon, lift out, draining well. Set aside.

Prepare a CHARCOAL or GAS grill for DIRECT grilling over MEDIUM-HIGH heat (page 18 or 22). Oil the grill rack. Brush the vegetables with butter and oil, and sprinkle with the rosemary, crumbling it with your fingers.

CHARCOAL: Grill the vegetables over the hottest part of the fire, turning as needed, until tender, 3–6 minutes for the carrots and parsnips and about 10 minutes for the rutabagas and butternut squash.

GAS: Grill the vegetables directly over the heat elements, turning as needed, until tender, 3–6 minutes for the carrots and parsnips and about 10 minutes for the rutabagas and butternut squash.

Transfer to a platter, sprinkle with the salt and cracked black pepper, and serve hot or warm with the aioli for dipping.

For the Aioli

4 egg yolks, at room temperature

2 tablespoons fresh lemon juice

3 cloves garlic, chopped

Sea salt and white pepper, preferably freshly ground

1 cup (8 fl oz/250 ml) extra-virgin olive oil

6 carrots, peeled and halved lengthwise

6 medium to large parsnips, peeled and halved lengthwise

2 rutabagas, peeled and sliced crosswise $1/2$ inch (12 mm) thick

1 butternut squash, peeled, halved lengthwise, seeded, and cut into 2-inch (5-cm) chunks

Melted unsalted butter and olive oil for brushing

1 teaspoon dried rosemary

Sea salt and freshly cracked black pepper

MAKES 6–8 SERVINGS

Asparagus with Lemon Butter and Pine Nuts

Look for medium-sized, bright green asparagus spears rather than very thick ones. Serve the asparagus over grilled toast for a lovely lunch dish. If you want to toast the pine nuts or almonds, place them in a cast-iron frying pan and put it on the grill rack directly over the fire or heat elements until the nuts just begin to color, 1–3 minutes.

In a shallow, nonreactive bowl, whisk together the oil, lemon juice, bay leaves, and $1/4$ teaspoon white pepper. Snap or trim off the tough ends of the asparagus, then, if desired, peel the bottom third of each spear with a vegetable peeler or paring knife. Add the asparagus to the marinade and turn to coat. Marinate at room temperature for 1–2 hours, turning once.

While the asparagus are marinating, make the lemon butter: In a small bowl, mix together the butter, lemon zest and juice, parsley, and hot-pepper sauce until well blended. Cover and refrigerate until needed. Bring to room temperature before serving.

Prepare a CHARCOAL or GAS grill for DIRECT grilling over MEDIUM-HIGH heat (page 18 or 22). Oil the grill rack or a vegetable-grilling basket.

CHARCOAL: Arrange the asparagus spears on the rack or in the basket over the hottest part of the fire. Cook, turning once, until tender-crisp, 2–4 minutes per side.

GAS: Arrange the asparagus spears on the rack or in the basket directly over the heat elements. Cook, turning once, until tender-crisp, 2–4 minutes per side.

Put the asparagus on a warmed platter, sprinkle with the pine nuts and lemon zest, and serve hot. Pass the lemon butter at the table.

$1/2$ cup (4 fl oz/125 ml) olive oil

Juice of 1 lemon

2 bay leaves

White pepper, preferably freshly ground

$1^1/2$ lb (750 g) asparagus

For the Lemon Butter

$1/2$ cup (4 oz/125 g) unsalted butter, at room temperature

1 tablespoon grated lemon zest, plus 1 teaspoon for garnish

2 tablespoons fresh lemon juice

2 tablespoons minced fresh flat-leaf (Italian) parsley

Dash of hot-pepper sauce such as Tabasco

$1/3$ cup ($1^1/2$ oz/45 g) pine nuts or slivered blanched almonds

MAKES 6 SERVINGS

Asparagus Rafts with Soy and Sesame Seeds

¹/₂ cup (4 fl oz/125 ml) soy sauce

2 tablespoons rice wine or dry sherry

1 tablespoon bottled oyster sauce

¹/₂ teaspoon Asian sesame oil

1¹/₂ teaspoons peeled and finely minced fresh ginger

1¹/₂ lb (750 g) pencil-thin asparagus

12 wooden cocktail picks, soaked in water for 10 minutes and drained

¹/₄ cup (1 oz/30 g) sesame seeds, toasted (see note)

MAKES 6 SERVINGS

In a small bowl, whisk together the soy sauce, wine, oyster sauce, sesame oil, and ginger to make a basting sauce.

Snap or trim off the tough ends of the asparagus. Line up 4–5 asparagus spears next to one another on a work surface. Insert a cocktail pick through the spears just below the asparagus tips. Insert a second pick about ¹/₂ inch (12 mm) from the ends of the stalks. There should be a small amount of space between the spears so the heat from the grill will reach all sides of the asparagus. Repeat with the remaining asparagus and cocktail picks. Brush the asparagus on all sides with some of the sauce.

Prepare a CHARCOAL or GAS grill for DIRECT grilling over MEDIUM-HIGH heat (page 18 and 22). Oil the grill rack.

CHARCOAL: Grill the bundled asparagus over the hottest part of the fire, turning once and brushing with the remaining sauce as you turn, until tender-crisp, 3–6 minutes total.

GAS: Grill the bundled asparagus directly over the heat elements, turning once and brushing with the remaining sauce as you turn, until tender-crisp, 3–6 minutes total.

Serve the asparagus on a warmed platter sprinkled with the sesame seeds.

Grilling asparagus mellows its herbaceous edge. Assembling asparagus spears into rafts makes them easy to handle on the grill and guarantees good grill marks.

To toast sesame seeds, put them in a dry frying pan and place over low heat on the stove top or the grill. Stirring frequently, heat them until they turn an even golden brown. Toasting brings out the flavor of the seeds.

Corn with Flavored Butters

For the Garlic-Parsley Butter

¹/₂ cup (4 oz/125 g) unsalted butter, at room temperature

¹/₄ cup (¹/₃ oz/10 g) finely minced fresh flat-leaf (Italian) parsley

1 teaspoon finely minced garlic

1 teaspoon finely minced shallot

1 teaspoon finely grated lemon zest

For the Honey-Tangerine Butter

¹/₂ cup (4 oz/125 g) unsalted butter, at room temperature

3 tablespoons wildflower honey

1 tablespoon fresh tangerine juice or orange juice

For the Pecan Butter

¹/₂ cup (4 oz/125 g) unsalted butter, at room temperature

¹/₃ cup (1¹/₂ oz/45 g) ground pecans

2 teaspoons grated orange zest

2 tablespoons Cognac

6–8 large ears white or yellow corn, husks intact

Ice water to cover

MAKES 6 SERVINGS

Prepare one or more of the flavored butters: To make the garlic-parsley butter, in a small bowl, mix together the butter, parsley, garlic, shallot, and lemon zest until well blended. To make the honey-tangerine butter, in a small bowl, mix together the butter, honey, and citrus juice until well blended. To make the pecan butter, in a small bowl, mix together the butter, pecans, orange juice, and Cognac until well blended. Cover and refrigerate until needed. Bring to room temperature before serving.

Carefully pull down the husk on each ear of corn, leaving it attached at the base. Remove and discard as much of the silk as possible. Pull the husks back up around each ear and tie the top with kitchen string. Soak the ears in ice water to cover for 30–60 minutes. Drain.

Prepare a CHARCOAL or GAS grill for DIRECT grilling over MEDIUM-HIGH heat (page 18 or 22).

CHARCOAL: Grill the corn over the hottest part of the fire, turning occasionally, until just tender, 30–35 minutes. The husks will char.

GAS: Grill the corn directly over the heat elements, turning occasionally, until just tender, 30–35 minutes. The husks will char.

Shuck the corn and serve it hot with the flavored butter(s).

When shopping for fresh corn, select ears that have pale yellow silk and evenly green husks with no signs of brown. Instead of pulling down the husk to expose the kernels, which can dry out the corn and affect the flavor, feel the kernels through the husk to determine that they are tightly packed, fairly evenly spaced, and are without dry patches between them. Have the flavored butters ready for slathering on the corn when it is piping hot off the grill. Other flavored butters (page 289) will also complement corn.

Corn, Arugula, and Cherry Tomato Salad

Corn can be grilled in two ways: in the husks, which essentially steams the kernels while imparting a smoky flavor; or out of the husks and directly on the grill, which chars the kernels and heightens their natural sweetness. The sugar in corn quickly turns to starch once the corn is picked, so always buy the freshest corn available and cook it as soon as possible for the best taste. Do not remove the husks until you're ready to fire up the grill.

Prepare a CHARCOAL or GAS grill for DIRECT grilling over MEDIUM-HIGH heat (page 18 or 22).

CHARCOAL: Place the bacon in a cast-iron frying pan over the hottest part of the fire. Cook the bacon until crisp, 7–9 minutes. Transfer to paper towels to drain. Oil the grill rack. Grill the corn over the hottest part of the fire, turning occasionally, until just tender, 10–12 minutes total. The corn will char.

GAS: Place the bacon in a cast-iron frying pan directly over the heat elements. Cook the bacon until crisp, 8–10 minutes. Transfer to paper towels to drain. Oil the grill rack. Grill the corn directly over the heat elements, turning occasionally, until just tender, 10–12 minutes total. The corn will char.

Transfer the corn to a cutting board and let cool just until it can be handled. Holding each ear stem end down on the board, carefully cut off chunks of the kernels. In a bowl, combine the corn kernels, bacon, tomatoes, arugula, cilantro, garlic, and lime juice and toss well. Season to taste with salt and pepper. Serve the salad warm.

5 slices lean bacon, chopped

6–8 large ears corn, shucked

2 cups (12 oz/375 g) cherry tomatoes

1 bunch arugula (rocket), tough stems removed

1/4 cup (1/3 oz/10 g) finely chopped fresh cilantro (fresh coriander)

2 cloves garlic, minced

1/4 cup (2 fl oz/60 ml) fresh lime juice

Salt and freshly cracked pepper

MAKES 6 SERVINGS

Ginger-Soy Eggplant

Salt

1 large globe eggplant (aubergine), about 1¹/₂ lb (750 g), peeled and cut crosswise into slices ¹/₂ inch (12 mm) thick

For the Ginger-Soy Marinade

¹/₃ cup (3 fl oz/80 ml) soy sauce

2 tablespoons *mirin* (Japanese rice cooking wine) or sherry

2 tablespoons rice vinegar

1 clove garlic, minced

2 teaspoons peeled and minced fresh ginger

2 teaspoons sugar

Freshly ground pepper

Chopped fresh flat-leaf (Italian) parsley for garnish

MAKES 6 SERVINGS

Lightly salt the eggplant slices on both sides and lay them in a single layer on paper towels. Let stand for 30 minutes. Rinse and pat dry.

To make the ginger-soy marinade, in a wide, shallow, nonreactive bowl, stir together the soy sauce, *mirin*, rice vinegar, garlic, ginger, sugar, and ¹/₈ teaspoon pepper. Slip the eggplant slices into the marinade and turn to coat both sides. Let stand for 1 hour, turning once. Drain and pat dry with paper towels.

Prepare a CHARCOAL or GAS grill for DIRECT grilling over MEDIUM-HIGH heat (page 18 or 22). Oil the grill rack.

CHARCOAL: Grill the eggplant slices over the hottest part of the fire, turning once, until soft when pierced with a knife, 5–8 minutes per side.

GAS: Grill the eggplant slices directly over the heat elements, turning once, until soft when pierced with a knife, 5–8 minutes per side.

Arrange the eggplant slices on a warmed serving plate, sprinkle with the parsley, and serve hot or at room temperature.

Eggplants come in many shapes, from round to cylindrical to oval. They can weigh more than 1¹/₂ pounds (750 g) each, or they can be the size of a fig. The color can vary from a rich, deep purple to lavender to green to glossy white. Salting and draining cut eggplants rids them of excess moisture and of the bitterness they sometimes carry. Grilling them infuses their creamy flesh with an appealing smoky flavor.

Fennel and Orange Salad

For the Orange Marinade

²/₃ cup (5 fl oz/160 ml) olive oil

¹/₂ cup (4 fl oz/125 ml) fresh orange juice

3 cloves garlic, minced

3 tablespoons chopped fresh flat-leaf (Italian) parsley

Salt and freshly cracked pepper

3 fennel bulbs, about 1¹/₂ lb (750 g) total weight, thinly sliced with a mandoline or sharp knife

3 navel or blood oranges, or a combination

Melted unsalted butter for brushing

1 bunch watercress, tough stems removed

Dried lavender flowers (pesticide-free) (optional)

MAKES 6 SERVINGS

Fennel, which is native to southern Europe, has a mild licorice taste, making it a particularly wonderful accompaniment to fish and pork. Grilling fennel brings out its creamy and earthy qualities.

To make the orange marinade, in a nonreactive bowl, whisk together the olive oil, orange juice, garlic, parsley, and salt and pepper to taste. Measure out ¹/₃ cup (3 fl oz/80 ml), cover, and refrigerate.

Trim off the stalks and fronds from the fennel bulbs and reserve for another use or discard. Trim away any bruised outer layers from the bulbs. Cut the bulbs lengthwise into slices ¹/₄ inch (6 mm) thick.

Arrange the fennel slices in a shallow, nonreactive dish and pour the remaining marinade over the slices. Turn to coat, then cover and refrigerate for at least 6 hours or for up to 8 hours, turning once. Drain just before grilling. Remove the reserved marinade from the refrigerator.

Working with 1 orange at a time, and using a sharp knife, cut a slice off both ends of the orange to reveal the flesh. Place the orange upright on the cutting board and, using the knife, cut downward to remove the peel, following the contour of the orange. Cut the orange crosswise into slices ¹/₄ inch (6 mm) thick.

Prepare a CHARCOAL or GAS grill for DIRECT grilling over MEDIUM-HIGH heat (page 18 or 22). Oil the grill rack or a vegetable-grilling basket. Brush the orange slices on both sides with the melted butter.

CHARCOAL: Arrange the fennel slices on the rack or in the basket over the hottest part of the fire. Cook, turning as necessary, until fork-tender, 15–20 minutes total. Put the orange slices on the grill near the end of the grilling time, and grill for 1 minute on each side until lightly branded with grill marks.

GAS: Arrange the fennel slices on the rack or in the basket directly over the heat elements. Cook, turning as necessary, until fork-tender, 15–20 minutes total. Put the orange slices on the grill near the end of the grilling time, and grill for 1 minute on each side until lightly branded with grill marks.

In a small saucepan, warm the reserved marinade over low heat just until it starts to steam. Divide the watercress among individual plates. In a bowl, toss together the warm orange and fennel slices with the warm marinade. Arrange evenly over the watercress. Sprinkle the salads with lavender flowers, if using, and serve warm.

Honey-Lime Sweet Potatoes

6 sweet potatoes, peeled and cut crosswise into slices ¹/₂ inch (12 mm) thick

Melted unsalted butter for brushing, plus 2 tablespoons

¹/₂ cup (6 oz/185 g) honey, at room temperature

¹/₄ cup (2 fl oz/60 ml) fresh lime juice

Salt and freshly ground pepper

MAKES 6 SERVINGS

Bring a saucepan three-fourths full of water to a boil. Add the sweet potato slices and parboil for 10 minutes. Drain and let cool.

Prepare a CHARCOAL or GAS grill for DIRECT grilling over MEDIUM-HIGH heat (page 18 or 22). Brush the potato slices with the melted butter.

CHARCOAL: Grill the potato slices over the hottest part of the fire, turning once, until fork-tender, 4–5 minutes per side.

GAS: Grill the potato slices directly over the heat elements, turning once, until fork-tender, 4–5 minutes per side.

While the potatoes are grilling, in a small saucepan over low heat, mix the honey and lime juice until smooth. Stir in the 2 tablespoons butter until melted. Season to taste with salt and pepper. Brush the sweet potatoes on both sides with the glaze and grill them briefly, turning once, about 30 seconds per side. Serve hot.

Often labeled "yam" in markets, the best sweet potato to use for this dish has dark reddish orange skin and vibrant orange, moist flesh. The smoke from the grill will permeate the potato's sweet flesh, while the heat will caramelize its natural sugars.

Balsamic Portobello Steaks

These meatlike portobello mushrooms can be eaten as a main course, or they can be used in a sandwich. For the latter, split squares of focaccia and toast lightly, cut sides down, on the grill. For added richness, crumble about 3 ounces (90 g) blue cheese over the cooked mushrooms and serve with arugula (rocket).

In a large, shallow, nonreactive bowl, stir together the vinegar, oil, lemon juice, parsley, and garlic. Add the mushrooms and turn to coat. Let stand at room temperature for 1 hour, turning once. Drain before grilling.

Prepare a CHARCOAL or GAS grill for DIRECT grilling over MEDIUM-HIGH heat (page 18 or 22). Oil the grill rack.

CHARCOAL: Place the mushrooms, gill side down, over the hottest part of the fire. Cook, turning once, until moist on the underside and just firm to the touch on the top, 4–6 minutes per side.

GAS: Place the mushrooms, gill side down, directly over the heat elements. Cook, turning once, until moist on the underside and just firm to the touch on top, 4–6 minutes per side.

Arrange the mushrooms on individual plates and serve hot.

$^{1}/_{2}$ cup (4 fl oz/125 ml) balsamic vinegar

$^{1}/_{2}$ cup (4 fl oz/125 ml) olive oil

$^{1}/_{4}$ cup (2 fl oz/60 ml) fresh lemon juice

$^{1}/_{4}$ cup ($^{1}/_{3}$ oz/10 g) chopped fresh flat-leaf (Italian) parsley

2 cloves garlic, minced

6 large, fresh portobello mushroom caps, each about $^{1}/_{4}$ lb (125 g), brushed clean

MAKES 6 SERVINGS

Radicchio and Endive
with Salsa Verde

For the Salsa Verde

2 anchovy fillets

$1/3$ cup ($1/2$ oz/15 g) chopped fresh flat-leaf (Italian) parsley

6 fresh basil leaves, chopped

1 teaspoon capers, plus 1 tablespoon brine

$1/4$ cup (2 fl oz/60 ml) olive oil

3 tablespoons red wine vinegar

3 heads radicchio, halved lengthwise

3 heads Belgian endive (chicory/witloof), halved lengthwise

Olive oil for brushing

Salt and freshly ground pepper

MAKES 6 SERVINGS

To make the *salsa verde*, in a food processor, combine the anchovy fillets, parsley, basil, capers and caper brine, oil, and vinegar. Process until the ingredients are finely minced. Spoon into a serving bowl, cover, and set aside until serving.

Brush the radicchio and endive halves generously with oil. Sprinkle with salt and pepper.

Prepare a CHARCOAL or GAS grill for DIRECT grilling over MEDIUM-HIGH heat (page 18 or 22). Oil the grill rack.

CHARCOAL: Grill the radicchio and endive halves, cut sides down, over the hottest part of the fire, turning once and brushing again with oil, until fork-tender, 4–6 minutes per side.

GAS: Grill the radicchio and endive halves, cut sides down, directly over the heat elements, turning once and brushing again with oil, until fork-tender, 4–6 minutes per side.

Arrange the radicchio and endives on a serving platter and serve hot. Pass the *salsa verde* at the table.

Salsa verde, literally "green sauce," refers to a paste made from a variety of green herbs or vegetables. Each Italian cook has his or her own recipe, altering the ingredients slightly depending on the region or the season. You can do the same at home by changing the types or proportions of herbs to suit your taste. Grilled radicchio and endive drizzled with this bold sauce are a fitting accompaniment to grilled veal chops and coarse country bread.

Grilled-Potato Salad

New potatoes are small, young, and usually round, and have thin skins and a waxy, firm texture. They have a short shelf life when compared to mature potatoes and are available in markets only in spring. Tossing the potatoes with the dressing while they are still warm helps them absorb the flavors. For a more colorful salad, use a mixture of red, white, and blue potatoes.

Bring a saucepan three-fourths full of water to a boil. Add the potatoes and parboil just until they can be pierced with a knife but are not completely tender, 5–7 minutes. Do not overcook. Drain and pat dry. Brush the potatoes with vegetable oil.

Prepare a CHARCOAL or GAS grill for DIRECT grilling over MEDIUM-HIGH heat (page 18 or 22).

CHARCOAL: Place the bacon in a cast-iron frying pan over the hottest part of the fire. Cook the bacon until crisp, 8–10 minutes. Transfer to paper towels to drain. Oil the grill rack. Grill the potatoes over the hottest part of the fire, turning once or twice, until tender when pierced with the tip of a knife, 15–20 minutes total, depending on the size of the potatoes.

GAS: Place the bacon in a cast-iron frying pan directly over the heat elements. Cook the bacon until crisp, 8–10 minutes. Transfer to paper towels to drain. Oil the grill rack. Grill the potatoes directly over the heat elements, turning once or twice, until tender when pierced with the tip of a knife, 15–20 minutes total, depending on the size of the potatoes.

Transfer the potatoes to a cutting board, let cool just until they can be handled, and then slice or cut into chunks, discarding any loose skin.

To make the mustard vinaigrette, in a small bowl, whisk together the olive oil, vinegar, mustard, pickle, and salt and pepper to taste.

In a large serving bowl, toss the warm potatoes, bell pepper, and onion with the vinaigrette until all the ingredients are evenly coated. Let stand for up to 30 minutes to blend the flavors. Crumble the bacon and mix it into the salad. Garnish with the parsley, if desired. Serve at room temperature.

2 lb (1 kg) red or white new potatoes, unpeeled

Vegetable oil for brushing

5 slices lean bacon

For the Mustard Vinaigrette

1/4 cup (2 fl oz/60 ml) olive oil

1/4 cup (2 fl oz/60 ml) white wine vinegar or red wine vinegar

2 teaspoons Dijon mustard

2 tablespoons chopped dill pickle

Salt and freshly ground pepper

1 cup (4 oz/125 g) chopped red bell pepper (capsicum)

1 small red onion, thinly sliced

1/3 cup (1/2 oz/15 g) chopped fresh flat-leaf (Italian) parsley (optional)

MAKES 6 SERVINGS

Smoky Potatoes with Cumin Rub

2 lb (1 kg) Yukon gold potatoes, each cut lengthwise into 6–8 spears

For the Cumin Rub

2 tablespoons ground cumin

1 tablespoon paprika

1 tablespoon firmly packed dark brown sugar

Salt and freshly cracked pepper

Olive oil for rubbing

3 handfuls hickory or mesquite chips, soaked if using charcoal (page 13)

MAKES 6 SERVINGS

Bring a saucepan three-fourths full of water to a boil. Add the potato spears and parboil just until they can be pierced with a knife but are not completely tender, about 10 minutes. Do not overcook. Drain and pat dry.

To make the cumin rub, in a small bowl, stir together the cumin, paprika, brown sugar, 1/2 teaspoon salt, and 1/4 teaspoon pepper. Rub the potato spears with oil. Then, rub the potato spears with the cumin rub.

Prepare a CHARCOAL or GAS grill for DIRECT grilling over MEDIUM-HIGH heat (page 18 or 22). Oil the grill rack or a vegetable-grilling basket.

CHARCOAL: Sprinkle the wood chips on the coals. Place the potatoes on the rack or in the basket over the hottest part of the fire. Cook, turning the potatoes occasionally, so that all sides brown, until fork-tender, 30–35 minutes total.

GAS: Add the wood chips to the grill in a smoker box or perforated foil packet (page 10). Place the potatoes on the rack or in the basket directly over the heat elements. Cook, turning the potatoes occasionally, so that all sides brown, until fork-tender, 35–40 minutes total.

Serve the potato spears piping hot.

Yukon gold potatoes are a good choice for the grill, as their buttery, succulent flesh stays moist during cooking. Look for potatoes that are uniform in size, so that they will cook at the same time. For additional flavor, mix the wood chips with an herb, for example, mesquite chips with dried sage leaves. A cooling dipping sauce of 1 cup (8 oz/250 g) sour cream mixed with 2 tablespoons minced fresh chives can be served with the potatoes.

Grilled Fruit

Fruits of all kinds can be successfully grilled, making dramatic and unusual desserts. Use firm fruit, as softer fruit can quickly turn mushy. Prepare a charcoal or gas grill for direct-heat cooking over medium to medium-high heat. Brush fruits with melted butter and place cut side down directly on the grill rack or on a grill screen, following the timing cues on the chart below. Serve grilled fruit with vanilla ice cream, custard sauce, chocolate sauce, berry purée, or chopped crystallized ginger.

FRUIT TYPE	PREPARATION	GRILLING TIME
Apples, Golden Delicious	Peel, cut in half lengthwise, and core	25–30 minutes, turning occasionally
Apricots, firm but ripe	Cut in half lengthwise, remove pit	1–2 minutes per side
Bananas, large, firm but ripe	Peel, cut in half lengthwise	4 minutes total, turning occasionally
Figs, firm but ripe	Cut in half lengthwise	3 minutes per side
Kiwifruits, ripe	Peel if desired, cut into $1/4$-inch (6-mm) slices	$1–1^1/2$ minutes per side
Mangoes, ripe	Peel, pit, and cut into $1/2$-inch (12-mm) slices	2 minutes per side
Nectarines, ripe	Cut in half lengthwise, remove pit	$1^1/2–2$ minutes per side
Oranges	Peel if desired, cut into $1/4$-inch (6-mm) slices	$1^1/2–2$ minutes per side
Papayas, firm but ripe	Peel, cut in half lengthwise, seed, cut into $1/2$-inch (12-mm) slices	2 minutes per side
Pears, firm, winter	Peel if desired, cut in half lengthwise, and core	25–30 minutes, turning occasionally
Pineapples, fresh	Peel, core, and cut into $1/2$-inch (12-mm) slices	2 minutes per side
Plums, firm but ripe	Cut in half lengthwise, remove pit	2 minutes per side

Barbecue

About Barbecuing

The techniques and equipment vary, but the guiding principle of barbecue remains the same: slowly cook a large cut of meat at a low temperature in a covered cooker, surrounded with fragrant hardwood smoke, until it is fall-off-the-bone tender and imbued with flavor.

Barbecuing was designed for tough cuts of meat, such as spareribs, pork shoulder, and beef brisket. These cuts contain a fair amount of connective tissue, or collagen. When you apply high heat to these cuts, the meat tightens, toughens, and dries out. At low temperatures, however, the collagen softens and becomes gelatin, resulting in tender and juicy meat when cooked to well done. The art of barbecuing involves keeping the heat low enough to melt the collagen for tenderness, but high enough to cook the meat through and to keep smoke flowing over it for flavor. To achieve the ideal low temperatures favored by most Southern pitmasters, you need specialized equipment, such as an offset smoker-cooker or a pit roaster. However, with care and attention, you can turn out good barbecued ribs and Texas-style brisket on a standard charcoal or gas grill.

PREPARING MEAT FOR BARBECUE

Another key to making great barbecue is flavoring the meat generously. Most barbecue begins with a dry spice rub applied liberally to the meat. For maximum flavor, it's best to let the seasoned meat sit for an hour or two before cooking or, even better, to rub the meat the night before and refrigerate overnight. This allows the spices and herbs to penetrate the surface and helps to create a savory crust on the meat.

You can also add flavor with wet ingredients, such as a paste of garlic and fresh herbs or a marinade of oil, herbs, and an acidic liquid such as wine or vinegar. Be sure to dry the meat thoroughly before barbecuing.

Some barbecue aficionados like to baste meat as it cooks with a mop or sauce made of beer, wine, or spirits mixed with vinegar, red pepper, and other seasonings.

Some longer-cooking barbecue recipes call for wrapping the meat in heavy-duty foil for part of the cooking time. This helps keep the meat from drying out during long cooking.

BEEF CUTS FOR BARBECUE

Tender steaks from the back, ribs, and loin are best cooked over high heat on the grill. Since they contain little collagen, they can be quickly cooked without the meat tightening and drying out. But tough cuts like brisket and ribs, and some tender but larger roasts such as tri-tip, are delicious when barbecued at low heat levels. See illustrations on pages 52–53.

Beef Rib Roast

While rib roast or prime rib is usually roasted in moderately high heat in an oven or by the indirect method on a charcoal or gas grill, it can be successfully smoke-roasted in low heat. Be sure to test the internal temperature with an instant-read meat thermometer and remove the roast when it is no more than medium-rare (about 130°F/71°C).

Beef Ribs

Beef ribs can be cooked over direct heat or slow-cooked in a covered barbecue. They should be cooked to the well-done stage (160°F/71°C) and are delicious seasoned with a spicy dry rub and basted with barbecue sauce during the latter stages of cooking. Look for ribs with plenty of meat and little fat.

Brisket

Brisket is a large, boneless muscle cut from under the shoulder of the steer. Since the muscle gets a lot of use, it is full of connective tissue and collagen and must be cooked for a long time to become tender. Like other tough cuts such as chuck or shoulder or short ribs, however, brisket has a wonderful beefy flavor. Brisket is sold whole or in smaller pieces. Try to get a piece of brisket that includes the succulent deckle, a cap of fat and meat much loved by brisket fanciers. Contrary to the usual practice when selecting meat, look for brisket with as much fat as possible, since the fat bastes the meat and keeps it juicy during long cooking. You can cut away most of the fat before serving.

Tri-Tip

Tri-tip, a triangular-shaped small roast from the sirloin, is delicious both when grilled and when slow-cooked in a covered charcoal or gas grill. In either case, do not cook tri-tip past the medium-rare stage (130°–135°F/54°–57°C), or it will toughen and dry out.

PORK CUTS FOR BARBECUE

Pork is the ideal meat for long, slow, and smoky cooking. The rich meat absorbs the smoke flavors, and fat and collagen in cuts from the rib and shoulder turn luscious and silky with long cooking at low temperatures. See illustrations on pages 124–25.

Baby Back Ribs

Baby back ribs are bones with meat attached that are trimmed from the rib section of the pork loin when the butcher cuts boneless pork loin roast or chops. Since they are essentially loin meat, baby back ribs are much more tender than true spareribs and can be cooked quickly with direct heat on the grill. They can also be cooked by long, slow cooking, but are done in about half the time of traditional spareribs. Look for lean racks of ribs with plenty of meat, the heavier the better.

Country-Style Ribs

Country-style ribs are butterflied or split chops from the shoulder end of the loin. Bone-in or boneless, they are usually quite meaty, with a moderate amount of fat. They can be grilled over direct heat using any pork chop recipe or cooked by the long and slow method in a charcoal grill or gas grill. Country-style ribs are inexpensive, easy to cook, and delicious.

Pork Shoulder

The shoulder has more internal fat and connective tissue than the pork leg or fresh ham and thus is best cooked long and slow. Professionals often cook the whole shoulder, but most home cooks prefer to barbecue half shoulders (about 5–7 pounds) or quarter shoulders. The best cut is the Boston butt, or pork cut from the top part of the shoulder.

Pork Loin

Pork loin is quite tender and can be cut into chops and cooked directly on the grill or slowly barbecued whole over low heat on a covered charcoal or gas grill. The loin will be done more quickly than shoulder. Care must be taken to avoid overcooking this cut. Since it is quite low in internal fat and connective tissue, it will dry out and toughen if the internal temperature rises over 150°F (65°C). Bone-in loin will stay moist on the grill longer than boneless; test with an instant-read meat thermometer to avoid overcooking.

Spareribs

Spareribs, cut from the belly of the hog, need long, slow cooking to become tender and juicy, but most true barbecue fanciers prefer these succulent ribs above all other cuts. There's nothing better than gnawing on a tender sparerib and savoring the combination of crisp brown surface and the luscious sweet meat next to the bone. Choose large slabs (13 ribs to a slab) with plenty of meat and a moderate amount of fat. Slabs run 2–3 pounds (1–1.5 kg) on average, and it's worth taking the time to choose large, meaty ribs.

Tri-Tip with Pinto Bean Salad

The triangular beef tri-tip roast gained its popularity as Santa Maria barbecue, named for a town on the coast of central California. It is a flavorful cut, but care must be taken not to cook it beyond medium-rare for the best texture and taste. A lengthy soak in a red-wine marinade tenderizes the meat before smoking it. Serve it hot or at room temperature with the zesty pinto bean salad, a variation on the classic accompaniments of pinto beans and salsa.

Combine the wine, vinegar, oil, mustard, oregano, peppercorns, onion, garlic, bay leaf, and $1/2$ teaspoon salt in a shallow, nonreactive dish just large enough to hold the roast and mix well. Add the beef to this marinade and turn to coat on all sides. Cover and refrigerate, turning occasionally, 6–8 hours. Remove the beef from the refrigerator 30 minutes before barbecuing.

Prepare a CHARCOAL or GAS grill for BARBECUING over MEDIUM-LOW heat (page 25 or 27). Oil the grill rack. Remove the meat from the marinade and discard the marinade. Pat the meat dry with paper towels.

CHARCOAL: Place a drip pan half full of water in the center of the fire bed. Sprinkle wood chips on the coals. After the chips start smoking, place the meat on the grill rack over the drip pan. Cover the grill and continue to cook, turning once at the midway point and adding more wood chips, more coals, and more water to the drip pan as needed, for $1^1/4$–$1^1/2$ hours total.

GAS: Place a shallow pan half full of water at the edge of the grill rack. Add wood chips to the grill in a smoker box or a perforated foil packet (page 27). After the chips start smoking, place the meat on the grill rack away from the heat elements, cover, and cook, turning once at the halfway point, adding more wood chips and more water to the pan as needed, for $1^1/4$–$1^1/2$ hours total.

To test for doneness, insert an instant-read thermometer into the thickest part of the roast; it should register 130°–135°F (54°–57°C) for medium-rare. The temperature will rise another 5°–10°F (3°–6°C) while the meat is resting.

While the meat is grilling, make the pinto bean salad. In a serving bowl, combine the beans, onion, cilantro, chile, tomato, oil, lime juice, pepper sauce, $1/4$ teaspoon salt, and pepper to taste and mix well.

Let the roast rest for 15 minutes. Carve across the grain into thin slices and serve with the salad.

1 cup (8 fl oz/250 ml) dry red wine

$1/4$ cup (2 fl oz/60 ml) red wine vinegar

2 tablespoons vegetable oil

1 tablespoon Dijon mustard

$1/2$ teaspoon dried oregano

8–10 peppercorns

1 yellow onion, thinly sliced

1 clove garlic, lightly crushed

1 bay leaf

Salt

1 beef tri-tip roast, 2–$2^1/2$ lb (1–1.25 g), trimmed of fat

1 or 2 handfuls mesquite or hickory chips, soaked if using charcoal (page 13)

For the Pinto Bean Salad

1 can (15 oz/470 g) pinto beans, drained and rinsed

$1/3$ cup minced yellow onion

$1/4$ cup ($1/3$ oz/10 g) lightly packed fresh cilantro (fresh coriander) leaves, chopped

1 jalapeño, seeded and minced

1 tomato, seeded and chopped

2 tablespoons vegetable oil

1 tablespoon fresh lime juice

$1/2$ teaspoon chipotle pepper sauce or other hot-pepper sauce, or to taste

Salt and ground black pepper

MAKES 4–6 SERVINGS

Texas-Style Brisket

--For the Hill Country Rub

2 tablespoons chili powder

1 tablespoon sweet paprika

1 teaspoon ground oregano

Salt

$1/2$ teaspoon ground cumin

$1/4$ teaspoon ground cayenne pepper

1 whole beef brisket, 5–6 lb (2.5–3 kg), trimmed to leave a thin layer of fat

3–4 handfuls hickory or mesquite chips, soaked if using charcoal (page 13)

For the Beer Barbecue Sauce

3 tablespoons vegetable oil

1 yellow onion, chopped

1 celery stalk, chopped

1 green bell pepper (capsicum), seeded and chopped

2 cloves garlic, minced

2 tablespoons chili powder

3 cups (24 fl oz/750 ml) bottled barbecue sauce

1 cup (8 fl oz/250 ml) beer

2 tablespoons prepared horseradish

2 tablespoons cider vinegar

2 tablespoons Worcestershire sauce

MAKES 8–10 SERVINGS

To make the Hill Country rub, in a small dish, stir together the chili powder, paprika, oregano, 1 teaspoon salt, the cumin, and cayenne. Sprinkle the mixture evenly on all sides of the brisket, patting and rubbing it into the meat. Tightly wrap the meat in a large piece of heavy-duty aluminum foil. Let the meat stand at room temperature for at least 15 minutes, or cover and refrigerate for up to 24 hours before barbecuing. If the meat is refrigerated, remove from the refrigerator at least 30 minutes before barbecuing.

Prepare a CHARCOAL or GAS grill for BARBECUING over MEDIUM-LOW heat (page 25 or 27).

CHARCOAL: Place a drip pan half full of water on the center of the fire bed. Sprinkle one-third of the wood chips on the coals. Place the foil-wrapped meat on the grill rack over the drip pan. Cover the grill and cook, adding more wood chips, more coals, and more water as needed, for 3 hours. Remove the meat from the grill and place it in a shallow pan. Unwrap the meat, allowing the juices to collect in the pan. Place the unwrapped meat on the grill over the drip pan, cover the grill, and continue to cook until the meat is very tender and black-ened on the outside, $2^1/2$–3 hours longer. Baste the meat several times with the reserved meat juices, and add wood chips, coals, and water as needed.

GAS: Place a shallow pan half full of water at the edge of the grill rack. Add half of the wood chips to the grill in a smoker box or perforated foil packet (page 27). Place the foil-wrapped meat on the grill away from the heat elements. Cover the grill and cook for 3 hours, adding more water as needed. Remove the meat from the grill and place it in a shallow pan. Unwrap the meat, allowing the juices to collect in the pan. Place the unwrapped meat on the grill and add the rest of the wood chips to the grill in a smoker box or perforated foil packet. Cover the grill and continue to cook until the meat is very tender and blackened on the outside, $2^1/2$–3 hours longer. Baste the meat several times with the reserved meat juices. Add more water as necessary.

To test for doneness, insert an instant-read thermometer into the thickest part of the meat; it should register 190°F (88°C).

In the Hill Country, believed by many to be the birthplace of real Texas barbecue, brisket is the only meat in town. Texans would never think of brushing a slow-cooking brisket with sauce. They might start with a peppery rub, but usually they let the wood and smoke do the job of turning a tough cut of beef into the most tender, flavorful meat in the world, or at least in Texas. Traditionally, barbecued brisket is served in big rolls, ideal for soaking up sauce and juices.

While the meat is cooking, make the beer barbecue sauce: In a saucepan over medium heat, warm the oil. Add the onion, celery, and bell pepper and sauté until softened, about 4 minutes. Stir in the garlic and chili powder and cook, stirring, for 1 minute. Stir in the barbecue sauce, the beer, the horseradish, the vinegar, and the Worcestershire sauce. Simmer, stirring often, until reduced by about one-fourth, about 20 minutes. Let cool, then cover and refrigerate for at least 2 hours or for up to 2 days before using.

Let the smoked brisket rest for at least 15 minutes. Carve across the grain into thin slices. Meanwhile, warm the sauce in a pan over medium-low heat or set the pan on the grill rack to warm. Serve hot.

Slow-Smoked Rib Roast

For the Garlic Rub

4 large cloves garlic, finely chopped

Coarse sea or kosher salt and freshly ground coarse pepper

2 tablespoons chopped fresh rosemary

2 tablespoons chopped fresh thyme

2 tablespoons Dijon mustard

1 standing 4-rib beef roast, 8–10 lb (4–5 kg), trimmed of excess fat

2–3 handfuls mesquite chips, soaked if using charcoal (page 13)

MAKES 8 SERVINGS

To make the garlic rub, in a small dish, use the back of a wooden spoon to mash together the garlic and 1 1/2 teaspoons coarse salt. Mash in 1 1/2 teaspoons pepper, the rosemary, thyme, and mustard. Rub the paste onto all sides of the roast. Let stand at room temperature for 30 minutes, or cover and refrigerate for up to 8 hours. If refrigerated, remove from the refrigerator 30 minutes before barbecuing.

Prepare a CHARCOAL or GAS grill for BARBECUING over MEDIUM-LOW heat (page 25 or 27). Oil the grill rack.

CHARCOAL: Place a drip pan half full of water in the center of the fire bed. Sprinkle wood chips on the coals. Place the roast, fat side up, on the rack over the drip pan. Cover the grill. Cook without turning, adding more wood chip, more coals, and more water to the drip pan as needed, until richly browned on all sides and cooked as desired, 2–3 hours for medium-rare.

GAS: Place a shallow pan half full of water at the edge of the grill rack. Add the wood chips to the grill in a smoker box or perforated foil packet (page 27). Place the roast, fat side up, away from the heat elements. Cover the grill. Cook without turning, adding more wood chips to the grill and more water to the pan as needed, until richly browned on all sides and cooked to your liking, 2–3 hours for medium-rare.

If the rib bones blacken during roasting, lightly cover them with aluminum foil. Do not open the grill cover more than necessary, or you will release the flavorful smoke and the temperature will drop.

To test for doneness, insert an instant-read thermometer into the thickest part of the roast away from the bone; it should register about 130°F (54°C). The temperature will rise another 5°–10°F (3°–6°C) while the roast is resting.

Let the roast rest for 15 minutes, then carve into thick slices on the bone, or cut away from the bone and carve into thinner slices.

Few culinary sights are more impressive than a standing rib beef roast. You can carve it into thick slices, bone and all, or, for a more elegant presentation, you can cut the roast away from the bone after grilling and then carve the meat into thinner slices. Wood chips will add deep flavor to the roast. For easy grilling and carving, ask the butcher to "french" the roast, that is, cut away the fat and meat from the ends of the bones. Grilled or roasted vegetables are the perfect accompaniment.

Creole Smoked Beef Ribs

Although beef ribs can be slowly cooked to tenderness in an indoor oven, the smoke of the grill and eating them outdoors are more in keeping with the spirit of the meal. Almost any rub and sauce that is good with beef will be good here, but a spicy Creole rub and a bourbon-spiked barbecue sauce seem more robust than most, and thus just right.

To make the Creole rub, in a small dish, stir together the paprika, thyme, brown sugar, onion and garlic powders, mustard, celery seeds, cayenne pepper, and $1^1/_2$ teaspoons each salt and black pepper.

To make the bourbon sauce, in a saucepan over medium heat, combine the chili and barbecue sauces, bourbon, vinegar, honey, and Worcestershire sauce. Cook, stirring occasionally, until slightly reduced, 5–10 minutes. Stir in the hot-pepper sauce to taste. The sauce can be made up to 2 days ahead and refrigerated. Reheat gently before using.

Pat the ribs on all sides generously with the rub. Let the ribs stand for 30 minutes at room temperature, or cover and refrigerate for up to 3 hours. If refrigerated, remove from the refrigerator 30 minutes before barbecuing.

Prepare a CHARCOAL or GAS grill for BARBECUING over MEDIUM-LOW heat (page 25 or 27).

CHARCOAL: Place a drip pan half full of water in the center of the fire bed. Sprinkle wood chips on the coals. Place the ribs on the grill rack over the drip pan. Cover the grill and cook, turning occasionally and adding more wood chips, more coals, and more water to the drip pan as needed, until the ribs are very tender and richly browned, about 2 hours. After about $1^1/_2$ hours, brush the ribs once or twice with the sauce.

GAS: Place a shallow pan half full of water at the edge of the grill rack. Add wood chips to the grill in a smoker box or perforated foil packet (page 27). Place the ribs on the grill rack away from the heat elements. Cover the grill and cook, turning occasionally and adding more wood chips and more water to the pan as needed, until the ribs are very tender and richly browned, about 2 hours. After about $1^1/_2$ hours, brush the ribs once or twice with the sauce.

Simmer any remaining sauce for at least 5 minutes before serving. Cut the ribs into pieces and serve with the sauce on the side.

For the Creole Rub

2 tablespoons paprika

1 tablespoon dried thyme

2 teaspoons brown sugar

$1^1/_2$ teaspoons onion powder

1 teaspoon garlic powder

1 teaspoon dry mustard

1 teaspoon ground celery seeds

$1/_4$ teaspoon ground cayenne pepper

Salt and freshly ground black pepper

For the Bourbon Sauce

$2/_3$ cup (5 fl oz/150 ml) bottled chili sauce

$2/_3$ cup (5 fl oz/150 ml) hickory-flavored bottled barbecue sauce

$1/_4$ cup (2 fl oz/60 ml) bourbon

3 tablespoons cider vinegar

3 tablespoons honey

1 tablespoon Worcestershire sauce

1–2 teaspoons hot-pepper sauce such as Tabasco

2 racks beef ribs, about 5 lb (2.5 kg) total weight

3–4 handfuls hickory chips, soaked if using charcoal (page 13)

MAKES 4 SERVINGS

Smoked Pork Loin

3 tablespoons chopped fresh rosemary

2 tablespoons finely chopped shallot

1¹/₂ tablespoons grated orange zest

1 tablespoon grated lemon zest

2 tablespoons olive oil

1 tablespoon thawed, frozen orange juice concentrate

Coarse sea or kosher salt and freshly ground coarse pepper

1 bone-in pork loin roast, about 3 lb (1.5 kg)

5 large fresh rosemary sprigs, each 6–8 inches (15–20 cm) long

4 or 5 handfuls wood chips, preferably apple or cherry, soaked if using charcoal (page 13)

MAKES 6 SERVINGS

In a small dish, stir together the chopped rosemary, shallot, orange and lemon zests, oil, orange juice concentrate, and 1 teaspoon each of the salt and pepper. Smear the mixture evenly over the pork loin. Place in a dish, cover, and refrigerate for at least 1 hour or for up to 3 hours. Remove from the refrigerator 30 minutes before smoking.

Prepare a CHARCOAL or GAS grill for BARBECUING over MEDIUM-LOW heat (page 25 or 27). Oil the grill rack.

CHARCOAL: Fill a drip pan half full of water and float 1 rosemary sprig in it. Place the pan in the center of the fire bed. Sprinkle wood chips on the coals. Place the pork, bone side down, on the grill rack over the pan. Cover the grill and smoke the pork without turning, adding more wood chips, more coals, another herb branch, and more water to the drip pan as needed, until done to your liking, about 2 hours for medium (slightly pink at the center and juicy). About 10 minutes before the pork is done, dampen the remaining rosemary sprigs in cold water and toss onto the coals.

GAS: Place a shallow pan half full of water at the edge of the grill rack and float 1 rosemary sprig in it. Add wood chips to the grill in a smoker box or perforated foil packet (page 27). Place the pork, bone side down, on the grill rack away from the heat elements. Cover the grill and smoke the pork without turning, adding more wood chips to the grill and another herb branch and more water to the pan as needed, until done to your liking, about 2 hours for medium (slightly pink at the center and juicy). About 10 minutes before the pork is done, dampen the remaining rosemary sprigs in cold water and toss onto the grill rack.

To test for doneness, insert an instant-read thermometer into the thickest part of the roast away from the bone; it should register 150°F (65°C). The temperature will rise another 5°–10°F (3°–6°C) while the meat is resting.

Let the pork rest for at least 5 minutes before slicing. Cut into thick slices to serve.

No meat lends itself better to smoking than pork. A bone-in pork loin roast can be smoked in about 2 hours, and the result is a woodsy aroma and juicy, sweet-smoky meat. The chips of choice are any fruitwood, such as apple or cherry, although mesquite is nice, too. Near the end of the smoking, add several large branches of fresh rosemary to the fire to emphasize that rosemary has been rubbed onto the pork. Serve the flavorful meat with herbed mashed potatoes.

North Carolina Pulled Pork

Pork shoulder, brisket, and ribs are the Big Three of American barbecue. Texas claims the brisket, and Memphis and Kansas City are still arguing over the ribs, but North Carolina is home to barbecued pork shoulder, and its traditional presentation, pulled pork. After hours of smoking, pork shoulder, also known as pork butt or Boston butt, becomes so tender that it can be shredded or "pulled" with an ordinary fork. The pulled pork is usually moistened with a peppery vinegar sopping sauce. Traditionally the pork and sauce are heaped into buns and topped with a spoonful of creamy coleslaw.

Trim the meat of excess fat. In a small bowl, combine the paprika, garlic and onion powders, celery seeds, mustard, thyme, cayenne, and 1 teaspoon salt and mix well. Reserve 2 teaspoons of the mixture, then rub the remaining mixture evenly over the pork. Place in a dish, cover, and refrigerate for at least 6 hours or for up to 24 hours.

To make the North Carolina mopping sauce, in a saucepan over medium heat, combine the vinegar, water, brown sugar, red pepper flakes, and 1 teaspoon salt. Bring to a simmer, stirring to dissolve the sugar. Remove from the heat and let cool. Measure and reserve 1 1/2 cups (12 fl oz/375 ml) of the mopping sauce to use for the sopping sauce.

Prepare a CHARCOAL or GAS grill for BARBECUING over MEDIUM-LOW heat (page 25 or 27). Oil the grill rack.

CHARCOAL: Place a drip pan half full of water in the center of the fire bed. Sprinkle wood chips on the coals. Place the pork on the grill rack over the drip pan. Cover the grill and cook, turning occasionally and brushing with the mopping sauce, adding more wood chips, more coals, and more water to the pan as needed, until the pork is fork-tender and richly browned, about 5 hours.

GAS: Place a shallow pan of water at the edge of the grill rack. Add wood chips to the grill in a smoker box or perforated foil packet (page 27). Place the pork on the grill rack away from the heat elements. Cover the grill and cook, turning occasionally and brushing with the mopping sauce, adding more wood chips and more water to the pan as needed, until the pork is fork-tender and richly browned, about 5 hours.

To test for doneness, insert an instant-read thermometer into the thickest part of the roast; it should register 190°F (88°C).

Transfer the pork to a carving board and let rest for at least 15 minutes. Using 2 forks, pull the pork apart into shreds, place them in a roasting pan or Dutch oven, and cover with aluminum foil to keep warm.

To make the sopping sauce, in a small pan over medium heat, combine the reserved mopping sauce, the ketchup, and the reserved spice mixture. Bring to a simmer, then pour over the pork. Serve at once.

1 bone-in pork shoulder roast, 5–6 lb (2.5–3 kg)

2 tablespoons sweet paprika

1 teaspoon garlic powder

1 teaspoon onion powder

1 teaspoon celery seeds

1 teaspoon dry mustard

1 teaspoon dried thyme

1/4 teaspoon ground cayenne pepper

Coarse sea or kosher salt

For the North Carolina Mopping Sauce

2 cups (16 fl oz/500 ml) cider vinegar

1 cup (8 fl oz/250 ml) water

1/3 cup (2 1/2 oz/75 g) firmly packed brown sugar

1 teaspoon red pepper flakes

Salt

5 or 6 handfuls hickory chips, soaked if using charcoal (page 13)

For the Sopping Sauce

1 1/2 cups (12 fl oz/375 ml) reserved North Carolina mopping sauce

1/4 cup (2 fl oz/60 ml) tomato ketchup

Reserved spice mixture

MAKES 8 SERVINGS

Memphis-Style Spareribs

For the Memphis Dry Rub

2 tablespoons sweet paprika

1¹/₂ tablespoons chili powder

2 teaspoons sugar

1 teaspoon onion powder

1 teaspoon garlic powder

1 teaspoon ground celery seeds

1 teaspoon ground cumin

1 teaspoon dry mustard

1 teaspoon dried oregano

1 teaspoon dried thyme

¹/₂ teaspoon ground cayenne pepper

Salt

4 lb (2 kg) trimmed pork spareribs, in slabs

1¹/₂ cups (12 fl oz/375 ml) barbecue sauce (page 169) (optional)

3 or 4 handfuls hickory chips, soaked if using charcoal (page 13)

MAKES 4 SERVINGS

In the opinion of many grill masters, including the legions of experts who trail the weekend barbecue contest circuit, Memphis is the only place to find real ribs. It's where the contest finalists gather each year for the big rib cook-off, and it's where enthusiasts come year-round for legendary ribs at world-famous restaurants. Ribs are done dry (dry rub, that is) in Memphis, and the sauce is served on the side.

To make the Memphis dry rub, in a small bowl, stir together the paprika, chili powder, sugar, onion and garlic powders, celery seeds, cumin, mustard, oregano, thyme, cayenne, and 1 teaspoon salt. Use the rub immediately, or cover tightly and store at room temperature for up to 1 week.

Using your fingers, pat the dry rub evenly over the spareribs, rubbing it in well. Place in a dish in a single layer, cover, and refrigerate for at least 1 hour or for up to 4 hours. Remove from the refrigerator 30 minutes before barbecuing.

Prepare a CHARCOAL or GAS grill for BARBECUING over MEDIUM-LOW heat (page 25 or 27). Oil the grill rack.

CHARCOAL: Place a drip pan half full of water in the center of the fire bed. Sprinkle wood chips on the coals. Place the ribs on the grill rack over the drip pan. Cover the grill and smoke the ribs, turning them every 30 minutes or so and adding more wood chips, more coals, and more water to the drip pan as needed, until the ribs are fork-tender, 2¹/₂–3 hours.

GAS: Place a shallow pan half full of water at the edge of the grill rack. Add wood chips to the grill in a smoker box or perforated foil packet (page 27). Place the ribs on the grill rack away from the heat elements. Cover the grill and smoke the ribs, turning every 30 minutes or so and adding more wood chips and more water to the pan as needed, until the ribs are fork-tender, 2¹/₂–3 hours.

If you are using the barbecue sauce, heat it in a saucepan on the grill rack or on the stove top, then pour into a bowl to serve alongside the ribs for dipping or for brushing onto the finished ribs. To serve, cut the slabs into separate ribs or into manageable 3- or 4-rib portions.

Kansas City–Style Spareribs

Kansas City barbecue sauce takes the best ingredients—tomatoes, vinegar, and molasses—from other popular styles and combines them in a thick, sweet, smoky sauce. These ribs are cooked in an apple cider–flavored liquid for the first 45 minutes to keep them moist, and then finished directly on the grill. Creamy coleslaw is a perfect partner. Leftover sauce is great with burgers or steaks.

To make the rub, stir together the paprika, garlic, 1 teaspoon salt, and $1/2$ teaspoon black pepper. Using your fingers, pat the dry rub evenly over the spareribs, rubbing it in well. Let stand at room temperature for 30 minutes before barbecuing.

To make the braising liquid, combine the vinegar, cider, water, and hot-pepper sauce in a heavy-duty aluminum foil roasting pan large enough to fit the ribs. Add the spareribs, bone side down, and cover the pan with heavy-duty aluminum foil.

Prepare a fire in a CHARCOAL or GAS grill for BARBECUING over LOW heat (page 25 or 27).

CHARCOAL: Place a drip pan half full of water in the center of the fire bed. Sprinkle wood chips on the coals. Place the pan with the ribs over the drip pan, cover the grill, and cook for about 45 minutes. Carefully remove the pan with the ribs from the grill and open the foil, allowing the steam to dissipate. Reserve the liquid and place the ribs on the grill rack directly over the drip pan. Cover the grill and continue to cook, turning the ribs every 15 minutes, basting with the reserved braising liquid, and adding more wood chips, coals, and water to the pan as needed, until the meat is browned and tender and has started to pull away to expose the ends of the bones, 1–$1^{1}/2$ hours longer. During the last 20 minutes of grilling, brush the ribs lightly with the sauce.

GAS: Place a shallow pan half full of water at the edge of the grill rack. Add wood chips to the grill in a smoker box or perforated foil packet (page 27). Place the pan with the ribs on the grill rack away from the heat elements, cover the grill, and cook for about 45 minutes. Carefully remove the pan from the grill and open the foil, releasing the steam. Reserve the liquid and place the ribs on the grill rack away from the heat elements. Cover the grill and continue to cook, turning the ribs every 15 minutes, basting with the reserved braising liquid, and adding more wood chips and more water to the pan as needed, until the meat is browned and tender and has started to pull away to expose the ends of the bones, 1–$1^{1}/2$ hours longer. During the last 20 minutes of grilling, brush the ribs lightly with the sauce.

Meanwhile, heat the barbecue sauce. Remove the ribs from the grill, generously brush them with some of the warm sauce, and let rest for 20 minutes. To serve, cut the slabs into manageable portions. Pass the remaining sauce at the table.

For the Rub

1 tablespoon sweet paprika

1 teaspoon granulated garlic

Coarse sea or kosher salt and freshly ground black pepper

4 lb (2 kg) trimmed pork spareribs, in slabs

For the Braising Liquid

$1/3$ cup (3 fl oz/80 ml) cider vinegar

$1/3$ cup (3 fl oz/80 ml) apple cider

$1/3$ cup (3 fl oz/80 ml) water

$1/4$ teaspoon hot-pepper sauce

4 handfuls hickory chips, soaked if using charcoal (page 13)

1 recipe Kansas City Barbecue Sauce (page 287)

MAKES 3 OR 4 SERVINGS

Baby Back Ribs
with a Mustard-Bourbon Mop

For the Rub

2 teaspoons sweet Hungarian paprika

1 teaspoon dry mustard

Coarse sea or kosher salt and freshly ground pepper

3–4 lb (1.5–2 kg) baby back pork ribs, in slabs

For the Mop

1/2 cup (4 fl oz/125 ml) bourbon whiskey

1/4 cup (2 oz/60 g) prepared mustard

2 tablespoons cider vinegar

2 tablespoons firmly packed golden brown sugar

1 tablespoon vegetable oil

1 tablespoon Worcestershire sauce

1/2 teaspoon hot-pepper sauce

Freshly ground pepper

2 or 3 handfuls hickory chips, soaked if using charcoal (page 13)

MAKES 4–6 SERVINGS

To make the rub, stir together the paprika, dry mustard, 1 teaspoon salt, and 1/2 teaspoon pepper. Using your fingers, pat the dry rub evenly over the spareribs, rubbing it in well. Let stand at room temperature for 30 minutes before grilling.

To make the mop, whisk together the bourbon, mustard, vinegar, sugar, oil, Worcestershire sauce, hot-pepper sauce, and 1/2 teaspoon pepper until the sugar dissolves.

Prepare a CHARCOAL or GAS grill for BARBECUING over MEDIUM-LOW heat (page 25 or 27). Oil the grill rack.

CHARCOAL: Place a drip pan half full of water in the center of the fire bed. Sprinkle wood chips on the coals. Place the ribs, meat side up, on the grill rack over the drip pan. Cover the grill and cook, turning the ribs over after 30 minutes. Continue to cook, basting the ribs with the mop every 15–20 minutes, turning the ribs 2 or 3 times more, and adding more wood chips, more coals, and more water to the drip pan as needed, until the meat is tender and has started to pull away and expose the ends of the bones, 1³/₄–2 hours longer.

GAS: Place a shallow pan half full of water at the edge of the grill rack. Add wood chips to the grill in a smoker box or perforated foil packet (page 27). Place the ribs, meat side up, on the grill rack away from the heat elements. Cover the grill and cook, turning the ribs after 30 minutes. Continue to cook, basting with the mop every 15–20 minutes, turning the ribs 2 or 3 times more, and adding more wood chips and more water to the pan as needed, until the meat is tender and has started to pull away to expose the ends of the bones, 1³/₄–2 hours more.

Let the ribs rest for 15 or 20 minutes. Cut the slabs into 2- or 3-rib portions and serve warm.

Though they can also cook quickly over higher heat, low and slow cooking makes for succulent baby back ribs. The mustard bourbon mop is generously applied every 15 minutes or so, contributing flavor and moisture to the ribs.

Dry Rubs

Meat, poultry, and meaty fish are often flavored before grilling with a dry rub, a mixture of herbs and/or spices that is pressed into their surface. Coat the food well with canola or olive oil, then use the following to flavor 2–3 pounds (1–1.5 kg) of food. All formulas yield 3–4 tablespoons.

All-Purpose Herb Rub

1 tablespoon dried basil

1 tablespoon dried thyme

1 tablespoon dried oregano

2 teaspoons dried rosemary

1 teaspoon coarse sea or kosher salt

¹/₂ teaspoon coarsely ground pepper

In a small bowl, stir together the basil, thyme, oregano, rosemary, salt, and pepper. Rub the mixture on all sides of the meat or poultry, rubbing well to cause some friction.

Dry Rub for Lamb

1 tablespoon dried marjoram

1 tablespoon dried summer savory

1 tablespoon dried thyme

2 teaspoons dried lavender

2 teaspoons dried oregano

2 teaspoons dried rosemary

1 teaspoon dried sage

¹/₂ teaspoon lightly crushed fennel seeds

¹/₂ teaspoon salt

¹/₂ teaspoon coarsely ground pepper

In a small bowl, stir together the marjoram, savory, thyme, lavender, oregano, rosemary, sage, fennel, salt, and pepper. Rub the mixture on all sides of the lamb, rubbing well to cause some friction.

Dry Rub for Beef

1 tablespoon cracked black peppercorns

1 tablespoon cracked white peppercorns

1 tablespoon cracked green peppercorns

1 teaspoon coarse sea or kosher salt

¹/₄ teaspoon red pepper flakes

In a small bowl, stir together the peppercorns, salt, and red pepper flakes. Rub the mixture on all sides of the beef, rubbing well to cause some friction.

Dry Rub for Meaty Fish

1 tablespoon paprika

1 teaspoon dried thyme

1 teaspoon dried oregano

1 teaspoon onion powder

1 teaspoon garlic powder

1 teaspoon coarsely ground black pepper

¹/₂ teaspoon coarsely ground white pepper

¹/₂ teaspoon celery seeds

¹/₂ teaspoon salt

¹/₈–¹/₄ teaspoon ground cayenne pepper

In a small bowl, stir together the paprika, thyme, oregano, onion and garlic powders, black pepper, white pepper, celery seeds, salt, and cayenne to taste. Rub the mixture on all sides of the fish, rubbing lightly to cause minimal friction.

Dry Rub for Pork

2 teaspoons dried thyme

2 teaspoons ground allspice

1 teaspoon onion powder

1 teaspoon sugar

¹/₂ teaspoon freshly grated nutmeg

¹/₂ teaspoon curry powder

¹/₂ teaspoon salt

¹/₄ teaspoon ground cinnamon

¹/₄–¹/₂ teaspoon ground cayenne pepper

¹/₈ teaspoon ground cloves

In a small bowl, stir together the thyme, allspice, onion powder, sugar, nutmeg, curry powder, salt, cinnamon, cayenne to taste, and cloves. Rub the mixture on all sides of the lamb, rubbing well to cause some friction.

Dry Rub for Poultry

1 tablespoon ground ancho chile powder

1 tablespoon ground cumin

2 teaspoons dried oregano

2 teaspoons garlic powder

1 teaspoon onion powder

1 teaspoon dry mustard

1 teaspoon sweet paprika

1 teaspoon salt

¹/₄–¹/₂ teaspoon ground cayenne pepper

In a small bowl, stir together the chile powder, cumin, oregano, garlic and onion powders, mustard, paprika, salt, and cayenne to taste. Rub the mixture on all sides of the chicken, rubbing well to cause some friction.

Basic Marinades

Marinades usually contain three types of ingredients: oil for moisture, acid for tenderizing, and herbs and/or spices for flavor. When using these, be sure to use a nonreactive dish. The yields range from 3/4–1 1/2 cups (6–12 fl oz/180–375 ml) and flavor 1–1 1/2 pounds (500–750 g) of food.

Basic Beef Marinade

1/2 cup (4 fl oz/125 ml) red wine vinegar

2 tablespoons extra-virgin olive oil

1/3 cup (1/3 oz/10 g) chopped fresh flat-leaf (Italian) parsley

2 tablespoons chopped fresh marjoram, thyme, or rosemary

2 tablespoons chopped shallot

6 cloves garlic, chopped

1/2 teaspoon red pepper flakes

1/2 teaspoon salt

In a small bowl, stir together the vinegar, oil, parsley, marjoram, shallot, garlic, red pepper flakes, and salt. Marinate beef for at least 2 hours or for up to 12 hours.

Basic Lamb Marinade

1/2 cup (4 fl oz/125 ml) dry red wine

1/4 cup (2 fl oz/60 ml) olive oil

2 tablespoons red wine vinegar

6–8 cloves garlic, chopped

3 tablespoons chopped fresh oregano

1/2 teaspoon salt

1/2 teaspoon coarsely ground pepper

In a small bowl, stir together the wine, oil, vinegar, garlic, oregano, salt, and pepper. Marinate chops for at least 1 hour; marinate a leg for up to 12 hours.

Basic Fish Marinade

1/3 cup (3 fl oz/80 ml) fresh lemon juice

1/4 cup (2 fl oz/60 ml) olive oil

1/4 cup (2 fl oz/60 ml) bottled clam juice

1 1/2 tablespoons Worcestershire sauce

2 teaspoons grated lemon zest

2 cloves garlic, finely chopped

1 teaspoon coarsely ground pepper

1/2 teaspoon salt

In a small bowl, stir together the lemon juice, oil, clam juice, Worcestershire sauce, lemon zest, garlic, pepper, and salt. Marinate fish for at least 15 minutes or for up to 1 hour.

VARIATIONS

- Add 2 tablespoons chopped fresh tarragon or basil

- Add about 1 tablespoon Dijon mustard

Basic Pork Marinade

1 cup (8 fl oz/250 ml) cider vinegar

1/2 cup (4 fl oz/125 ml) apple juice

3 tablespoons firmly packed brown sugar

1 yellow onion, chopped

2 tablespoons vegetable oil

1–2 tablespoons hot-pepper sauce such as Tabasco

1/2–1 teaspoon red pepper flakes

1/2 teaspoon salt

In a saucepan over medium heat, combine the vinegar, apple juice, and sugar and stir until the sugar is dissolved. Remove from the heat and stir in the onion, oil, hot-pepper sauce, red pepper flakes, and salt. Marinate pork chops and boneless tenderloin for at least 1 hour or for up to 3 hours. Marinate larger roasts for at least 2 hours or for up to 12 hours.

Basic Poultry Marinade

1/3 cup (3 fl oz/80 ml) dry vermouth

1/3 cup (3 fl oz/80 ml) tarragon wine vinegar

1 tablespoon Dijon mustard

1 tablespoon olive oil

2 tablespoons chopped fresh tarragon

1/2 teaspoon salt

1/2 teaspoon coarsely ground pepper

In a small bowl, stir together the vermouth, vinegar, mustard, oil, tarragon, salt, and pepper. Marinate chicken breasts for at least 1 hour or for up to 3 hours. Marinate chicken thighs or drumsticks for at least 1 hour or for up to 4 hours.

VARIATIONS

- Substitute whole-grain mustard, a flavored mustard, or honey mustard for the Dijon mustard.

- Substitute Champagne vinegar or balsamic vinegar for the tarragon wine vinegar.

- Substitute chopped fresh thyme, summer savory, oregano, or rosemary for the tarragon.

Bold Marinades

Below are some highly flavored, fiery hot marinades from India, Jamaica, China, and Cuba that will add kick to beef, lamb, pork, or chicken. All marinades will flavor 2½–3 pounds (1.25–1.5 kg) of food. Be sure to use a nonreactive dish for marinating the foods.

Tandoori Spice Marinade

1 cup (8 oz/250 g) whole-milk or low-fat plain yogurt

2 tablespoons fresh lemon juice

3 tablespoons peeled and chopped fresh ginger

2 teaspoons ground cumin

1 teaspoon ground turmeric

1 teaspoon ground coriander

1 teaspoon salt

³/₄ teaspoon ground cinnamon

¹/₂ teaspoon ground allspice

¹/₂ teaspoon ground cayenne pepper

¹/₄ teaspoon ground cloves

3 cloves garlic, finely chopped

In a bowl, stir together the yogurt, lemon juice, ginger, cumin, turmeric, coriander, salt, cinnamon, allspice, cayenne, cloves, and garlic. Coat the food and refrigerate for at least 1 hour or for up to 4 hours.

Chile-Orange Marinade

Juice of 1 navel orange

¹/₄ cup (2 fl oz/60 ml) rice vinegar

¹/₄ cup (2 fl oz/60 ml) soy sauce

1¹/₂ tablespoons chile oil

2 tablespoons peeled and chopped fresh ginger

4 small, dried red chiles, lightly crushed

3 cloves garlic, sliced

In a small bowl, stir together the orange juice, vinegar, soy sauce, chile oil, ginger, chiles, and garlic. Coat the food and marinate at room temperature for 30 minutes, or in the refrigerator for up to 2 hours.

Mango Jerk Paste

1 cup (8 oz/250 g) mango pulp (about 2 small mangoes)

1 small yellow onion, finely chopped

¹/₄ cup (2 fl oz/60 ml) fresh lime juice

¹/₄ cup (2 fl oz/60 ml) soy sauce

2 tablespoons peeled and grated fresh ginger

2 tablespoons firmly packed dark brown sugar

2 cloves garlic, chopped

1 habanero chile, chopped

1 teaspoon ground allspice

³/₄ teaspoon dried thyme, crumbled

¹/₂ teaspoon freshly ground pepper

In a food processor, combine the mango, onion, lime juice, soy sauce, ginger, sugar, garlic, chile, allspice, thyme, and pepper. Process until fairly smooth. Coat the food and marinate at room temperature for up to 2 hours.

Mojo Marinade

¹/₃ cup (3 fl oz/80 ml) fresh orange juice

¹/₃ cup (3 fl oz/80 ml) fresh lime juice

¹/₃ cup (3 fl oz/80 ml) red wine vinegar

2 tablespoons rum

3 tablespoons olive oil

5 cloves garlic, finely chopped

¹/₄ cup (¹/₃ oz/10 g) chopped fresh flat-leaf (Italian) parsley

1 tablespoon chopped fresh oregano

1 tablespoon chopped fresh thyme

1 teaspoon ground cumin

1 teaspoon grated orange zest

1 teaspoon grated lime zest

¹/₂ teaspoon salt

¹/₂ teaspoon freshly ground pepper

In a bowl, mix together the orange and lime juices, vinegar, rum, oil, garlic, parsley, oregano, thyme, cumin, orange and lime zests, salt, and pepper. Coat the food and refrigerate for at least 3 hours or for up to 12 hours.

Staple Sauces

Zesty sauces are familiar companions to grilled food, accenting everything from ribs and burgers to duck and salmon. Consider the following recipes as versatile staples, using them to enhance the flavor of your grilled foods.

Kansas City Barbecue Sauce

2 tablespoons vegetable oil

1 yellow onion, finely chopped

1 small celery stalk, finely chopped

1 tablespoon chili powder

1 tablespoon dry mustard

1 teaspoon fennel seeds

1 teaspoon celery seeds

1 1/2 cups (12 fl oz/375 g) tomato ketchup

1/2 cup (4 fl oz/125 ml) bottled chili sauce

1/4 cup (2 fl oz/60 ml) cider vinegar

1/4 cup (2 oz/60 g) firmly packed brown sugar

3 tablespoons molasses

2 tablespoons Worcestershire sauce

1–2 teaspoons hot-pepper sauce such as Tabasco

In a saucepan over medium heat, warm the oil. Add the onion and celery and cook, stirring often, until softened, about 5 minutes. Stir in the chili powder, mustard, and fennel and celery seeds. Cook and stir for 1 minute. Stir in the ketchup, chili sauce, vinegar, brown sugar, molasses, and Worcestershire sauce. Bring to a boil, then reduce the heat to medium-low and simmer, stirring occasionally, until lightly thickened, about 15 minutes. Stir in the hot sauce to taste.

Makes about 3 cups (24 fl oz/750 ml)

Quick Horseradish Sauce

1/3 cup (3 oz/90 g) sour cream

1/3 cup (3 oz/90 g) mayonnaise

1/4 cup (3/4 oz/20 g) chopped green (spring) onion, including tender green tops

2 tablespoons freshly grated or prepared horseradish

In a small bowl, stir together the sour cream, mayonnaise, green onion, and horseradish. Cover and refrigerate for at least 30 minutes before using.

Makes about 3/4 cup (6 fl oz/180 ml)

Sweet-and-Sour Sauce

1/2 cup (5 oz/155 g) Chinese plum sauce or sweet-and-sour sauce

2 tablespoons soy sauce

2 tablespoons rice vinegar

1 tablespoon Asian sesame oil

1 tablespoon peeled and chopped fresh ginger

2 large cloves garlic, finely chopped

1/4 teaspoon red pepper flakes

1/4 cup (3/4 oz/20 g) thinly sliced green (spring) onion, including tender green tops

In a small saucepan, combine the plum sauce, soy sauce, vinegar, sesame oil, ginger, garlic, and red pepper flakes. Place over medium heat and bring to a simmer, stirring occasionally. Simmer gently for about 2 minutes to blend the flavors. Just before serving, stir in the onion.

Makes about 1 cup (8 fl oz/250 ml)

Chunky Tomato Ketchup

2 tablespoons mixed pickling spices

6 whole cloves

1 cinnamon stick, broken in half

3 lb (1.5 kg) firm, ripe tomatoes, seeded and coarsely diced

1 large yellow onion, chopped

3 cups (24 fl oz/750 ml) spicy vegetable juice such as V-8

1/2 cup (4 fl oz/125 ml) red wine vinegar or cider vinegar

1/3 cup (2 1/2 oz/75 g) firmly packed brown sugar

1 teaspoon dry mustard

1 teaspoon sweet paprika

1/2 teaspoon salt

1/4–1/2 teaspoon red pepper flakes

Place the pickling spices, cloves, and cinnamon on a square of cheesecloth (muslin), bring the corners together, and tie securely with kitchen string. Set aside.

In a 3-qt (3-l) nonreactive saucepan, combine half of the tomatoes, all of the onion, the vegetable juice, vinegar, brown sugar, mustard, paprika, 1/2 teaspoon salt, and red pepper flakes. Bring to a boil over medium heat, stirring to dissolve the sugar. Add the spice bag, reduce the heat to medium-low, and simmer, uncovered and stirring often, until the mixture is reduced by about half and has thickened, 45–60 minutes.

Add the remaining tomatoes and simmer for 10 minutes until very thick. Watch carefully near the end of cooking to prevent scorching. Remove from the heat and let cool.

Remove and discard the spice bag. Transfer the ketchup to a covered container and refrigerate for at least 4 hours, or preferably for 12 hours, before using.

Makes about 3 cups (24 fl oz/750 ml)

Salsas and Relishes

Piquant salsas and sweet, mellow relishes pair equally well with the smoky flavors of grilled meat, poultry, and seafood. The salsas below are great companions to direct-grilled foods such as steaks and chops, while the sweet onion relish complements slow-roasted pork and duck.

Fruit Salsa

1 large mango

1 green bell pepper (capsicum), seeded and coarsely chopped

1/2 cup (2 oz/60 g) chopped red onion

1–2 jalapeño chiles, seeded and finely chopped

3 tablespoons chopped fresh cilantro (fresh coriander) or mint

1 teaspoon grated lime zest

2 tablespoons fresh lime juice

Salt and freshly ground pepper

Place the mango on a cutting board, resting it on one of its narrow edges, and, using a sharp knife, cut lengthwise slightly off center, cutting off all the flesh from one side of the pit. Repeat on the other side. Hold one of the slices, flesh side up, in your hand, and score the flesh lengthwise and then crosswise, forming 1/2-inch (12-mm) cubes and taking care not to cut through the peel. Press against the center of the peel to force the cubes upward, then slice along the peel, releasing the cubes into a bowl. Repeat with the remaining slice.

In a bowl, combine the mango, bell pepper, onion, chiles, cilantro, and lime zest and juice and toss gently to mix. Season to taste with salt and pepper. Let stand at room temperature for at least 20 minutes before using.

VARIATION

■ Substitute 1 cup (6 oz/185 g) chopped fresh peach, pineapple, or orange flesh for the mango

Makes about 2 cups (12 oz/375 g)

Pico de Gallo

2 tomatoes, seeded and coarsely chopped

1 small yellow onion, coarsely chopped

2 cloves garlic, finely chopped

1–2 jalapeño chiles, seeded and finely chopped

1/4 cup (1/3 oz/10 g) chopped fresh cilantro (fresh coriander)

3 tablespoons fresh lime juice

Salt

In a bowl, stir together the tomatoes, onion, garlic, chiles, cilantro, and lime juice. Season to taste with salt. Let stand at room temperature for at least 15 minutes.

Makes about 1 1/2 cups (9 oz/280 g)

Tomatillo Salsa

1/2 lb (250 g) tomatillos, husks removed and chopped

1 jalapeño chile, seeded and chopped

3/4 cup (1 oz/30 g) chopped fresh cilantro (fresh coriander)

2 tablespoons fresh lime juice

2 tablespoons extra-virgin olive oil

1 teaspoon sugar

In a bowl, combine the tomatillos, jalapeño chile, cilantro, lime juice, oil, and sugar and toss to mix. Cover and refrigerate for 2 hours to allow the flavors to blend; drain before serving.

Makes about 2 cups (12 oz/375 g)

Caramelized Onion Relish

2 tablespoons olive oil

1 tablespoon unsalted butter

2 large yellow onions, very thinly sliced

1 teaspoon sugar

1 teaspoon salt

1/2 teaspoon coarsely ground pepper

3 cloves garlic, finely chopped

2 tablespoons chopped fresh thyme

1 tablespoon white wine vinegar or other white vinegar

FRYING PAN METHOD: In a large frying pan over medium heat, warm the oil and butter. Add the onions and cook, stirring often, until softened, about 5 minutes. Stir in the sugar, salt, and pepper. Reduce the heat to medium-low and cook, stirring often, until the onions are golden, about 10 minutes. Stir in the garlic and thyme, reduce the heat to low, and cook the onions, stirring occasionally, until they are dark golden brown and very soft, 15–20 minutes more. Stir in the vinegar and cook, stirring, for 3 minutes.

OVEN METHOD: Preheat the oven to 400°F (200°C). Place the oil and butter in a rimmed baking sheet and place in the oven to melt the butter. Add the onions and roast, stirring often, until softened, about 5 minutes. Stir in the sugar, salt, and pepper. Roast, stirring often, until the onions are golden, about 8 minutes. Stir in the garlic and thyme, then reduce the heat to 350°F (180°C) and roast the onions, stirring occasionally, until they are dark golden brown and very soft, 15–20 minutes more. Stir in the vinegar and roast for 3 minutes.

Makes about 1 1/2 cups (7 1/2 oz/235 g)

Other Sauces and Flavorings

Use the following to enhance grilled foods. For example, guacamole is a great accompaniment for Mexican-style dishes. Fresh herb pastes add pizzazz to plain grilled poultry, meat, and seafood, while flavored butters, melted over a hot steak, are perhaps the simplest sauces of all.

Guacamole

1 large, ripe avocado, preferably Hass, halved and pitted

2 tablespoons sour cream

1 tablespoon fresh lime juice

2 or 3 dashes hot-pepper sauce such as Tabasco

Salt

Scoop out the avocado flesh into a small bowl. Mash the flesh with a fork, then add the sour cream, lime juice, and hot-pepper sauce and salt to taste. Cover and set aside at room temperature for 15 minutes before serving.

Makes about 1 cup (8 oz/250 g)

Mediterranean Garlic and Herb Paste

2 tablespoons olive oil

1 tablespoon fresh lemon juice

2 tablespoons chopped fresh flat-leaf (Italian) parsley

2 teaspoons grated lemon zest

2 cloves garlic, finely chopped

2 tablespoons chopped fresh herbs of choice such as parsley, basil, thyme, and/or mint

$^{1}/_{2}$ teaspoon each salt and ground pepper

In a small bowl, stir together the oil, lemon juice, parsley, lemon zest, garlic, herbs, salt, and pepper. Use sparingly to flavor grilled meat, poultry, or seafood.

Makes about $^{1}/_{2}$ cup (4 fl oz/125 ml)

Cilantro Pesto

2 cups (2 oz/60 g) firmly packed fresh cilantro (fresh coriander) leaves

3 cloves garlic, chopped

3 tablespoons pine nuts

$^{1}/_{2}$ cup (4 fl oz/125 ml) extra-virgin olive oil

$^{1}/_{2}$ cup (2 oz/60 g) grated Parmesan cheese

Salt and freshly ground pepper

In a food processor, combine the cilantro, garlic, pine nuts, and oil. Process until a smooth paste forms. Spoon the pesto into a bowl and stir in the cheese. Season to taste with salt and pepper. Cover and refrigerate until ready to serve. Stir again just before serving.

Makes about 1 cup (8 fl oz/250 ml)

VARIATIONS

- Replace the cilantro with basil, mint, arugula (rocket), or watercress leaves

- Replace the pine nuts with almonds, walnuts, pistachio nuts, or cashew nuts

- Replace the Parmesan with pecorino Romano, aged Asiago, dry Jack, or other hard grating cheese

- Add about 1 tablespoon dry white wine

- Add 1 teaspoon grated lemon or orange zest

- Add red pepper flakes to taste

Lemon-Parsley Butter

$^{1}/_{2}$ cup (4 oz/125 g) unsalted butter, at room temperature

2 tablespoons finely chopped fresh flat-leaf (Italian) parsley

1 tablespoon finely chopped shallot

2 teaspoons fresh lemon juice

2 teaspoons grated lemon zest

$^{1}/_{2}$ teaspoon salt

$^{1}/_{2}$ teaspoon freshly ground pepper

In a small bowl, mix together the butter, parsley, shallot, lemon juice and zest, salt, and pepper until well blended. Let stand at room temperature for at least 15 minutes before using, or cover and refrigerate for up to 12 hours. If refrigerated, return to room temperature before using.

Makes about $^{1}/_{2}$ cup (4 oz/125 g)

VARIATIONS

For different flavors, replace the shallot, lemon juice, and lemon zest with the following:

- 1 tablespoon freshly grated or well-drained prepared horseradish

- 1–2 tablespoons chopped fresh herb such as basil, thyme, tarragon, savory, mint, or cilantro (fresh coriander), or a mixture

- 2–4 uncooked or roasted cloves garlic

- 1 teaspoon curry powder or garam masala

- 2 tablespoons finely chopped oil-cured black or green olives

- 3 tablespoons softened blue cheese

- 2 tablespoons grated Parmesan cheese

- $^{1}/_{4}$–$^{1}/_{2}$ teaspoon ground cayenne pepper

- 1 or 2 jalapeño chiles, seeded and finely chopped

- 1 teaspoon grated orange, lime, or grapefruit zest

Basic Techniques

TRUSSING POULTRY

1 Place the bird breast side up on the work surface. Bring a long piece of kitchen string under the tail, cross it over once, then bring it up and around the legs, pulling the string tight.

2 Pull each end of the string up toward the breast. Turn the bird breast side down, bringing each string end over each wing. Cross the string ends and hold them securely.

3 Turn the bird breast side up and ensure that it sits in a compact shape. Tie the strings securely at the top of the neck. Cut the ends of the strings close to the knot.

BUTTERFLYING POULTRY

1 Place the bird breast side down on a cutting board. Cut along one side of the backbone with kitchen shears or a large knife.

2 Pull open the halves of the bird. Cut down the other side of the backbone to free it. Discard the backbone or save it for stock.

3 Turn the chicken breast side up, opening it as flat as possible. Press it firmly to break the breastbone and flatten the bird.

CUTTING POULTRY INTO PARTS

1 Cut through the skin between the thigh and body. Locate the joint by moving the leg, then cut through the joint to remove the leg. Repeat on the other side.

2 Turn the chicken slightly on the board, Move a wing to locate its joint with the body. Cut through the joint to remove the wing. Repeat with the other wing.

3 Starting at the neck opening, cut along both sides of the chicken, separating the breast section from the remainder of the bird. Discard the backbone or save it for stock.

4 Place the breast skin side down on the cutting board. Cut along the center of the breast to split it in half.

5 If desired, separate the legs from the thighs by cutting through the joints. A whole chicken will yield 6–8 pieces, depending on whether you separated the legs and thighs.

Basic Techniques

FRENCHING MEAT BONES

1 After trimming most of the external fat from the lamb rack or roast, insert a sharp boning knife into the meat and tissue on each side of the bones to mark what should be cut away.

2 Use the knife or your fingers to cut and/or pull out the meat and tissue from between the bones, up to 2–3 inches (5–7.5 cm) from the ends of the bones.

3 Using the back of the knife, scrape off any remaining meat or tissue to leave the bones clean. Or, use a kitchen towel to rub off the remaining meat and tissue.

CUTTING A POCKET IN A PORK OR VEAL CHOP FOR STUFFING

1 Using a small, sharp knife, cut a deep, wide horizontal pocket into each chop, taking care not to cut through the top or bottom.

2 Use a small spoon or your fingers to insert the filling into each chop, packing it firmly into the pocket.

3 Secure the opening closed with a toothpick or small metal skewer. Remember to remove the toothpick before serving.

SLICING MEAT

Use a carving fork to steady the meat and cut it crosswise, against the grain, into slices with a sharp knife. The leaner the meat to be carved, the thinner the slices should be.

INSERTING FLAVORINGS UNDER POULTRY SKIN

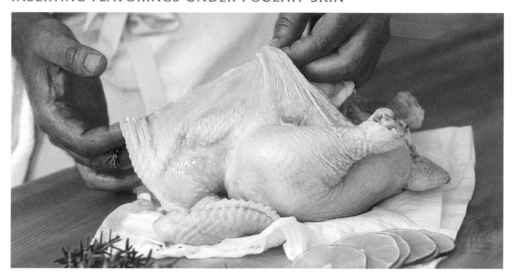

Using your fingers and starting at the tail cavity, carefully loosen the skin of the bird over the breasts and thighs. Insert the herbs, spices, citrus slices, flavored butters, or other flavorings under the skin, spreading them as evenly as possible.

REMOVING SILVER SKIN FROM A PORK TENDERLOIN

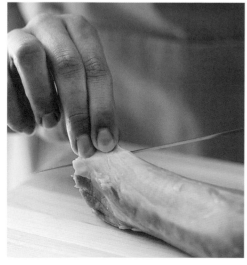

1 Locate the thin, white membrane (silver skin) that runs the length of the tenderloin. Slide a thin, sharp knife under the silver skin.

2 Keeping the knife pointed slightly upward, and pulling the silver skin taut, cut along the silver skin to separate it from the meat.

APPLYING A DRY RUB

Pat the mixture on all sides of meat or poultry, rubbing well to cause some friction. When applying a rub to fish, use minimal friction.

Glossary

AHI TUNA Hawaiian for yellowfin tuna, ahi boasts deep red, meaty, firm, oily flesh that takes well to grilling. Its flavor and texture are reminiscent of red meat, and, like steak, it can be served rare or medium-rare. Be sure to purchase sashimi-grade tuna if planning to serve it undercooked.

AIOLI A pungent garlic-flavored mayonnaise popular in the south of France. The word derives from a combination of the Provençal dialect words for garlic, *aïl*, and oil, *oli*.

BAKER'S PEEL A thin-edged wooden or metal paddle used for transferring pizzas into or removing them from the oven or grill. It slides easily under a pizza crust, making for smooth, mishap-free moving.

BARBECUING Although many people use this term interchangeably with grilling, the two are not the same. Barbecuing is cooking meat out-doors in a closed chamber by indirect heat. A low temperature is maintained for a long time, using fragrant, smoky wood or high-grade charcoal. The sauce served with barbecue is determined by region—from a vinegar-based sauce in North Carolina to a mustard-based sauce in South Carolina to a sweet, thick tomato-based sauce in Kansas City.

BEARD The little tuft of fibers a mussel uses to connect to rocks or pilings. To remove it, cut and scrape it with a knife or scissors. You may also pull it sharply down toward the hinged point of the shells with your fingers.

BEEFSTEAK TOMATO A large, meaty, round tomato about 5 inches (13 cm) in diameter and bright red to orange.

BELGIAN ENDIVE Also known as witloof or chicory, this small, white (or sometimes red-tipped), tightly furled, bullet-shaped member of the chicory family is widely grown in Belgium. Its expensive price is due to its painstaking cultivation and its fragility during transport.

BISTECCA The Italian word for "beef."

BREAD FLOUR An unbleached, hard-wheat flour whose high protein content creates an elastic dough for higher rise and more structure in breads and pizza crusts.

BRINING Soaking meat or poultry in brine to enhance its juiciness is an old-fashioned cooking technique that is now regaining popularity. Depending on the food, brining can take from 30 minutes to 2 days. The brine must contain salt—specifically kosher salt, which is free of additives—but other flavorings can be added, such as garlic, red pepper flakes, sugar, or honey. The brine can also include flavorful liquids, such as apple cider, vinegar, beer, or wine. As the meat soaks, the salt penetrates it, drawing in moisture and flavor.

BUTTERFLYING The technique of cutting food nearly all the way through so that, instead of being split into two pieces, it can be opened up to lie relatively flat. Butterflying allows fast, even cooking of foods. It also allows meat to be stuffed, rolled up, and tied before cooking.

CAPER The small, unopened flower buds of a shrub native to the Mediterranean, capers are unpleasantly bitter when raw. Once dried and packed in brine or salt, however, they add a pleasantly pungent flavor and a light crunch to dishes. Capers are usually sold in vinegar brine and sealed in glass jars. Salted capers are harder to find, but they are usually carried in well-stocked Italian markets in bulk or in jars.

CAPER BERRY The fruit of the same shrub that produces capers. Olive shaped and with long stems, caper berries are pickled or salted and must be rinsed before use.

CARAMELIZE To cook foods until their natural sugars, which caramelize when exposed to heat over a relatively long time, are accentuated.

CHEESES

Asiago An Italian cow's milk cheese that is pleasantly sharp tasting and covered with an inedible rind. The longer it ages, the sharper the cheese will taste.

Camembert This cow's milk cheese, similar to Brie, has a pale yellow interior and edible rind. Camembert should be as soft as bread dough when ripe and ready to eat.

Fontina A mild, fruity Italian cow's milk cheese with a pleasing firmness and light but heady aroma.

Gorgonzola A cow's milk blue cheese from Italy with a moist, creamy texture and a complex, pleasantly pungent flavor.

Pecorino Romano A pleasantly salty Italian sheep's milk cheese with a grainy texture; primarily used for grating.

Reggiano Parmesan Produced in the Emilia-Romagna region of Italy, Reggiano Parmesan is true Parmesan. Look for an aged, firm cheese with a pale yellow to medium straw color and a piquant, slightly salty flavor. To tell it from imposters, look for "Parmigiano-Reggiano" stenciled vertically on the rind.

CHIPOTLE A dried and smoked jalapeño chile, with lots of flavor and lots of heat. These dark brown chiles are about 4 inches (10 cm) long and may be bought dried, or in cans or jars in an oniony tomato mixture called adobo sauce.

CRÈME FRAÎCHE A soured, cultured cream product, originally from France, crème fraîche is similar to sour cream. Silken and thick, it is tangy and sweet, with a hint of nuttiness.

DIRECT-HEAT GRILLING An intense, high-heat cooking method, in which foods are placed directly over a heat source. Direct-heat grilling is used for searing and for cooking small or thin food items, including steaks, chops, burgers, sausages, some poultry pieces, fish fillets, and kabobs. In general, foods cooked over direct heat are ready in less than 25 minutes.

DRIED LAVENDER FLOWERS Fresh, these small blossoms of the lavender plant are purple, but when dried they take on a gray cast. A signature seasoning of southern France, the flowers have a sweet and mildly lemony flavor and fragrance.

DRUMETTES These meaty third segments of chicken wings are often sold separately from the wings, sometimes labeled "chicken wing drumettes."

FISH SAUCE A clear liquid, ranging from amber to dark brown, fish sauce is famous for its pungent aroma and strong, salty flavor. Southeast Asians use fish sauce in much the same way Westerners use salt, as a seasoning both at the stove and at the table. The best-quality fish sauce is pressed from small fish, commonly anchovies, that have been salted, packed in barrels, and fermented for several months. Look for fish sauce, known as *nam pla* in Thailand and *nuoc mam* in Vietnam, in Asian food stores and the international food aisle of the supermarket.

FIVE-SPICE POWDER Sometimes labeled "Chinese five-spice powder," this potent spice blend varies in its makeup—and often in its number of spices—but usually contains cloves, anise seeds or fennel seeds, star anise, cinnamon, Sichuan peppercorns, and sometimes ginger. It lends a haunting flavor and fragrance to Chinese- and Southeast Asian–style dishes.

FLANKEN STYLE A way of cutting beef short ribs across the rib bones. This cut can be done accordion style, as cooks do in Korea, to make short ribs that can be quickly cooked over direct heat.

FRENCH, TO A process of cutting meat and connective tissue away from the end of a rib or chop so that a portion of the bone is exposed, giving the finished product an elegant look.

FRENCHED A rib or chop that has had the meat and connective tissue removed at its end, giving it an elegant appearance after cooking.

FRUITWOOD Wood from fruit trees such as apple, cherry, and plum. Turned into chips, these hardwoods lend subtle smoky flavor to grilled and smoked foods.

GARAM MASALA An aromatic blend of roasted, ground spices popular in Indian cooking. Each region or cook has a different recipe, but each is composed of "warm" spices, lending a touch of heat to dishes in which it is used. Common additions are peppercorns, cardamom, cinnamon, cloves, coriander, nutmeg, turmeric, fennel seeds, and dried chiles.

GRAPE LEAVES Primarily used as edible wrappers for appetizers. Purchase jars of brined leaves at specialty-food stores or in the international section of the local grocery. Rinse the leaves before using.

GRAPEVINE CUTTINGS Grapevines that have been cut into small pieces and dried, for adding to fires to flavor foods with aromatic smoke. Available at specialty-food stores or through mail order.

HARICOTS VERTS Small, slender, dark green, young pod beans favored in France. Delicately flavored, they are more elegant, and expensive, than other green beans.

HEIRLOOM Refers to a fruit or vegetable grown from seeds that have never been hybridized or otherwise altered by humans. Look for heirloom produce in farmers' markets and upscale food stores.

HERBES DE PROVENCE A blend of dried herbs, traditionally thyme, summer savory, basil, fennel seeds, and lavender, traditionally used in France's Provence region to flavor meats, poultry, and vegetables.

HIBACHI A small, inexpensive uncovered square-cornered grill. Although good for picnics and for grilling in tight spaces, it can hold only a few servings at a time.

HOISIN A thick, sweet, reddish brown sauce made from soybeans, sugar, garlic, and spices. Used throughout China, hoisin sauce is used as a glaze or sauce for meats and poultry. Use sparingly, as it has a strong flavor.

HORSERADISH, FRESH A thick, gnarled root of a plant in the cabbage family. The root has a refreshing, spicy bite, and must be peeled first to reveal the creamy white, edible flesh below the brown skin. Look for fresh horseradish in the produce section of a specialty-food store or well-stocked supermarket.

INDIRECT-HEAT GRILLING A method of cooking that uses moderate to low reflected heat in a covered grill, much like roasting in an oven. The heat that circulates inside the grill cooks the food more slowly and evenly than direct heat. Use this method for cooking large pieces, such as a pork loin or a whole chicken or turkey, that take 25 minutes or more to cook.

INSTANT-READ THERMOMETER This type of thermometer is inserted into foods toward the end of the cooking period to test for doneness. Instant-read thermometers are more accurate than probe-type thermometers and make a smaller hole in meat or poultry, thus releasing fewer juices.

KETTLE GRILL The design of this popular spherical, covered grill promotes good heat circulation. The grill's domed lid efficiently directs heat back down to the food. Most kettle grills use charcoal, but gas models are also available.

KOSHER SALT A favorite of many cooks, kosher salt has large flakes that are easy to handle. The coarse salt, made by compressing granular salt, is also free of additives. Since it is not as salty as table salt, and has a superior flavor, it can be used more liberally.

LEMONGRASS An aromatic herb used in much of Southeast Asia, lemongrass resembles a green (spring) onion in shape. The slender, gray-green stalk has a fresh lemony aroma and flavor. Use only the pale bottom part of the stalk for cooking, removing the tough outer leaves before crushing it with a pestle or the side of a knife blade and then chopping. Since its fibers are tough, lemongrass needs to be minced finely or removed from a dish before serving, much like a bay leaf.

MADEIRA A fortified wine from Portugal, made in versions from dry to sweet.

MANDOLINE A flat, rectangular tool ideal for cutting food quickly and easily, with precision and uniformity.

MARBLING The white streaks of fat found throughout meat that contribute to its flavor, tenderness, and juiciness.

MIRIN A sweet, syrupy Japanese rice wine used in Asian-style marinades, glazes, and sauces. It is available in Asian markets and well-stocked grocery stores.

MISO A staple food in Japan, this fermented soybean paste is used to flavor robust dishes. Miso comes in two main types: sweet, mild light (or yellow) miso; and strong, salty dark (or red) miso.

MOPPING SAUCE A flavorful sauce applied generously to slow-cooked and smoked meats. The name comes from the old barbecue tradition of using a clean cotton dish mop to apply sauce to large portions of smoked meats or ribs.

MORTAR AND PESTLE Traditional implements that grind, purée, and blend ingredients. Some cooks argue that using a mortar and pestle is essential to gain the true flavor and retain the necessary texture of an authentic sauce or herb paste. A bowl-shaped mortar holds the ingredients, while the club-shaped pestle crushes and grinds them. These tools are made from a variety of materials and in a number of different sizes.

MUSHROOMS

Cremini Also known as common brown mushrooms and Italian or Roman mushrooms, these small cultivated mushrooms mature to become portobellos.

Oyster Cream to pale gray, oyster mushrooms have a fan shape and a subtle flavor of shellfish. Look for small, young mushrooms, as they become tough and bitter as they grow older.

Portobello Cultivated mushrooms, portobellos are cremini mushrooms that have been allowed to grow until their caps are about 6 inches (15 cm) wide and dark brown. They have a rich, smoky flavor and meaty texture.

Shiitake The most popular mushrooms in Japan and now widely cultivated. Buff to dark brown, fresh shiitakes should have smooth, plump caps. Remove their thin, tough stems before using.

NEW POTATO An immature potato, usually of the round red or round white variety. Most often available in spring and early summer, new potatoes are low in starch and perfect for grilling. Be aware that not all small red and white potatoes are new. A true new potato is freshly harvested, will have a thin skin, and will not keep long.

NONREACTIVE DISH A dish made of or lined with a material—most commonly stainless steel, enamel, or glass—that will not react with acidic ingredients.

OYSTER SAUCE A thick, dark brown Chinese sauce made from oysters, salt, and water. With its distinctive smoky-sweet flavor, this all-purpose seasoning is used to give body, deep color, and rich flavor to sauces and marinades.

PANCETTA This flavorful Italian bacon, which derives its name from *pancia*, the Italian word for "belly," has a moist, silky texture. It is made by rubbing a slab of pork belly with a simple mixture of spices, then rolling the slab into a tight cylinder and curing it for at least 2 months.

PARBOIL To cook food partially in boiling water, sometimes as a preparatory step before combining ingredients with different cooking times or finishing with another cooking method.

PATHOGEN A disease-causing microorganism.

PLANKING A method of cooking oily fish on a board, which imparts its wood flavor to the flesh. Cedar and alder planks or untreated shingles are popular choices.

POLENTA Cornmeal that is cooked in liquid until it thickens and the grains become tender. The Italian term *polenta* is used both for the grain and the finished dish, a specialty of northern Italy.

POMEGRANATE MOLASSES Concentrated pomegranate juice, which is an essential ingredient in many eastern Mediterranean cuisines. Look for it in Middle Eastern groceries and in specialty-food stores.

PORK LOIN, BONELESS ROLLED A lean and tender boneless roast formed from two top loins tied together with string. The butcher's removal of the animal's backbone makes the meat easier to carve and serve, but it can also lead to drier meat, which is why this cut is often stuffed before cooking.

PROSCIUTTO Seasoned, salt-cured, air-dried rear leg of pork. Aged from 10 months to 2 years, it boasts a distinctive fragrance and a subtle flavor. Although it is made in many parts of Italy and elsewhere in the world, most authorities agree that the best prosciutto comes from Parma, in the Italian region of Emilia-Romagna.

RADICCHIO A member of the chicory family native to Italy and characterized by its variegated purplish red leaves and pleasantly bitter taste.

RESTING To allow food to sit undisturbed for a period of time during the course of preparing a dish. A resting period allows cooked meat juices to redistribute themselves through the meat, making it uniformly juicier. During resting, the internal temperature of meat and poultry will rise 5° to 10°F (3° to 6°C).

ROMESCO A classic Spanish sauce made by puréeing together tomatoes, red bell peppers (capsicums), onions, garlic, and olive oil, and then thickening the mixture with ground almonds. *Romesco* is a common accompaniment to grilled foods.

ROSEMARY BRANCHES Long, sturdy sprigs of rosemary. They can be used as skewers for poultry or seafood, imparting their flavor to the food as it cooks.

ROTISSERIE A spit that rotates food, commonly whole chickens, whole ducks, legs of lamb, or beef roasts, in front of a heat source. The food self-bastes as it turns.

RUB A mixture of spices and herbs, often in the form of a powder or paste, that is pressed or massaged onto the surface of meat or poultry for flavor.

SATAY Popular in Southeast Asian countries, satay are strips of meat or poultry threaded on skewers, grilled, and served with a spicy peanut-based dipping sauce.

SEA SALT Naturally evaporated, and containing no additives, sea salt adheres well, dissolves quickly, and has a unique flavor. Many prefer it to table salt for cooking.

SMOKING To give a smoky flavor to foods cooked on an outdoor grill. Also known as hot smoking, it is done by adding wood chips, dried herbs, or other flavoring materials to the charcoal or gas fire and covering the grill during cooking.

SOBA Thin, flat Japanese noodles made from buckwheat flour.

SOMEN Thin Japanese noodles made from wheat flour.

SRIRACHA A bright red, hot chile sauce from Thailand, used to add zest to many Southeast Asian dishes.

STAR ANISE Brown, star-shaped pods with an aniselike flavor from a Chinese evergreen tree. They are a main ingredient in Chinese five-spice powder.

TAHINI A paste popular in Middle Eastern cuisines made from ground sesame seeds. It has a rich, creamy flavor and a concentrated sesame taste.

TAPENADE A classic Provençal caper and olive paste. Usually made from black olives, it can also be made from green olives, sun-dried tomatoes, and other piquant ingredients. Garlic and anchovies are common accents.

TRICHINOSIS A disease caused by microscopic parasites. For many years trichinosis was a health concern in the United States, where it was discovered in some pork. Today the incidence of trichinosis is rare, but it is still wise to cook pork, and other meats and poultry, to a safe temperature before eating.

TZATZIKI A garlicky Greek sauce, spread, or dip made by combining cucumber, drained yogurt, and fresh dill.

WASABI Similar to horseradish, this Japanese root is commonly sold in two forms, as a green powder and as a green paste. It adds fiery flavor to recipes.

YUKON GOLD POTATOES Thin-skinned potatoes with yellowish skin and golden, fine-grained, buttery-tasting flesh. These all-purpose potatoes hold their shape well when cooked.

ZEST The colored portion of citrus peel, which is rich in flavorful oils.

Index

PHOTOGRAPHS

JASON LOWE

Pages 4, 6, 32 (left and right), 35–39, 40 (right), 41–42, 50, 55–69, 75–76, 80–81, 86, 87 (left and right), 90–92, 98 (left, center), 102–05, 110–112, 114–22, 129–130, 141, 149–65, 166 (left, center), 168–75, 179, 183–218, 222–24, 226–56, 260, 271–79, 292 (bottom row), 293 (top left)

MAREN CARUSO

Endpapers; pages 8–13, 15, 16, 18–20, 22–23, 28, 48–49, 87 (center), 290–91, 292 (top row)

HOLLY STEWART

Pages 2, 14, 17, 21, 29, 30, 32 (center), 40 (left), 45, 46–47, 54, 72, 83, 88, 95, 96–97, 98 (right), 108–09, 113, 134–35, 166 (right), 167, 259, 264 (left), 269, 293 (top right, bottom row)

DAVID MATHESON

Cover image; 24–27, 60, 71, 79, 84–85, 106, 126, 133, 136, 139, 142–46, 176–77, 180, 221, 225, 262, 264 (center, right), 266, 280–83

ACKNOWLEDGMENTS

Weldon Owen would like to acknowledge the following people for their gracious assistance in producing the first and second editions of this book: our late Chief Operating Officer Larry Partington; Associate Creative Director Leslie Harrington; Copy Editor Sharon Silva; Consulting Editors Laurie Wertz and Sarah Putman Clegg; Consulting Senior Art Director Emma Boys; Designer Charlene Charles; Designer Briar Levit; Photographer's Assistants Tom Hood and James Thomas; Food Stylist Kevin Crafts; Assistant Food Stylist Luis Bustamente; Prop Stylists Carol Hacker, Amy Denebeim, and Leigh Noe; Proofreaders Desne Ahlers, Vené Franco, and Sharron Wood; Indexer Ken DellaPenta; and Production and Shipping Coordinator Libby Temple.

OXMOOR HOUSE INC.

Oxmoor House books are distributed by Sunset Books
80 Willow Road, Menlo Park, CA 94025
Telephone: 650-321-3600 Fax 650-324-1532
Vice President/General Manager: Rich Smeby
National Accounts Manager/Special Sales: Brad Moses

Oxmoor House and Sunset Books are divisions of
Southern Progress Corporation

WILLIAMS-SONOMA, INC.
Founder & Vice-Chairman: Chuck Williams

WELDON OWEN INC.
Chief Executive Officer: John Owen
President and Chief Operating Officer: Terry Newell
Chief Financial Officer: Christine Munson
Vice President International Sales: Stuart Laurence
Creative Director: Gaye Allen
Publisher: Hannah Rahill
Series Editor: Jennifer Newens
Assistant Editor: Donita Boles
Production Director: Chris Hemesath
Color Manager: Teri Bell
Production and Reprint Coordinator: Todd Rechner

THE ESSENTIALS SERIES
Conceived and produced by
WELDON OWEN INC.
814 Montgomery Street, San Francisco, CA 94133
Telephone 415-291-0100 Fax: 415-291-8841
In collaboration with Williams-Sonoma Inc.
3250 Van Ness Avenue, San Francisco, CA 94109

A WELDON OWEN PRODUCTION
Copyright © 2006 Weldon Owen Inc.
and Williams-Sonoma Inc.
All rights reserved, including the right of
reproduction in whole or in part in any form.

ISBN 13: 978-0-8487-3133-5
ISBN 10: 0-8487-3133-6

First printed in 2005

10 9 8 7 6 5

Printed by Midas Printing Limited
Printed in China